DATE

EDUCATION AND WORK

EDUCATION AND WORK

Eighty-first Yearbook of the
National Society for the Study of Education

PART II

By

THE YEARBOOK COMMITTEE
and
ASSOCIATED CONTRIBUTORS

Edited by

HARRY F. SILBERMAN

Editor for the Society

KENNETH J. REHAGE

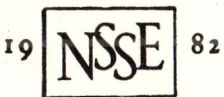

19 NSSE 82

University of Charleston Library
Charleston, WV 25304
Distributed by THE UNIVERSITY OF CHICAGO PRESS • CHICAGO, ILLINOIS

The National Society for the Study of Education

Founded in 1901 as successor to the National Herbart Society, the National Society for the Study of Education has provided a means by which the results of serious study of educational issues could become a basis for informed discussion of those issues. The Society's two-volume yearbooks, now in their eighty-first year of publication, reflect the thoughtful attention given to a wide range of educational problems during those years. A recently inaugurated series on Contemporary Educational Issues includes substantial publications in paperback that supplement the yearbooks. Each year, the Society's publications contain contributions to the literature of education from more than a hundred scholars and practitioners who are doing significant work in their respective fields.

An elected Board of Directors selects the subjects with which volumes in the yearbook series are to deal, appropriates funds to meet necessary expenses in the preparation of a given volume, and appoints a committee to oversee the preparation of manuscripts for that volume. A special committee created by the Board performs similar functions for the Society's paperback series.

The Society's publications are distributed each year without charge to approximately 4,000 members in the United States, Canada, and elsewhere throughout the world. The Society welcomes as members all individuals who desire to receive its publications. For information about membership and current dues, see the back page of this volume or write to the Secretary-Treasurer, 5835 Kimbark Avenue, Chicago, Illinois 60637.

The Eighty-first Yearbook includes the following two volumes:

Part I: Policy Making in Education
Part II: Education and Work

A complete listing of the Society's previous publications, together with information as to how earlier publications still in print may be obtained, is found in the back pages of this volume.

Library of Congress Catalog Number: 81-85131
ISSN: 0077-5762

Published 1982 by
THE NATIONAL SOCIETY FOR THE STUDY OF EDUCATION

5835 Kimbark Avenue, Chicago, Illinois 60637
© 1982 by the National Society for the Study of Education

First Printing, 7,500 Copies

Printed in the United States of America

Officers of the Society
1981-82

(Term of office expires March 1 of the year indicated.)

LUVERN L. CUNNINGHAM

(1984)
Ohio State University, Columbus, Ohio

MARGARET J. EARLY

(1982)
Syracuse University, Syracuse, New York

ELLIOT W. EISNER

(1983)
Stanford University, Stanford, California

JOHN I. GOODLAD

(1983)
University of California, Los Angeles, California

PHILIP W. JACKSON

(1982)
University of Chicago, Chicago, Illinois

RALPH W. TYLER

(1984)
*Director Emeritus, Center for Advanced Study in the Behavioral Sciences
Stanford, California*

KENNETH J. REHAGE

(Ex-officio)
University of Chicago, Chicago, Illinois

Secretary-Treasurer

KENNETH J. REHAGE

5835 Kimbark Avenue, Chicago, Illinois 60637

▼

The Society's Committee on Education and Work

HARRY F. SILBERMAN

(Chairman)
Professor of Education
Graduate School of Education
University of California
Los Angeles, California

SAM BARRETT

Director of Vocational Education
California State Department of Education
Sacramento, California

JOHN I. GOODLAD

Dean, Graduate School of Education
University of California
Los Angeles, California

RALPH W. TYLER

Director Emeritus, Center for Advanced Study
in the Behavioral Sciences
Stanford, California

Associated Contributors

RICHARD J. BECKER

Graduate Student, Graduate School of Education
University of California
Los Angeles, California

ASSOCIATED CONTRIBUTORS

SUSAN REDELMANN BERG

Instructor/Coordinator, Co-op Work Experience
Coastline Community College
Fountain Valley, California

SUE E. BERRYMAN

Social Scientist, Rand Corporation
Santa Monica, California

LOIS-ELLIN DATTA

Associate Director, Program on Teaching and Learning
National Institute of Education
Washington, D.C.

MARCIA FREEDMAN

Senior Research Associate
Conservation of Human Resources, Columbia University
New York, New York

EDWIN L. HERR

Professor and Head
Division of Counseling and Educational Psychology
Pennsylvania State University
University Park, Pennsylvania

BEATRICE G. REUBENS

Senior Research Associate
Conservation of Human Resources, Columbia University
New York, New York

BENJAMIN SHIMBERG

Senior Program Research Scientist
Educational Testing Service
Princeton, New Jersey

GORDON I. SWANSON

Professor and Director of Graduate Studies
University of Minnesota
St. Paul, Minnesota

ROBERT TAGGART

Director, Youth Knowledge Development Project
National Council on Employment Policy
Washington, D.C.

WELLFORD W. WILMS

Assistant Professor of Education
University of California
Los Angeles, California

JULIA WRIGLEY

Assistant Professor of Education
University of California
Los Angeles, California

Editor's Preface

The Congress of the United States is preparing new vocational education legislation designed to effect closer ties between schools and the private sector, between the Comprehensive Employment and Training Act (CETA) and vocational education, and between basic literacy and occupational programs. It is trying to insure that all students are better served, including those who are handicapped or disadvantaged. It is also trying to insure a better match between the educational system and the changing demands of the labor market.

The issues being considered in the new legislation mirror the problems in the larger society. Reduced federal budgets will mean higher unemployment, and in times of high unemployment there is always a greater emphasis on job training and on closer connections between education and work. The economy of the United States is also beginning to feel the competition from other industrial countries that are challenging our position as one of the most productive nations in the world. Concern over our declining industrial preeminence raises questions about the productivity and skill level of our workforce, which comes back to the effectiveness of our training programs.

Another problem that has emerged in the past few decades is that young people are growing up too fast, too soon, with too many possessions, and with too little opportunity to feel needed by adults. The separation of youth from adults is a product of the decline of the family and the separation of school and work. It is becoming increasingly apparent that the educational development of youth cannot succeed solely through the efforts of the schools. Learning must be enhanced through exposure of young people to a variety of opportunities to test themselves in the community and in the workplace alongside supportive adults. Schools must find ways of working together with other organizations in the community to make this possible.

It is in the context of such issues at the forefront of current events that this yearbook examines the relationships between education and work. We begin with a historical analysis of legislation, noting major policy issues, and we review the current status of vocational education and the structure of work in the United States. Contrasts are made with other industrialized countries, and special chapters are included on the topics of licensure, guidance, basic literacy, evaluation, problems of cooperation, the employment problems of black youth, and what we have learned from employment and training programs. The chapters on these topics are crucial to an understanding of the problems of education and work. We hope that this volume will contribute a broadened perspective from which to view these problems.

HARRY F. SILBERMAN
Los Angeles, January 1982

Acknowledgement

The subject of the relationship between education and work has been addressed in a number of previous yearbooks of the National Society for the Study of Education, beginning in 1905 with a volume on *The Place of Vocational Subjects in the High-School Curriculum*. The most recent comprehensive treatment in the Society's series of yearbooks appeared in the Sixty-fourth Yearbook entitled *Vocational Education*. Many of the issues that have engaged the attention of educators persist, as the present volume amply demonstrates. But some of these concerns have taken on new dimensions in the light of developments in the past two decades.

The Society is greatly indebted to Professor Harry F. Silberman, editor of this volume, and to his associates for a yearbook that will surely help all educators come to a broadened and deepened understanding of the current issues involved in efforts to assist youth in making the transition from education to work.

KENNETH J. REHAGE
Editor for the Society

Table of Contents

CHAPTER I

Education and Work: A Historical Perspective

RICHARD J. BECKER

Introduction

While vocationalism in American education has its roots in the Manual Training Movement of the 1880s, the great debate over "education and work" was argued in the early 1900s. Especially in the hearings and final report of the Commission on Vocational Education (1914), the accompanying public debate, and the Chicago conflict over a dual system of education, the relation between education and work was thoroughly discussed.[1] The Smith-Hughes Act of 1917 set the course of public policy with federal funds for vocational education. Yet today, after sixty years of federal involvement in the area of education and work, the discussion is still going on over many of the same themes and arguments of that earlier era.

Most recently the debate was waged in the policy analysis process for the Youth Act of 1980 (H.R. 6711). This bill was drafted for Congress by the Carter Administration in February 1980, after a full year of intense activity by the Vice President's Task Force on Youth Employment. With a budget of more than $1 million, the Task Force commissioned issue papers, conducted meetings of researchers, employers, educators, and administrators of programs under the Comprehensive Employment and Training Act (CETA) and solicited opinions of all who are concerned with the issues centering around education and work. Subsequent action by the House of Representatives (where the bill passed) and by the Senate (where the bill died) enlarged the discussion.

---

1. Marvin Lazerson and W. Norton Grubb, eds., *American Education and Vocationalism: A Documentary History, 1870-1970* (New York: Teachers College Press, 1974), pp. 17-41.

As a means to some historical perspective on American attitudes toward education and work, this chapter compares arguments of that earlier era with contemporary views as reflected in President Carter's Youth Initiative of 1980. Three issues are singled out: (a) equality of opportunity and a more democratic system of education, (b) the relation of education to economic growth and productivity, and (c) the control of vocational training.

Equality of Opportunity

In the American experience, the most self-evident truth has always been that all men are created equal. Formulating public policy consistent with this ideal has often been a problem. The concern in the early 1900s was how to provide "the children of the plain people" with an educational opportunity equal to that of the small elite who in earlier days had been the only participants in secondary education. In 1890, less than 4 percent of the high school age population was enrolled in secondary schools; by 1920 the secondary enrollment had reached 28 percent.[2] In an effort to adapt the secondary curriculum to the influx of working-class children, a new concept of democracy in education emerged. The underlying principle was that while all children are equal, they are not all the same. The traditional "common school" curriculum with a single program of literary instruction was viewed as ill-suited to the "masses" who were destined for work in industry or a more scientific agriculture. Real equality of opportunity in education could only be achieved through the introduction of vocational training into the curriculum. There was no mincing of words in the way the argument was stated. For example, in 1908 Charles W. Eliot stated:

The teachers of the elementary schools ought to sort the pupils and sort them by their evident or probable destinies. I am afraid that strikes you at once as an undemocratic idea, but let us see whether it is undemocratic or not. Does democracy mean that all people are alike? Does it mean that all children are equal? We know they are not. . . . We have learned that the best way in education is to find out what the line is in which the child can do best, and then to give him the happiness of

2. Ibid., p. 22.

achievement in that line. Here we come back to the best definition of democracy.[3]

A report of the Commission on Vocational Education in 1914 put it this way:

The social and educational need for vocational training is equally urgent. Widespread vocational training will democratize the education of the country . . . by recognizing different tastes and abilities and by giving an equal opportunity to all to prepare for their life work.[4]

There were dissenting voices at the time to this approach. John Dewey was the most articulate adversary to segregated vocational programs, which he regarded as class-biased and subservient to the interests of employers. Dewey stated his objections in an article entitled "An Undemocratic Proposal":

Those who believe in the continued separate existence of what they are pleased to call the "lower classes" or the "laboring classes" would naturally rejoice to have schools in which these "classes" would be segregated. And some employers of labor would doubtless rejoice to have schools supported by public taxation supply them with additional food for their mills.[5]

Dewey was not objecting to vocational education but to splitting it off from the rest of the school system. His main thesis was: "Democracy has to be born anew every generation, and education is its midwife."[6] His view was that vocational education, properly integrated into the curriculum, could be a powerful means to equality of opportunity.

In the Youth Initiative of 1980, we find equality of opportunity still a primary concern. If anything, the belief that upward

3. Charles W. Eliot, "Equality of Educational Opportunity," in *American Education and Vocationalism*, ed. Lazerson and Grubb, pp. 136-38.

4. Report of the *Commission on National Aid to Vocational Education together with the Hearings Held on the Subject*, U.S. House of Representatives, 63d Congress, 2d Session, Doc. No. 1004 (Washington, D.C.: U.S. Goverment Printing Office, 1914), vol. 1, p. 12. Hereafter cited as *Report of the Commission on Vocational Education.*

5. John Dewey, "An Undemocratic Proposal," in *American Education and Vocationalism*, ed. Lazerson and Grubb, pp. 143-47.

6. John Dewey, "The Need of an Industrial Education in an Industrial Society," *Proceedings of the Second Pan-American Scientific Conference*, vol. 4, 1915, p. 222.

mobility is tied to educational achievement runs stronger than in that earlier era, buttressed with statistics about the relation between schooling and employment benefits. The entire focus of the Youth Act of 1980 was on young people who either drop out of high school or earn a diploma without acquiring the skills they need for employment. The Vice President's Task Force on Youth Employment called attention to these youth in its summary report:

There are nearly 44 million Americans ages fourteen to forty-five. Of those, 24 million are in the critical sixteen- to twenty-one-year age span, the period of "transition" from school to work. For the vast majority of these young people . . . that transition is made reasonably well. . . . For almost four million others, though, things do not go so smoothly. Their transition is bumpy and difficult, and they face a serious risk of not completing it successfully.[7]

Earlier efforts of the Carter Administration in 1977 to deal with this problem population had concentrated on creating employment and training programs under CETA through the Youth Employment and Demonstration Projects Act (YEDPA). These programs were administered by "prime sponsors" and channeled largely through community-based organizations. The Youth Initiative of 1980 began with a new approach that gave a larger role to the school system. Essentially the decision was to focus more on a preventive effort aimed at younger people in junior and senior high school. The Youth Act of 1980 envisioned a federal allocation of approximately $1 billion for the education system to match another $1 billion for the CETA system. Significantly, however, the main thrust of this educational solution was not vocational education but basic skills. The Secretary of Education, Shirley Hufstedler, described the approach succinctly in her testimony before Congress:

The young people most at risk are the children of the poor, a disproportionate number of whom are minorities. They are failing to enter the labor force primarily because they reach young adulthood without basic skills, including the ability to read, write, and compute. They are further handicapped by the lack of any real work experience, and by

7. The Vice President's Task Force on Youth Employment, *A Summary Report of the Vice President's Task Force on Youth Employment* (Washington, D.C.: The White House, 1980), p. 11. Hereafter cited as *Summary Report of the Vice President's Task Force.*

the lack of opportunity to develop the skills and attitudes necessary to get and keep a job.[8]

Vocational education was pushed by some as the most important remedy for easing the transition from school to work for this problem population. Gene Bottoms, Executive Director for the American Vocational Association, argued strongly that opportunities for vocational training in depressed communities are not equal to those in the nation at large.[9] In the Administration draft of the Youth Act of 1980, 25 percent of the education funds were earmarked for vocational programs. Whereas in an earlier era vocational education was perceived as the foundation of equal opportunity, the "great and crying need" of the 1980s was for basic skills.

The movement for vocational education in 1915 drew some of its strongest support from the business community. The drive for basic skills in 1980 had equally strong support from the same quarter. It is interesting to contrast the attitudes of business in that earlier era with those of today. For example, in 1913 the National Association of Manufacturers expressed its views on the purpose of vocational education as follows:

It is the purpose of vocational education to save, educationally, that 50 percent of the children of the land who now leave school by the end of the sixth grade, undirected, unskilled, uninformed, and to train them and others of all ages in the essentials of successful and happy workers in their chosen occupations, in commerce, manufacturing, in agriculture, and in home making.[10]

In 1980, however, the Vice President's Task Force on Youth Employment reported a different kind of concern on the part of employers:

At Task Force Roundtables around the country, employers told the same story—that a high school diploma no longer is a good indicator

8. Shirley Mount Hufstedler, "Statement on the Youth Act of 1980" (S. 2385) before the Subcommittee on Education, Arts, and Humanities of the Committee on Labor and Human Resources, U.S. Senate, 96th Congress, 2d Session, March 7, 1980.

9. Gene Bottoms, "Statement on the Youth Act of 1980" before the Subcommittee on Employment Opportunities of the Committee on Education and Labor, House of Representatives, 96th Congress, 1st Session, June 26, 1979.

10. *Report of the Commission on Vocational Education*, vol. 2, p. 101.

of the skills of job applicants. High school students cannot even fill out application forms correctly. Employers say their concerns are not about whether young people have been trained for specific jobs. What they do want, and must have, are employees who can add and subtract, read and write.[11]

The extent to which employers influenced the policy process in favor of vocational education in 1914 has been well documented. That was the whole basis for Dewey's opposition to the Commission on Vocational Education. The same strong influence of employers is evident in the policy analysis for the Youth Act of 1980. Since employers hold the strings to job opportunities, they set the tone for equality of educational opportunity. This is starkly apparent in statements by the key policy formulators for the education component of the Youth Act of 1980:

You'd go around the country and these employers would say over and over again: "Hey, these kids don't have what we need. They can't do the things we need done." The first or fifth or tenth time, you're skeptical. You think it's an excuse of employers who just don't want to hire inner-city kids, and it clearly is some of that. But when you hear it everywhere in the country, over and over again, they clearly can't be making it up. It was an insistent drumbeat, and we had to attend to the fact that the schools, in the minds of the employers of this country, are producing too many kids who don't have the necessary tools to hold a job.[12]

The most useful thing we did was the Roundtables where we sat down with small business people in the morning and large business people in the afternoon, and asked them about youth employment, the minimum wage, vocational education. We would not have had the emphasis on basic skills if it was not for the Roundtables. You just can't sit through three hours and then three more hours, in five cities across the country and hear employers say "I just can't find kids who can read and write," without it having an impact.[13]

The most suasive evidence that came out of all the Vice President's Task Force stuff came from the anecdotal records with the private quar-

11. *Summary Report of the Vice President's Task Force,* p. 20.

12. Interview with Peter Edelman, Consultant to the Vice President's Task Force on Youth Employment, Washington, D.C., June 25, 1980.

13. Interview with Thomas Glynn, Executive Director, Vice President's Task Force on Youth Employment, June 19, 1980.

ter. Basically they were saying the kids can't handle the stuff—reading, writing, arithmetic. For many jobs you don't have to know how to read and write and compute except in emergencies, but then you need to know how to understand the emergency instructions. You can't afford to have someone who can't communicate that way.[14]

Perhaps the most significant lesson from this historical contrast is not the shift from vocational education to basic skills in the quest for equal opportunity. Rather, it is the continuity of approach in allowing employers to prescribe the kind of education that will provide opportunity. The solution, both then and now, is devised in terms of fitting the peg to the hole, or assisting the individual to meet the demands of the employer. Dewey's plea for a broader educational quest to develop the person first, leaving the employer with the task of adapting the job opportunity to the needs and abilities of the worker, remains more than ever a Utopian dream.

The Relation of Education to Economic Growth

While social concerns were important for the 1914 Commission on Vocational Education, the main argument for federal aid to vocational education was "the crying economic need":

There is a great and crying need of providing vocational education of this character for every part of the United States—to conserve and develop our resources; to promote a more productive and prosperous agriculture; to prevent the waste of human labor; to supplement apprenticeship; to increase the wage-earning power of our production workers; to meet the increasing demand for trained workmen; to offset the increased cost of living. Vocational education is therefore needed as a wise business investment for this Nation, because our national prosperity and happiness are at stake and our position in the markets of the world can not otherwise be maintained.[15]

The argument was developed in great detail, even to the point of a cost-benefit analysis which showed the return on vocational training over a lifetime to be six times the cost. The rhetoric often verged on hyperbole, describing vocational education as a panacea

14. Interview with Marshall Smith, Assistant Commissioner of Education for Policy Studies, U.S. Department of Education, Washington, D.C., June 20, 1080.

15. Report of the Commission on Vocational Education, vol. 1, p. 12.

for all the economic problems of the nation. Reasons other than economic ones were advanced by the 1914 Commission, particularly the social and educational need and the overwhelming public sentiment in favor of vocational education. But in justifying federal aid, the first and strongest argument was in terms of what vocational training would do for the economy.

The Youth Initiative of 1980 presents an interesting contrast. The entire *Summary Report* of the Vice President's Task Force is written from the vantage point of helping disadvantaged youth achieve personal fulfillment through meaningful employment. The report begins and ends on this note:

In November of 1979, 2,695,000 young people actively looked for work for fifteen weeks or more, but could not find it. Many more were too discouraged to look. When young people go without jobs, all of us are hurt. Youth unemployment touches us in many different ways. For a teenager trying to get a start, it's a stone wall of failure, and for the young adult, it's a closing out of life's options. . . . "Dreams are a terrible thing to waste," President Carter said. "We cannot let the dreams of our young people die."[16]

Throughout the entire report, and indeed throughout the year-long process of policy analysis of the Task Force, the implications of youth unemployment for the nation's economy were scarcely mentioned. None of the issue papers commissioned by the Task Force dealt with that problem. The need was viewed predominantly as a "festering social problem." The Administration's motivation stemmed both from a genuine concern for this unfortunate segment of American society, and from a desire to satisfy certain political constituencies. A White House memorandum to the Vice President in the early stages of the Task Force indicates this clearly:

Despite Administration efforts, youth unemployment remains a festering social problem. . . .
The three objectives indicated above would allow us to provide leadership on a bread and butter issue that is of central concern to the Black leadership, the Chicano and Puerto Rico leadership, big city Mayors,

16. *Summary Report of the Vice President's Task Force*, front and back covers.

particularly in the Northeast, and people concerned about education all over the country.[17]

This focus on the social need was, of course, totally consistent with the Carter Administration's approach. The Youth Employment Initiative was President Carter's main domestic policy issue in 1980. In retrospect, this may have been one cause of his political demise: the voting public was more concerned with the economy.

This analysis is not suggesting that either economic or social considerations are more important in addressing the problems of education and work. Rather the lesson seems to be that political considerations inevitably exert a dominant influence on public policy whenever the issues of education and work are confronted.[18]

Control of Vocational Training

In the early debate over vocationalism in the schools, the question of control was pervasive. Initially the conflict was between labor unions and employers. Labor feared the establishment of private vocational schools under the control of employers, offering a narrow trade training suitable to the needs of business but detrimental to the broader educational development of young workers:

There is also evident some apprehension that this proposed industrial education may ultimately give way to an attempt on the part of large commercial interests, whereby the opportunities of the workers' children for a general education will be limited, and which will tend to make the workers more submissive and less independent.[19]

To circumvent domination of vocational training by business

17. Stuart Eizenstat, Assistant to the President for Domestic Affairs and Policy, William Spring, Domestic Policy Staff, and Kitty Higgins, Domestic Policy Staff, "Memorandum to Walter Mondale, Vice President of the United States, January 31, 1979."

18. It is interesting to contrast the congressional testimony of the American Vocational Association on the Youth Act of 1980 with their more recent statements before Congress on the reauthorization of the Vocational Education Act under the Reagan administration. There is a noticeable shift in the arguments for vocational education on the basis of bolstering the nation's economy. By the same token, the position papers for the Vocational Education Act reauthorization drafted by the U.S. Department of Education in late 1980 have been discarded and a whole new set of papers focusing on the implications for the national economy is being formulated.

19. "Report of the Commission on Industrial Relations, American Federation of Labor (1915)," in *American Education and Vocationalism*, ed. Lazerson and Grubb, pp. 110-14.

interests, labor supported public rather than private vocational education. Ultimately this approach was endorsed by labor, employers, and educators, and the issue became the control of publicly sponsored vocational programs. This battle was waged at the local level as many school districts instituted separate vocational schools. Proponents of these separate vocational schools argued that vocational training should be kept out of the control of academic educators lest it be "watered down" and cease to be truly vocational. On the other hand, the opponents of a separate vocational system argued that separate systems would be divisive and would promote inequality and class distinctions. In the end, the country settled for a differentiated curriculum within comprehensive high schools.[20]

In the Youth Initiative of 1980, the question of who should control vocational training was still being debated. Equality of opportunity was again the underlying issue, but new dimensions were added to the argument, among them competition for funds among education interest groups and a struggle for control of vocational training between the school system and community-based organizations (CBOs).

The labor unions were relatively passive in the Youth Initiative of 1980. The AFL-CIO testified briefly at the congressional hearings, supporting federal funds to create more jobs, opposing a subminimum wage, and rejecting any infringement on the opportunities of adult workers for employment. Compared with the vigorous role played by the unions in the 1915 debate on vocational training, the unions of today were almost silent bystanders.

Employers were more involved than the unions, but their position had changed radically from that earlier era. There was no single strong voice speaking for employers reminiscent of the National Association of Manufacturers in 1915. Nor did they appear to place their hopes in any federally sponsored employment and training legislation. They certainly were not promoting vocational education as essential for the national economy. Their influence on policy was significant (as mentioned above), but their posture was more one of willingness to cooperate with the Youth Initiative rather than a militant effort to control the policy process. They

20. Lazerson and Grubb, *American Education and Vocationalism*, pp. 33-40.

urged that the limited resources of the public schools be used to provide sound fundamental skills and good work habits, and manifested a readiness to invest in their own training programs for the people they hire. Underlying their position was the fact that many large employers already maintain their own vocational skill training programs.

The struggle for control of the education component of the Youth Act of 1980 was waged among the many education interest groups, and between the education groups and the CBOs. In the Hearings of the Commission on Vocational Education in 1914, there were only two education groups involved; in 1980 there were more than twenty education groups actively vying for control of the funding and programs. The American Vocational Association (AVA) was active early in the policy process, testifying before Congress on other employment and training bills in early 1979, and even drafting their own bill advocating that all the education funds for youth employment be channeled through an amendment to the Vocational Education Act. The American Federation of Teachers (AFT) became involved in June, 1979, arguing that the public school system should control the education component of employment and training programs. In October, 1979, when it became evident that the Administration was planning a major education effort to address the problem of youth employment, a coalition of eleven major education groups known as "The Forum" entered the fray. Organizing their own "Education Task Force on Youth Policy," they joined forces with AVA and other education groups to present a united education front for lobbying with the Administration and Congress.

Within the education coalition there was a struggle between AVA and the other groups over the proportion of funds to be allocated to vocational education and whether the funds would be administered by the State Boards of Vocational Education or by the Local Education Agencies (LEAs). AVA feared that vocational programs would be "watered down" if the academic people got control of the administration of funds. A further problem stemmed from the existence of many "area vocational centers" serving more than one school district. The Administration proposal to channel funds through the LEAs left problems with how such institutions would be included. In the end, AVA agreed to reduce their claims on the education funds from 50 to 25 percent, but the vocational education funds were left under the control of the State Boards of Vocational Education.

A more bitter struggle for control of the education programs under the Youth Act of 1980 was between the education groups and the CBOs. Many of the education groups felt that CETA employment and training programs were creating a parallel education system in competition with the public schools. They viewed this new system as less accountable, as not tied into a governance structure that was democratic, and as encouraging students to leave school. The strongest voice against CETA-supported education and training programs run by CBOs was that of Albert Shanker, President of AFT:

We have watched with dismay over the years the development of what we consider to be a federally funded alternative series of school systems . . . where the Federal government has essentially set up institutions other than the public schools, and I might say, pretty much on the assumption that because test scores are going down and we have problems with truancy and other problems in the public schools, that therefore, the public schools are not good, and we ought to try some other way to provide these various educational services. . . .
The federal government has no business providing direct grants to storefront operations to provide educational services.[21]

On the other side, opponents of the school system were indeed charging that the schools have failed the disadvantaged poor. They claimed it was absurd to expect dropouts to return happily to the very institutions which had failed them. The Youth Act of 1980 basically opted to give the school system another chance, but opponents criticized it as a "teacher employment initiative" that would be used "to minimize teacher lay-offs, not to develop innovative programs."[22] Representative Shirley Chisholm of New York, one of the foremost critics of public school control over "education and work" programs, introduced her own bill to establish

21. Albert Shanker, Statement before the Subcommittee on Education, Arts, and Humanities of the Committee on Labor and Human Resources on S. 2385, U.S. Senate, 96th Congress, 2d Session, June 17, 1980.

22. *Education Daily*, 7 March 1980.

local alternative education programs which would be run by non-profit community-based organizations.

In summary, the issue of who should control "education and work" programs was every bit as important in 1980 as in 1915. The role of labor unions and employers was much diminished, and there was the new element of partisan squabbles among interest groups over how to divide the funds. But the basic issue of equality of opportunity still lay at the heart of this struggle for control. Some, like Representative George Miller of California, feared that the vocational education establishment could not be trusted to serve the needs of minorities. Others feared that the public schools at large were failing disadvantaged groups and dropouts. The issue was whether the schools or the CBOs were better able to provide a more equal educational opportunity to disadvantaged youth.

Conclusion

The relationship between education and work was a major problem in the early years of America's industrial development and remains such today. In 1915, the problem was seen in terms of both the national economy and social needs. In 1980, the focus was on social concerns. In both eras, the social concern was basically the same: equality of opportunity measured in terms of employment, with education as the stepping stone to upward mobility. Employers in both eras played a decisive role in prescribing the kind of education required. In 1915, they were strong advocates of vocational training; today they are more concerned about functional literacy. In 1915, all hopes settled on the public school system; today this confidence is diminished, although most people still feel the public school system is our best chance and worth trying to reform.

This brief historical contrast has touched on only a few of the issues relating to education and work; others can only be alluded to here. In 1915, the discussion included a good deal of concern about how children learn, various theories of educational psychology, and philosophical arguments over the objectives of education. Today the tenor of the discussion is devoid of such issues; education is presumed to be simply a matter of skills to be acquired. In 1915, attitudes and moral values were a major concern. Today there is no mention of morals or values but the issue is still discussed in terms of work attitudes. The Youth Act of 1980 preferred to speak of these attitudes as "employment skills," but the legislation had difficulty defining them and was curiously silent about how they would be taught.

In 1915, the idea of allocating public funds to create jobs for the unemployed was never mentioned. That strategy was born in Roosevelt's "New Deal" and remains a major issue today. The approach to counseling has certainly become more sophisticated in the contemporary discussion, although in practice teachers may still be "sorting" students as much as ever. In short, there are numerous issues related to education and work in the early years of America's industrial development which are still vital today. The discussion of "education and work" is apparently destined to be perennial.

CHAPTER II

Vocational Education Patterns in the United States

GORDON I. SWANSON

Introduction

The greatest documents of American history are those conveying the great promises made to Americans—immigrants and each succeeding generation borne of either immigrants or native Americans. The greatest of these documents involve the promise of freedom, equality, and opportunity combined with diminishing burdens associated with class, religion, or ethnic origin. The magnificence of these promises is unmatched in all of western tradition.

But promises are not enough; individuals and communities need blueprints for their hopes. They are necessary for exercise of the promised freedoms and for developing the avenues leading to opportunities. In one form or another, vocational education emerged early and securely to a central position on the public agenda as one of the blueprints. From its early beginnings in an evolving nation, vocational education has been held loosely in the net of the constitutional base, albeit firmly in the grip of a statutory base.

The amendments to the United States Constitution came in two batches. The first ten grew out of the grievances of the colonists against the dominant and arbitrary power of the state—imprisonment by executive order, taxation without legislative authorization, interference with the rights of individuals, and the like. They stressed noninterference with what were regarded as the *natural* rights of all people.

The subsequent batch of sixteen amendments became possible only after citizens were willing to regard the federal government as a nonhostile agent and as a tolerable intruder into private or community affairs to promote the general welfare. The second batch represented a shift from natural rights to *human rights*, the latter requiring widespread performance for their realization (for example, abolition of slavery, assurance of no sex discrimination, elimination of poll taxes, and so forth).

While vocational education is not mentioned in the amendments, the spirit or the dynamic which guided both batches of amendments had a powerful influence on the origin of vocational education and on its current status. In the early "noninterference" stage of the first ten amendments, decisions were made about vocational education which were just as inalienable as if they had been included in the Bill of Rights. In the spirit of rejecting interference, they rejected, for example, the European style of the system of apprenticeship training. Indeed, by the time of the revolution, apprenticeships in the United States had already been reduced to five years from the standard seven-year pattern of Europe, and the craft guild system, which survived for another seventy-five years in Europe, was already dead in America.

In the spirit of noninterference that surrounded the first ten amendments, the system of apprenticeship was seen as an exercise of power, a submission to indenturing involving a master's domination over orphans, bastards, the poor, and those who were required to accept such a circumstance owing to their subservient station in life or to repay the costs of passage to America. It was a system from which individuals sought to escape. It appeared inimical to the promise of freedom. From this early repute, the system of apprenticeship in America never recovered. An entire institutional framework emerged to take its place and the American and European patterns of preparing a work force were soon on different tracks.

A second decision was made about vocational education in this early period of self-determination and rejection of interference from dominant authority. It was to choose occupation-specific rather than employer-specific preparation for all or most preemployment preparation for work. From the very beginning, Americans were imbued with the Horatio Alger mentality; they built their hopes on the possibility of moving up the rungs on occupational ladders. While employer-specific kinds of on-the-job training emerged as a very important type of postemployment training, institutionally-based, occupation-specific preparation at the preemployment level emerged as the highly preferred format. It appeared to offer the hope of wider choice among potential employers and a clearer view of the stratification within the occupational structure. Even the labor union movement in America appeared to be influenced by these early decisions. Unions in America are industry-wide in their organization rather than job-specific as they are in many European countries.

A REVOLUTION IN THINKING

It would be a mistake to assume that a framework for thinking about past and present vocational education grew solely, or even mainly, out of political revolution or the desire to reject prerevolutionary patterns of education or training. It also grew out of a revolution in thinking about the human condition and the promises which could, in fact, be included in the blueprints for the hopes that each generation had for the next.

Crucial to this revolution was the writing of three individuals—Jean Jacques Rousseau (1712-1778), John B. Basedow (1724-1790), and Johann Heinrich Pestalozzi (1746-1826). Their work had an important impact on the conceptual framework of vocational education and training in America, on the long struggle to link general and vocational education and to minimize school-subject segregation, and on the tenuous task of separating the vocational/occupational orientation from welfare-oriented income maintenance or charity.

Rousseau's writing influenced all aspects of French life and culture including the French Revolution itself. He shocked his countrymen, his colleagues, and his other readers when he urged in *Emile* (1762) that work experience become a part of general education for developing intelligence, skills of observation, persistence, and skill. In this view he was soon joined by an admirer, Basedow, whose volume entitled *Appeal to the Friends of Mankind and to Men of Power Concerning School and Studies and Their Influence on Public Welfare* (1768) became the rage of his contemporaries along with many new friends. In it he urged a blending of the training of hand and mind. He was hailed as a champion, and he was urged onward and enriched by the voluntary contributions given him to support his work.

Pestalozzi first tried to demonstrate his educational ideas by creating a school. It attracted very little attention. In disappointment, he wove his ideas into a romantic novel, *Leonard and Gertrude* (1782), which catapulted the ideas into popular conversation. Tears flowed on the cheeks of readers as they identified with a teacher, Gertrude, whose teaching included the development of self-respect, craft skills, character, and the general skills of literacy. It was a testimony for the need to revolutionize general education by including vocational training, to regard such training as something other than the exercises then commonly conducted in poor houses, on poor farms, and in general to accommodate the children of the poor.

This was revolutionary thinking. The writings of Rousseau, Basedow, and Pestalozzi were not unknown to the framers of the American Constitution and the Bill of Rights. They continued as powerful influences over the thinking, writing, and acting of such individuals as Horace Mann, Justin Morrill, David Snedden, John Dewey, Charles Prosser, and many others. To mention this background is not merely to recount historical milestones but to emphasize that the revolution which began more than 200 years ago is still underway, that there are many for whom the revolution is still an unacceptable aberration, and many others for whom the revolution is the act of creating an acceptable future.

Types of Education

The structures and practices of education are not easily altered, however, even with widespread acceptance of principles implying the ease of change. A pluralistic society tends to opt for structures and practices of education that reflect the accepted pluralism. Accordingly, four main types of education appeared on the American scene.

The first type includes the instructive activities—often informal —developed in basic communities or work settings: families, villages, apprenticeships, voluntary organizations, factories, farms, and business settings. This type of education imparts knowledge, skill, and attitudes of great value to the recipient and to the community. Its main characteristics are that it is work-oriented, it is not driven by formulas that require generation of enrollments, and it fits those receiving it to the existing social, economic, and occupational structure. It does very little to motivate recipients to change such structures.

The second type is a system of formal education intended to produce and reproduce a social and economic setting in which an educated elite performs the leadership role. The emphasis is placed on knowledge, often symbolic or scientific and abstract, which is detached from the exigencies identified with work or work roles. Its examples include the liberal arts tracks at various levels of education, with completion occurring after a rather long period of study.

A third type combines education with training and emphasizes technological knowledge and skill as essential requirements for transforming as well as accommodating the current occupational structure. It produces technocrats, engineers, planners, and skilled workers. It is rarely an independent system; it is composed of vocational education, university-level technological education, and various other forms of instruction for increasing the efficiency of the different sectors of agriculture and industry. It is often associated with, and dependent upon, other types of education.

A fourth type is agency-oriented and is identified with the missions of government agencies, with its strongest identity at the federal level and, in a few instances, with a linkage to parallel agencies at state levels. Although the government agencies are involved in the task of carrying out the intent of legislative authorization, the central focus is neither on education nor on training; it is on addressing the immediate problems of the agency or the remedial problems of special target groups as these problems or groups are assigned by statute to the purview of the agency. Most of the activities involve means-oriented benefits such as employment, veterans' retraining, job search, military preparedness, civil rights, and various programs intended to assist special groups. With few exceptions, the fourth type tends to reinforce the current occupational structure and the current status of the recipients of program benefits. Most of the education and/or training programs are for a relatively short duration. The extent of this fourth type is seen in table 1.

Vocational education has not developed solely or mainly within

TABLE 1

FEDERAL OUTLAYS AND OBLIGATIONS FOR WORK AND TRAINING
PROGRAMS, BY AGENCY AND PROGRAM, FISCAL YEAR 1979
($ IN MILLIONS)

AGENCY AND PROGRAM	OBLIGATIONS	OUTLAYS
Total, all agencies	$15,257.6	$14,452.5
Department of Agriculture		
Youth Conservation Corps	60.0	62.7
Department of Commerce		
Job Opportunities Program	0.0	2.0
Department of Health and Human Services (HHS)		
Social Services Training and Employment	223.0	223.0
HHS Vocational Rehabilitation	1,018.8	965.9
Subtotal, HHS	1,241.8	1,188.9
Department of Interior		
Indian On-the-Job Training	1.2	1.2
Indian Institutional Training	17.6	17.6
Indian Direct Placement	14.2	14.2
Indian Action Teams	22.4	22.4
Subtotal, Interior	55.4	55.4
Department of Justice		
Prisoner Training	5.0	1.9
Department of Labor		
Older Americans	220.6	207.8
Work Incentive (WIN) Program	380.1	385.0
Employment Services		
ES Services	696.9	696.9
Food Stamp Recipient Placement	28.7	25.4
Employment Security Automation		
Program (ESAP)	22.7	22.7
Subtotal, ES	748.3	745.0
Employment and Training Assistance (CETA)		
Title II - A, B, C	1,910.1	1,801.5
Title II - D	2,442.8	1,755.4
Indians	73.2	66.1
Migrants	91.8	90.2
Other national programs	168.3	122.9
Program support	57.5	46.5
Summer Youth Employment Program	622.2	659.5
Job Corps	400.8	379.6
Young Adult Conservation Corps	226.7	273.2
Youth Community Conservation and		
Improvement Projects (YCCIP)	81.9	90.7
Youth Incentive Entitlement Pilot Projects	82.7	76.6
Youth Employment and Training		
Programs (YETP)	427.3	480.1
Skill Training Improvement Program	34.0	136.5
Help through Industry Retraining		
and Employment	4.5	47.3

TABLE 1—*(Continued.)*

AGENCY AND PROGRAM	OBLIGATIONS	OUTLAYS
Migrant Initiative	0.1	16.2
Indian Initiative	2.1	15.6
Private sector program	32.6	3.7
Labor PRM	0.0	0.0
YCCIP R & D	11.5	12.7
YETP R & D	67.3	75.4
Targeted Jobs Tax Credit		
Administration (TJTC)	10.3	5.8
Welfare Reform Demonstration	23.5	2.4
CETA Outlay Shortfall	0.0	0.0
Subtotal, CETA	6,811.2	6,157.9
Temporary Employment Assistance (Title VI)	3,317.2	3,285.2
Other, Department of Labor		
Antidiscrimination (Employment Service Assistance)	5.5	5.5
Labor Market Information (Bureau of Labor Statistics)	36.9	36.2
Program Administration (Employment and Training Administration)	114.0	113.8
Contract Compliance (Employment Service Assistance)	41.5	39.5
Subtotal, Other Department of Labor	197.9	194.5
Subtotal, Labor	**11,675.3**	**10,975.4**
Department of Education		
College Work-Study	574.0	542.0
Vocational Education	682.9	680.7
Education PRM	0.0	0.0
Subtotal, Education	**1,256.9**	**1,222.7**
Department of Housing and Urban Development		
Community Development	**30.0**	**20.4**
Veterans Administration (VA)		
Veterans Skill Training	505.8	508.3
Veterans Assistance Centers	11.0	11.0
Veterans Vocational Rehabilitation	109.1	109.6
Subtotal, VA	**625.9**	**628.9**
Other Independent Agencies (OIA)		
Equal Employment Opportunity Commission	105.6	92.5
Other Contract Compliance	0.0	0.0
Agency Federal Youth Programs (AFYP)		
Summer Aides	36.2	36.2
Stay-in-School	92.8	92.8
Federal Summer Employment	72.7	72.7
Subtotal, AFYP	201.7	201.7
Subtotal, OIA	**307.3**	**294.2**

SOURCE: U. S. Office of Management and Budget. This table was published in National Commission for Employment Policy, *Sixth Annual Report* (Washington, D.C.: National Commission for Employment Policy, 1980), pp. 138-39.

any of the four types of education. It has developed as an accommodation to all of them. One might think that it would have fitted automatically into the third type, the combination of education and training. Here the limitations have been the existence of federal statutes, which have consistently defined vocational education as instruction at "less than baccalaureate level." Vocational education is therefore a proper description of the preparation of such workers as tool makers, mechanics, nurses' aides, sales clerks, printers, and computer programmers. On the other hand, the preparation for such occupations as engineering, dentistry, architecture, forestry, and nursing is properly described as professional.

Vocational education has not developed as a system but rather as a collection of enterprises identified to a greater or lesser degree with every type of education and most types of institutions. Yet the most distinguishable characteristic of the various forms of occupational preparation is not the type of education chosen but rather its duration or length.

Long and Short Education

For administrative and organizational convenience, American education is classified as elementary, secondary, and higher education. A formal educational structure has risen to accommodate this classification. Yet for those who enter the occupations there is a de facto classification that is much closer to reality. It is, simply, *long* education and *short* education. Long education requires a much higher level of public expenditure per student; it allows the acquisition of more employability skills, and it leads to the status and rewards of a higher position in the occupational structure. Short education consumes a lower level of public expenditure per student; it has a disproportionate number of the poor and otherwise disadvantaged, and it leads to the status and rewards associated with the lower positions in the occupational structure. Included among those who receive a short education are the drop-outs, about 25 percent of the teenage population.

Although long and short education have not emerged as terms in the lingua franca of educational planning or the design features of educational reform, there is no way to disguise the reality of the differentials that exist in the cost, consequences, and groups served by the two kinds of education. Nor is there any way of disguising the fact that much employment-related education and training, including vocational education, is conventionally designed and planned as short education.

Sharp contrasts between the design and organization of long versus short occupational preparation can be seen by looking at the consequential effects of the two best known pieces of work-oriented enabling legislation, the Morrill Act (1862) and the Smith-Hughes Act (1917). Along with their follow-up amendments and attachments, both pieces of legislation had as much effect on the design and organization of occupational education as on its delivery.

The Morrill Act had the effect of extending a number of occupations to full professional status, particularly in engineering and agriculture, although perhaps as much in the extent to which other professional schools also grew out of the movement. The effect, therefore, was to provide a long education to some who previously had access to only a short education, including, inter alia, teachers. It generated some novel educational structures, one of which accommodated the Agricultural Extension Service, the only effective, inquiry-informed, lifelong education system in the United States.

In contrast, the Smith-Hughes Law created, and subsequent legislation maintained, a limit on the extent of training. Moreover, it was swept into a bureaucratic system which had been designed, organized, and rule-governed to focus on nonvocational education. To symbolize accommodation and custody, many state boards of education designated themselves as a "State Board of Vocational Education." Such actions served administrative convenience, but ordinarily they kept vocational education as a peripheral responsibility. Meanwhile, other state boards or agencies emerged to claim competence for providing employment-related education and training. The consequences are what might be expected; there are few, if any, states in the United States that have a state governing body possessing the convening authority and the creative leadership needed to prepare people to do society's work, which is the purpose of all education, and to carry out such a mission without adhering to the traditional conventions of long and short education.

If racial segregation in the public schools of the United States is contrary to constitutional rights, an absurd notion only a generation ago, how long will it be before the amendments covering life, liberty, and property are invoked to ensure guarantees against the segregating influences of education or training programs designed for some to be short, less expensive, and in many forms as acts of charity? Can a Constitution that guarantees "liberty" be interpreted to allow any of the education and/or training conditions that deprive individuals of autonomy, freedom, and ultimately, self-respect? In its design features, vocational education and/or training remains unfinished as a blueprint for the hopes of many individuals or the promises of the great American documents. The revolution in thinking about these issues has not been followed by revolutionary experiments to test the possibilities in the hopes, the strength in the promises, or the absurdities in both.

During the last half of the twentieth century, the American educational enterprise has intensified its tracking of students by ability. The National Longitudinal Study data shown in table 2 are revealing and irrefutable. Vocational education students are significantly lower in both socioeconomic class and ability than other students.

When confronted by the paradox between the promise of opportunity and practice of grouping students, most educators avoid the paradox and attempt to evade the implied accusation that it is the American educational enterprise itself which harbors the problems and remains indifferent to it. The usual response is that the school and the myriad of government programs in and out of the school are neutral; they merely serve to accommodate the natural segregation of students that is associated with subject matter or lifestyle. Not generally acknowledged are any of the effects of the organization of education or of instructional method, including the expanding propensity of federal legislation to resort to methodological solutions, which often consume so much time in compliance management that the time left for education is diminished.

It is not unfair to say, in summary, that American education is design-poor and that it suffers from a condition in which there is an abundance of superordinates preoccupied with fine-tuning and a dearth of leaders. Meanwhile, vocational education and training appears to have a residual claim on, or assignment to, marginality with respect to both students and resources.

TABLE 2

PERCENT OF SECONDARY SCHOOL STUDENTS IN THREE PROGRAM
AREAS, BY PERSONAL CHARACTERISTICS (SEX, PLACE OF RESIDENCE,
FAMILY INCOME, ACADEMIC ABILITY, AND ETHNIC BACKGROUND)[a]

CHARACTERISTIC	POPULATION DISTRIBUTION	PROGRAM AREA		
		Academic	General	Vocational
Sex				
Male	49.6	45	34	21
Female	50.4	41	30	29
Place of Residence				
Rural Area	22.2	30	38	32
Small City (50,000)	26.4	45	30	25
Medium City/Suburb	20.0	43	32	25
Suburb of Large City	16.5	58	26	16
Large City (100,000+)	14.8	47	29	24
Family Income				
Less than $7,500	27.9	28	38	34
$7,500 – 10,499	22.1	40	32	28
10,500 – 14,499	26.1	48	31	21
15,000 – 17,999	9.0	56	29	15
Over 18,000	14.9	65	24	11
Academic Ability[b]				
Low	29.8	17	45	38
Medium	44.3	44	33	23
High	25.9	77	16	7
Ethnic Category				
White	81.8	45	32	23
Black	13.4	33	33	34
Hispanic	4.8	29	41	20

SOURCES: William B. Fetters, *National Longitudinal Study of the High School Class of 1972: Student Questionnaire and Test Results by Sex, High School Program, Ethnic Category, and Father's Education* (Washington, D.C.: U.S. Government Printing Office, 1975); idem, *National Longitudinal Study of the High School Class of 1972: Student Questionnaire and Test Results by Academic Ability, Socioeconomic Status, and Region* (Washington, D.C.: U.S. Government Printing Office, 1976).

[a] Data used to construct this table were gathered by the National Longitudinal Study of the High School Class (twelfth grade) of 1972. Over 1,000 public and nonpublic schools participated in the study. The questionnaire was completed by 16,409 students.

[b] Academic ability was determined by combining test scores in four areas: Vocabulary, Reading, Mathematics, and Letter Groups. (The Letter Group test measures ability to find general concepts in a nonverbal context.) The High and Low groups represent the highest and lowest quartiles respectively and the Medium group includes the middle two quartiles.

Patterns of Organizing the Transitions from School to Work

The period of transition from school to a full-time, reasonably stable job in the adult work force or, if one prefers, the period of adolescence, is a mounting concern in the United States. The high unemployment rate for youth, particularly of minorities, is a major cause of the concern. This transitional period is much longer in the

United States than in most other western countries. The phenomenon of this prolonged transition has attributes worthy of careful examination and review; they are the consequences of decisions or traditions that are among the unexamined "givens" of the transition process. These attributes will be examined in the following paragraphs.

As has already been mentioned, Americans made an early decision to opt for institutionally based, occupation-specific preparation for work rather than the European style of apprenticeship training. Coupled with this decision is a requirement that all registered apprentices be high school graduates or possess certificates of General Education Development and be a minimum of sixteen years of age. In practical terms, this requires that all entrants to apprenticeships be a minimum of seventeen to eighteen years old and products of a prior selection process rather than members of the fifteen-year-old age category as is the case in much of Europe. The transition becomes much prolonged, accordingly, for those who choose the apprenticeship route as well as for those who do not.

The added value of remaining in the institutional setting until high school graduation may not be commensurate with the added penalty of failing to complete high school or even some post-high school training. Employing officers have come to use educational certificates and diplomas as screening devices and as bases of attaching penalties to those who do not possess them.

Certainly the transition has also been prolonged by the myriad of government-sponsored programs for youth. Often these programs offer incentives in the form of stipends, transportation, and other support services that delay the transition and leave individuals no better prepared for completing it.

The most important characteristic of this prolonged transition, especially for those remaining in school, is that it is a mixture of education and work. Part-time jobs are common for many, even in the early years of high school. This expands and becomes a normative pattern, a movement to and from education and work, by the late teens and into the early twenties. Almost three-quarters of all twelfth-grade students are employed part-time, with students enrolled in vocational courses working significantly more than nonvocational students. Twelfth-grade students enrolled in vocational education courses work in excess of twenty hours per week.[1]

Although this pattern of student employment (or the massive movement between education and work) has become a normative exercise, very little is known about it except, quite obviously, its existence. It is totally unorganized and unstructured. Virtually all of the employment is student initiated and unsupervised by school staff. Again, indifference marks the role of the school. The extent to which various types or intensities of student employment may offer advantages or disadvantages to subsequent employment or education is relatively unknown. Whether such part-time work opportunity is equally available to disadvantaged students and whether it compounds or alleviates their disadvantages are likewise unknown.

While the great majority of American youth graduates from high school, about 25 percent drop out without graduating, a figure that rises to as much as 55 percent in some of the inner cities. The national dropout figures are likely to be highly conservative because of the difficulty of getting accurate data and because all school finance formulas offer powerful incentives for maximizing school enrollment. Moreover, it has been estimated that as many as 700,000 minority youth have virtually "disappeared" from the system because they are neither counted among the employed, nor among the unemployed, nor are they in school.[2]

Efforts are made to encourage dropouts to return to schools, colleges, or special training programs. Most remain on the "outside" as a result of having missed the crucial qualification of high school graduation or its equivalent outside the schools, the general education diploma. In 1978, the 2670 GED Centers tested 640,000 persons, of whom 59 percent received a passing grade. Those taking the test had an average age of 25.5 years and an average of 9.9 years of formal school.[3] It is quite apparent that these individuals have an

1. Samuel S. Peng, William B. Fetters, and Andrew J. Kolstad, *High School and Beyond: A National Longitudinal Study for the 1980s* (Washington, D.C.: National Center for Educational Statistics, U.S. Department of Education, 1981), p. 19.

2. Organization for Economic Cooperation and Development, *Review of Youth Employment Policies in the United States* (Paris: Organization for Economic Cooperation and Development, 1980), p. 5.

3. American Council on Education, *The GED Statistical Report, 1978* (Washington, D.C.: American Council on Education, 1979).

exceedingly long transition from school to work and an education which has all of the limiting attributes, except for its duration, of being exceedingly "short."

The influence of vocational education and training on school dropout rates is a matter of great speculation. One form of argument holds that the presence of vocational education in schools is a strong incentive for teenagers to remain in school and, if this incentive were not present, the dropout rate would be much higher. Another form of argument holds that the employment programs conducted outside the school such as the youth programs of the Comprehensive Employment and Training Act (CETA) provide strong incentives (for example, stipends, health care, residence opportunities) to drop out of school, thus increasing the dropout rate. There are few data to support either argument, but there is clear evidence to show that national dropout rates have not fallen in the past decade.

Organizational Structure

The organizational structure of vocational education and training in the United States has many of the characteristics of assembled patchwork. Though it is intended to ease the movement of people toward their goals, this organizational patchwork can also lead to misdirection or mistake. Individuals moving through their formative years and on to a reasonably stable position in the work force are influenced by at least three important types of social institutions—the informal (family, community, voluntary activities, and so forth), the schools, and the work place. These institutions have their share of within and between system conflicts that influence all who pass through and, more importantly, each type of institution tends to operate as an entity that is sovereign and isolated. Follow-up studies of school graduates tend, for example, to emphasize the independent influence of the school rather than the interactive effects of the three institutions. Placement records tend to show only initial, postschool placement rather than work sequences related to family, part-time work, or school-related work experience.

There is at least one additional kind of structural barrier confronted by our example: the students attempting to move through the structure. Students are encouraged to acquire a rather clear view of a career path, a vertical movement with minimum delays and obstructions. What they actually encounter, however, is a sequence of horizontal barriers, different types of institutions at a succession of educational levels. What appears to be vertically oriented career paths turns out to be a horizontally organized educational structure where they encounter delay, redundancy, and problems of access.

The foregoing identifies some organizational considerations that are revealed neither in organizational charts nor in descriptions of institutional offerings. The following describes the organizational structure for the attendance functions of vocational education.

The formal educational enterprise of the United States consists of over 16,000 autonomous school districts that operate a combined total of over 88,000 public elementary and secondary schools. In addition, there are about 18,000 private elementary-secondary schools and more than 9,000 postsecondary institutions, two-thirds of which are privately operated. The detail of this structure is shown in table 3.

Almost all of the 24,000 high schools offer some mixture of general and vocational courses, even though the vocational offerings may be as limited as a casual approach to career education. About 6,000 of these high schools provide five or more sequential vocational programs and are thus often referred to as high schools with comprehensive vocational programs.

There are two types of secondary schools that specialize in vocational education at the secondary level—the area secondary vocational schools (ASVS) and the technical high schools. There are almost 1250 area secondary vocational schools (or centers), which may serve several attendance units within a single district or they may serve multidistricts. In a sense, they are adjuncts to their home high schools. Students may voluntarily transfer from a home school to an ASVS on a full-time basis or on a shared-time basis. Students may enroll in a choice of programs that may number as high as thirty or forty.

The 225 technical high schools are found in most of the major cities. Often they are specialized, rigorous, and enjoy enviable reputations. Ordinarily students attend on a full-time basis, taking

TABLE 3

A Selective Institutional Profile of Vocational Education
in the United States Including Elementary, Secondary,
and Postsecondary Institutions, 1978

Level	Approximate Number of Institutions Providing Programs		Comments
Elementary (grades 7-8)	all		Some combination of course work in career exploration or guidance, industrial practical arts, or home economics. Provided as separate courses or integrated grade courses.
Secondary (grades 9-12) Regular or comprehensive public schools			
Offering one to four sequential vocational programs	19,125		Programs one to four years in length, most frequently in business, home economics, and industrial courses, and/or personal skills courses on a one- to two-semester basis.
Offering five or more sequential vocational programs	4,875		Programs one to four years in length at a single school location.
Area vocational schools	1,250		Shared-time schools providing full-and/or part-time vocational instruction to students from feeder high schools. Multiple vocational offerings, frequently in excess of twenty-five per school, generally two to three years in length.
Specialized vocational schools	225		Specialized full-time schools for vocational instruction. Programs include both academic and vocational course work. Schools may specialize in a single area such as commerce or trade.
Postsecondary	Public	Private	
Vocational/technical	506	112	There are 1,955 public (enrollment, 712,150) and 7,382 private (enrollment, 991,805) post secondary schools, many of which offer advanced levels of instruction in vocational subjects. Many of these schools provide instruction that, with respect to level and content, is commonly found in secondary schools. Such programs are provided because the schools enroll (a) graduates of secondary schools and dropouts who were not previously enrolled in vocational programs, either by choice or because the programs were not available; (b) students whose occupational plans have changed; (c) students in shared-time programs who are dually enrolled in a secondary school and a postsecondary school.
Technical Institute	122	113	
Junior/Community College	788	201	
University/College	254	241	
Business/Commercial	4	1,297	
Cosmetology/Barber	0	2,163	
Flight School	5	1,059	
Hospital School	147	770	
Allied Health	114	245	
Arts/Design	0	254	
Trade School	14	736	
Other	1	191	

academic and occupational courses in the same school. The number of technical high schools has remained rather constant while the number of area vocational secondary schools has increased rapidly during the past decade or two.

At the postsecondary level the extent of the patchwork mentioned earlier becomes transparently obvious. More than 9,000 institutions, most of them private, compete for students. The range and complexity of this structure are shown in table 3.

An examination of table 3a will help to complete the picture of facilities for education and training. This table shows the extent of participation in various "nontraditional" vocational training programs operated by the U.S. Department of Labor. These programs are generally aimed at youth sixteen to twenty-one years of age, many of whom are secondary school dropouts.

Although it is possible to describe the general pattern of the organization of vocational education, further generalizations are risky. Variations among states in governance, funding, interinstitutional coordination, administration, and control are so great that even a very common type of institution, say a postsecondary technical institute, may be quite different from one state to another. Indeed, the terms "secondary," "postsecondary," "technical," and "comprehensive" lack descriptive precision as one looks at their use to identify programs in different states.

Left until the end of the discussion of organizational structure, but of sufficient importance to be at the beginning, is adult vocational education. It is the best illustration of the patchwork orientation of the structure and organization of vocational education. Illustrations are numerous. At the federal level there are separate advisory committees for adult education on one hand and vocational education on the other. Since each group courteously avoids the domain of the other, courtesy prevails over common sense and adult vocational education is avoided by both groups.

SOURCES FOR TABLE 3: W. Vance Grant and C. George Lind, *Digest of Education Statistics 1979* (Washington, D.C.: National Center for Education Statistics, 1979); Evelyn R. Kay, *Directory of Postsecondary Schools with Occupational Programs 1978* (Washington, D.C.: National Center for Education Statistics, 1978); Nickolas A. Osso, *Directory of Secondary Schools with Occupational Curriculums, Public-Nonpublic 1971* (Washington, D.C.: National Center for Education Statistics, 1973); National Center for Education Statistics, *Statistics of Public Elementary and Secondary Day Schools 1977-78, Final* (Washington, D.C.: National Center for Educational Statistics, 1978); Allan Woodruff et al., *National Study of Vocational Educational Systems and Facilities,* vol. 2 (Rockville, Md.: Westat, Inc.; 1978); U.S. Department of Labor and U.S. Department of Health and Human Services, *Employment and Training Report of the President* (Washington, D.C.: U.S. Government Printing Office, 1980).

TABLE 3a

APPROXIMATE NUMBER OF PARTICIPANTS IN VOCATIONAL
TRAINING PROGRAMS IN NONTRADITIONAL SECONDARY/
POSTSECONDARY ESTABLISHMENTS AND IN APPRENTICESHIP
PROGRAMS, 1979

U.S. DEPARTMENT OF LABOR PROGRAMS	NUMBER OF PARTICIPANTS	COMMENTS
Job Corps	85,000	Ninety-three residential centers; 83 percent of participants are nineteen years of age or younger; 86 percent are school dropouts; strong trade training component.
Youth Incentive Entitlement Pilot Projects	53,400	Provides the incentive of a guaranteed public job to assist disadvantaged students to remain in school or to return to earn a secondary school diploma.
Youth Employment Training Programs	413,600	Various approaches for dropouts and high-risk students, including educational vouchers. Seventy-six percent of participants are under the age of nineteen and 14 percent are under the age of fifteen. All are disadvantaged.
Youth Adult Conservation Corps	67,200	Work on conservation/water projects to provide employment to youth.
Youth Community Conservation and Improvement Programs	38,500	Community improvement work programs. Supervised work experience on community projects. Eighteen percent of participants have completed high school.
Summer Youth Employment Program	888,000	Summer employment with a nominal training and educational component. Eleven percent of participants have completed high school.
Title II B and C Activities		
Classroom training	569,425	Approximately half of the participants in Title II B and C programs were under twenty-two years of age and 48 percent were dropouts from elementary or secondary schools. Program objectives are marketable skill development and full-time unsubsidized employment.
On-the-job training	156,787	
Work experience	391,243	
Public service jobs	10,461	
Apprenticeship Training (Department of Labor, Bureau of Apprenticeship Training)	395,000	Receiving training under state and national apprenticeship programs in conjunction with trade unions; 131,000 new apprentices were registered/indentured in 1978.

SOURCES: See Table 3.

In federal appropriations, adult vocational education is combined in a "set-aside" allocated to postsecondary education. Since it has no natural institution-based nor client-based constituency, vocational adult education becomes a residual claimant to appropriations. At the local level, any type of eligible institution may initiate programs of adult vocational education. Most of the state regulations are, however, adapted from, or identical to, the operating regulations for the secondary or postsecondary level of vocational education. Vocational adult education remains, therefore, as the most patched-together part of vocational education and a further illustration of the condition described earlier as bureaucratically traditional and design-poor.

A Search for Definition

No educational endeavor matches or exceeds vocational education in its problems of definition. As a term, vocational education is sometimes employed to justify the limits of what may be funded and thus included as appropriate activities. Sometimes the term is used so broadly that it is almost limitless. Most uses of the term imply a diverse set of programs serving a wide range of students at different intensities and for different purposes.

THE STATUTORY BASIS OF DEFINITION

For many years, vocational education has been defined by the federal statutes which also provide funds to states and local communities. To obtain federal funds, states must apply to the federal level by submitting an application known as the State Plan, an agreement to accept the federal definition of vocational education as stated in federal law and as implemented in its funding formulas. The statutory basis of definition, though broad in principle, is more limited in implementation; it is limited to the scope and intensity of activities authorized in funding formulas, and it is limited to a federal description of who is permitted to be an administrative authority at the state level.

THE CLIENT BASIS OF DEFINITION

Individuals and groups in local communities have their own perceptions of what constitutes vocational education. The indicators of these perceptions are few but highly instructive. There is the willingness, for example, to support, through local tax levies, the programs that have been perceived locally as vocational education. When the 16,000 secondary school students participating in the National Longitudinal Study (see table 2) were asked to classify themselves by program, 43 percent of the students classified themselves in the college preparatory or academic program, 33 percent in general programs, and 24 percent in vocational programs of study. The reliability of self-classification is, of course, highly questionable. It is not known whether students classified themselves by the nature of their goals or by the nature of their course enrollments. Almost 90 percent of those classifying themselves in vocational programs were enrolled in only one course in vocational education, and the chances were rather good that the course did not qualify, by statutory definition, as an occupational course. Nevertheless, it is clear that there are prevailing perceptions of what constitutes vocational education and that these perceptions may have much or little relationship to any of the usual definitions.

THE PROGRAM BASIS OF DEFINITION

It is estimated that there are more than 400 different programs of instruction offered in vocational education. These are classified under eight major fields or areas—agriculture, distributive, health, occupational home economics, business and office, technical, trade and industry, and vocational consumer and homemaking education. There is, first of all, no natural cohesiveness for holding together such a diverse set of categories. There are enormous differences among the categories in subject matter, nature of clients, and in approach to instruction. Second, there are no standards for determining what constitutes a program—for example, standards involving organization, amount, level, or intensity of instruction. The difficulties in defining programs lead to further problems in describing enrollment. If one were to describe a program as a sequence of courses leading to some occupationally oriented goal, thus omitting enrollments in vocational courses taken as exploratory electives, the enrollment problem becomes somewhat more describable though not necessarily clear. There is still no assurance that course sequences in one category of instruction have any equivalence in terms of "time-on-task" with course sequences in another nor that the plural nature of courses is more programmatic than single courses. The difficulty of defining programs and their enrollments is shown in table 4, which shows three different enrollment counts by three different federal agencies.

TABLE 4

VOCATIONAL EDUCATION NATIONAL ENROLLMENTS, 1978, 1979
(IN MILLIONS)

LEVEL	ENROLLMENTS[a]		
	1978 BOAE Data	1979 VEDS	1979 OCR
Total enrollment	16.7	17.3	8.3
Total occupational enrollment	10.4[b]	7.7[b]	5.0
Secondary			
Occupational	4.9	3.1	
Consumer and Home Economics	2.8	2.7	1.0
Industrial Arts	1.5	1.7	0.6
Other nonoccupational	1.0	2.9[c]	1.4
Total secondary enrollment	10.2	10.4	5.7
Postsecondary			
Occupational	2.0	1.9	1.8
Nonoccupational	0.1	0.2	0.4
Total postsecondary enrollment	2.1	2.1	2.2
Adult			
Occupational	3.5	2.9	0.4
Nonoccupational	0.9	1.9	- -
Total adult enrollment	4.4	4.8	0.4

SOURCE: National Institute of Education, *The Vocational Education Study: Interim Report* No. 3 (Washington, D.C.: National Institute of Education, 1981), Section VI, p. 4.

[a] Bureau of Occupational and Adult Education (BOAE) and the Vocational Education Data Systems (VEDS) data include only enrollments in federally funded programs; Office of Civil Rights (OCR) data include only enrollments in institutions with five or more programs plus other institutions.

[b] Includes short-term adult enrollments.

[c] Includes all high school enrollments below grade eleven.

A PURPOSE-FOCUSED DEFINITION

Vocational education offers the hope of having positive effects on people (individuals and groups), families, and on communities. These expectations include: a widening latitude for job choice, initial and/or subsequent placement, opportunity for occupational mobility, movement upward on occupational ladders, and increased productivity as an employee or employer. But these hopes and expectations are interpreted quite differently at the various levels of decision making—local, state, and federal. There is an ongoing process of reconciling differences in the ways in which the purposes of vocational education may be viewed, differences in focus, as well as differences identified with different levels of administration and control.

It seems incredulous that the search for a definition of vocational education is still underway and that there is such diversity of perceptions about what it is or should be. Part of the reason may be that vocational education operates as a collection of overlapping democracies—local, state, and federal. Constituents at the local level (for example, families, communities, work sites) are also closer to the representatives elected to serve local jurisdictions (for example, school boards). Other levels of democratic governance, such as the state and the federal, are confronted by different lobbies and by different goal-setting forces. The tensions that arise among levels have a significant influence on evaluation of vocational education. Educational and/or training activities, which are difficult to define in generic terms, are also difficult to evaluate through any use of broad generic classifications. Vocational education is an evolving concept as well as an ongoing collection of enterprises serving multiple purposes existing at many different levels of government and/or human interaction.

Allocation of Funds

The allocation of funds to vocational education should mirror the goals and processes of the enterprise at all levels. It should be one of the ways of describing policy choices and the specific steps taken to implement such policies. One should also expect that such policy choices for vocational education are not independent, that is, not unconnected in some way with other forms of employment-related education and training. An overview of the total federal investment is the first step, therefore, in this discussion of vocational education funding.

As shown in table 1, the overall federal investment in all programs of work and employment and training programs is about $15 billion. As a proportion of this total, the federal allocation to vocational education is only 4.7 percent. This percentage appears miniscule in relation to the total federal investment. Not shown in table 1 is the extent to which revenues of local and state governments are joined to supplement and to complement the federal outlays. Here the story becomes dramatic. With only two exceptions—vocational education and vocational rehabilitation—local and state governments do not generate revenues for any of the training programs of the federal government shown in table 1. In the case of vocational education, the local and state allocations exceed the federal outlays by about ten multiples. If the local and state allocations were added to the federal outlays shown in table 1, the total investment would be about 30 percent of the national outlay for all employment-related education and training, rather than the mere 4.7 percent ($681 million) shown in table 1.

A critical question is one of whether the federal allocations to vocational education are rising or falling in relation to other expenditures at the federal level. In short, is the federal commitment to vocational education a stable commitment or is it changing? In dollar amounts, uncorrected for inflation, the allocations have risen modestly. In constant dollars (that is, corrected for inflation), the allocations show a steady decline. When compared to other federal expenditures or indices such as gross national product (GNP), allocations to nonvocational education or to other forms of vocational training, the federal commitment to vocational education shows a sharp decline. Expressed in another way, it can be said that during the past decade the growth of the GNP and the growth of federal expenditures on nonvocational education as well as on alternative forms of vocational training have occurred at almost twice the rate of the growth of vocational education expenditures.

What have been the trend lines at the state and local levels? Here the variation among states and local communities is so great that an aggregate figure has little meaning. It is well known, however, that state and local allocations have increased significantly in the past decade, but in relation to most other public expenditures they too have declined.

Next, it is useful to understand how vocational education allocations are distributed to states and within states. The distribution system is very complex and the explanation which follows gives only a general picture, including its complexity.

All of the sums appropriated by Congress are distributed to states with the exception of very small amounts, usually less than 5 percent, which are available to the Secretary of Education for what are known as "programs of national significance" (for example, data collection, research, and information-related activities). The remaining sum is available to states on the basis of population in certain age categories and on the basis of a measure of per capita income in states. Fifty percent of the allocation to states is available to states in proportion to their shares of the national population between the ages of fifteen and nineteen, 20 percent in proportion to their shares of the population between the ages of twenty and twenty-four, 15 percent in proportion to their shares of the population between ages twenty-five and sixty-five and 15 percent in proportion to their shares of the population between ages fifteen and sixty-five. The allotments are then readjusted to provide poor states with a larger allotment and richer states with a smaller sum by using a weighting factor involving the ratio of state to national median for per capita income. A separate appropriation for consumer and homemaking education follows the same distributional plan.

There is an implied priority imbedded in the above allocation formula; it is to focus most of the resources on the young, those under the age of twenty-four, and on the jurisdictions with the lowest median per capita income. But the allocation to states is not automatic. States must apply for their allocations, and numerous guarantees must accompany the application. They must agree to prepare a plan and to some federally established procedures for developing the plan, to regular accountability reports, to federal definitions, to federal specifications for allocating funds within states, to the nature and use of funds generated by state and local levies, to the use of funds seen as federal priorities, to a federally determined approach to state administration, and many others.

Federal vocational education funds used in states are crosssectioned in many ways. First, they are divided into what is known as basic grants and program improvement with 80 percent going to basic grants (mainly instruction) and 20 percent going to program improvement (curriculum development, guidance, research, and so forth). The total allocation is then cross-sectioned again, with 10 percent allocated to programs for the handicapped, 20 percent to programs for the disadvantaged, and 15 percent to programs for postsecondary students and adults.

State agencies distribute funds to eligible local education agencies, in turn, on the basis of applications for funds. Applications are approved on the basis of priorities established in the federal law. In approving applications, state agencies must demonstrate that a higher priority is given to depressed areas, areas with high unemployment, programs serving new or emerging job opportunities, applicants with crucially limited resources, areas having a high concentration of low-income families and/or a large number of students whose education imposes higher than average costs. State agencies are prohibited from allocating funds to local applicants solely on the basis of enrollment or on the basis of an ability to achieve a certain level of matching funds.

This brief description of fund allocations is incomplete and unfinished; it does not describe the total fund flow nor a number of the exceptions and variations. It is sufficient, nevertheless, to indicate that there can be enormous variations among states as well as a great many unfortunate uniformities. It is unfortunate, for example, that the set-asides for the disadvantaged and handicapped are implemented as if uniformity of these conditions prevailed among states.

It is also clear that allocations are made and data assembled in accordance with federal purposes rather than state and local purposes. Fund allocation data are not ordinarily classified by program areas except for those programs having separate identity in authorization and in allocation formulas (for example, consumer and homemaking programs). Their use includes evaluation of compliance and adherence to definitions established at the federal level.

Some Areas Needing Strengthening

Before discussing the areas of vocational education which need strengthening, it would be well to highlight some areas of current strength. As a field of service, vocational education has won acclaim in local communities. It has done well in the dual role of serving individuals and serving communities. It has improved the ability of individuals to adjust and advance in different work roles, and it has enhanced the ability of communities to utilize or accommodate a growing array of vocational skills. These somewhat disparate roles and goals are unique to vocational education and undoubtedly account in part for the high level of acceptance at community levels.

The field of vocational education has remained close to industry, commerce, and agriculture through many different kinds of advisory bodies and reference groups. The field's use of methodological approaches involving youth organizations, work experience, competitions, and voluntary organizations is spectacular though largely unheralded. It has similar successes in providing both long- and short-term instructional programs in a number of fields. A considerable amount of the part-time work of high school and postsecondary vocational students is preceded, for example, by some type of skill training.

Much of the success of vocational education is not shown in the typical approach to evaluation. As mentioned previously, vocational education is not a system; it is a collection of enterprises in different types of institutions, at different levels, for varying purposes, and available to different definitions. Attempting to aggregate evaluative data across such a wide spectrum is often an exercise in using ill-fitting paradigms or inappropriate matrices; precise statements of conclusions are made about imprecise categories of information.

In spite of high marks received by vocational education in local communities, there are some dimensions of vocational education which need strengthening in the next decade. These will be discussed in the following paragraphs.

INSTRUCTOR OR TEACHER PREPARATION

The area of emphasis that can contribute most to strengthening vocational education is instructor or teacher preparation. It may not be the most conspicuous because it is a weakness that is most easily obscured and about which there is a great deal of indifference. It is obscured by the ineffectiveness of certification or licensing procedures in serving as indicators of quality. Certification standards are notoriously adaptable to the conditions of supply and demand of vocational teachers. They easily obscure the need for improving the process of preparing teachers.

Indifference is a disincentive to a recognition of the need for improved instructor updating and retraining. Instructor updating and retraining in vocational education occurs only when employed instructors are willing to subsidize the system—to make a personal investment in such things as tuition, per diem, travel, and time for the hope of some equally personal, but rarely obtainable, reward. Where a personal subsidy is required to serve the public interest, there is an expected amount of indifference.

The need for added strength in the preparation of instructors is further observed by the rapid rise in enrollments over the past decade and even more by the increase in the number of vocational programs. The categories of instructor preparation have not had a parallel growth nor the needed changes in design to accommodate the growth. To rely on transfers into vocational teaching by individuals from industry or commerce is not an acceptable way of viewing the problem. After all, it is industry and commerce that have begun to suffer from lowered productivity. Instructors from industry may be no better prepared to define this problem. The preparation of the work force should remedy, not reinforce, this condition.

The preparation of vocational teachers and instructors is an area that obviously needs strengthening. The added strength should not be in technique nor in fine-tuning; it should involve a renewal of the overall design of the process.

INQUIRY AND LEADERSHIP

The entire domain of employment-related education and training suffers from a paucity of intellectual leadership. Present and future leaders need to be informed by inquiry and the nation deserves leaders who can function within the climate of inquiry.

As mentioned previously, vocational education is design-poor; it is preoccupied with "short" education, and it functions as a system of structural "patchwork." In most situations it also functions for a short year, thus leaving its facilities and personnel idle for three months out of each year.

Visible on the horizon are many new clients including the sons and daughters of many new immigrants. Also on the horizon are many new problems that will strain the present patchwork structure of vocational education and training. The costliness of trial and error solutions can be reduced only by economy and the strength of relying on inquiry and the leadership that emerges from the climate which surrounds inquiry. It is an area needing strength in vocational education.

SCIENCE AND TECHNOLOGY

Sooner or later all fields of instructional endeavor are struck with the realization that their past records have been influenced by forces that cause emphasis or deemphasis, inclusion or exclusion, and high priorities or low priorities. Such forces are operative in all of American education and no less in vocational education. In vocational education these forces are often associated with such labels as "national priorities" or "programs of national significance."

If one were to identify a curriculum area in American education that has suffered from neglect, indifference, or exclusion, it would be the area of instruction that should be elevating scientific literacy and the technological competence to accompany it. Preoccupation with other matters has diminished America's claim on leadership in these areas.[4]

Vocational education and training has been particularly vulnerable to this indifference and neglect. Its preoccupation with "short" education, its accommodation to marginal students and marginal resources, and its indifference to instructor training has compounded the problem. Scientific literacy and technological competence is important in the work force as well as in research laboratories. It is an area needing much strengthening in vocational education.

One could mention many other areas that need attention and strengthening such as equipment, facilities, organization, or plan-

4. National Science Foundation, *Science and Engineering Education for the 1980s and Beyond* (Washington, D.C.: National Science Foundation, 1980).

ning. All are important but not as critical as those which affect the design and focus of the field, specifically instructor training, inquiry, and the routes to scientific and technological literacy.

Closely related to the needs for strength are the focus and the quality of the policy debates that are ongoing in vocational education, which is the subject of the next section.

Vocational Education Policy Debates

Every society attempts to give its members a framework for thinking about what should be most valued and most sought. There are few aspects of human endeavor that are more important than establishing the standards for such a framework. It is the unfinished business of every society. It involves the unfinished task of differentiating between ends and means along with the assurance that inquiry is free to inform both. It also requires a parallel assurance that means will neither dominate nor become substitutes or surrogates for ends.

A role of education is to search for standards in such a framework for thinking and, further, to insure that they are utilized in carrying out education's most challenging task, namely, preparing people to do society's work. Preparing people to do society's work is also the process of allocating, indeed rationing, the statuses, rewards, and awards that members of society accord to each other. As an enterprise engaged in preparing individuals to do society's work, vocational education has been thrust upon the public agenda and into a central position in policy debate. Much is on the agenda and much is involved in the debate. This concluding section will mention a few of the agenda items and comment on the debate.

THE QUESTION OF CONTROL

The Tenth Amendment to the U.S. Constitution provides the guarantee that the power of education will be reserved to the states, respectively, or to the people. State responsibility for education, coupled with local control, has been an accepted fact of educational life for two centuries. It is a highly prized characteristic of the enterprise of vocational education.

The smaller of the local jurisdictions, the districts which are often the most limited in resources, are usually the ones that are most concerned with exercising their powers identified with local control. They have a highly developed sense of community, a record of relying on a great deal of local initiative, and ordinarily they have the lowest dropout rate. This helps to explain why vocational education enrollment rates are higher in rural areas. It also helps to explain why rural schools have fewer difficulties with mainstreaming; they did not remove as many students from the mainstream in the first place, and thus they have fewer students to return to the mainstream.

The question of control is, however, a growing debate. The federal government has become a more dominant actor on the educational stage. While education continues to be regarded as a function reserved to the states, the federal government has assumed the functions of maintaining national security, the distribution of income (through such devices as a graduated income tax, welfare, and public service employment), employment, and general economic health. None of the four responsibilities of the federal government can be separated from employment-related education and training. What appeared to be a clean separation of function when the Tenth Amendment was adopted is no longer clean.

Yet the debate about control is not solely about the locus of responsibility; it is also about methodology. Increasingly the Congress has become an implementer of its own experiments rather than a creator of the conditions needed for defining and solving the nation's problems. In this role as an implementer it has legislated a great deal of educational methodology. In order to carry out this methodology, it has mandated that compliance with its own experimental treatments be regarded as synonymous with educational merit—a leap of faith and a confusion of ends and means.

Governance at the state level is, however, the locus of the liveliest debate. Many states have created separate and multiple governing boards for various levels and functions of education and training. These boards have executive officers who have accepted a role as high priests in the seminaries of structural faith. They are entirely absorbed by the drama of permanent crisis and the threat of external reform. Since employment-related education and training transcends many different levels and functions, the basis for conflict is no longer hypothetical; it is real. State level governance and its various related policy issues will undoubtedly be a major battleground during the decade of the 1980s.

There has always been a debate about whether vocational education should be included among the offerings at the secondary level. A rapid increase in enrollments at the postsecondary level, coupled with problems of articulating programs at the two levels, has heightened this concern.

The debate was renewed when a policy report of the Carnegie Council on Policy Studies in Higher Education included recommendations that compulsory education not be extended beyond the age of sixteen and that all vocational education be eliminated from the high school except home economics and clerical skill training.[5] Unfortunately, the report did little to inform the debate; it merely intensified a number of ensuing exhortations. Most of all, it served as a reminder that there is no general purpose data base to inform the recommendations made in the report nor even to offer much assurance of the ensuing consequences of accepting the recommendations.

Yet it is possible to ask some "what if" questions. What if, for example, the recommendations were adopted at federal and state levels? Enumerated below are some possible consequences:

1. Local control would become an immediate crisis. Local districts have always provided the most generous support and mainly because they have regarded their degree of control as ostensible if not real. Any requirement to the contrary would generate a crisis of control.

2. The program of *general* education in high schools would grow in enrollment by about 25 percent. Most students would be of low or average academic ability and a high proportion would be poor and minority students.

3. American society would become increasingly stratified and divided: the rich from the poor, the more academically talented from the less academically talented, and those with a "short" educa-

---

5. Carnegie Council on Policy Studies in Higher Education, *Giving Youth a Better Chance: Options for Education, Work, and Service* (San Francisco: Jossey-Bass, 1979), p. 345.

tion from those with a "long" education. The system would enforce and reinforce a permanent underclass.

4. The costs of employment-training programs would rise sharply. At least in the past, the alternative training programs conducted outside the community's normative institutional framework have been very costly.

The suggested "what if" consequences are very reasonable possibilities. It is not necessary to defend the effectiveness of vocational education at the secondary level in order to reject the consequences of its elimination combined with early dropouts. Important policy decisions in the United States should be based on better information than has informed the Carnegie recommendations.

THE LIBERAL ARTS/HUMANITIES WORK NEXUS

To some degree the old cleavage separating vocational education and the liberal arts/humanities tradition had appeared to be closing. The appearance of closing the gap was, however, deceiving. It was not accomplished by a mutual embrace; it was accomplished by mutual disdain and distance. Disdain grew out of the earlier efforts to identify vocational education as the common enemy of the liberal arts/humanist tradition and distance was easily possible when the liberal arts/humanities orientation attached itself comfortably, though not popularly, with "long" education and very uncomfortably to "short" education.

The debate was renewed with the publication of a report of the Commission on the Humanities.[6] The report was a hand-wringing approach to an undefined problem. It proposed a reform of most of American education, but it left the liberal art/humanities tradition almost intact and unreformed. With conciliatory unimaginativeness the Commission accepted the assertion that "study of the humanities is neither possible nor appropriate in all areas of vocational education—for example, in short-term training for specific technical occupations."[7] They hastened to add, however, that it was possible in postsecondary vocational education where

6. Commission on the Humanities, *The Humanities in American Life* (Berkeley, Calif.: University of California Press, 1980).

7. Ibid., p. 118.

enrollments have grown rapidly and training appears to be longer.

One wonders what would be observable if one tried to subtract the corpus of what can be defined as the humanities from the preparation of people for the vocations or from the lives of workers. Most vocational educators would probably agree that what could be subtracted would be considerable, both in scope and in importance. They would also agree that the amount subtracted would not have been initially added, and thus available for later subtraction, through the efforts of public investments in the humanities (for example, the National Endowment for the Humanities) or by those who otherwise represent such interests. It would have been added by the efforts of vocational educators to improvise by creating exposure to the humanities.

The humanities are still represented by those who prefer an organization of courses, by lesson-giving, and by traditional approaches to scheduling subject-matter requirements. Those whose preparation involves short periods of education or training must rely on other approaches. The debate is likely to continue at varying levels of intensity and with little to inform it except disdain and distance, both in the elitist climate in which the humanities function most comfortably.

A Final Thought

The pattern of vocational education in the United States should be viewed as many different types of journeys taken to multiple destinations. It involves numerous enterprises that are deeply imbedded in an assortment of agencies and institutions. It is an important part of the evolving blueprint for the hopes of many individuals and groups as well as the nation itself.

This chapter has not dealt with the patterns of vocational education as a phenomenon illuminated solely by taxonomic descriptions or by organizational claims. Nor has it dealt with the topic solely in terms of problems to be solved. It has accepted the premise that vocational education is inseparable from the larger context of employment-related education and training, and it has assumed that most of the problems of vocational education are still undefined within this larger context.

The patterns are, therefore, unfinished and incomplete. Defining and addressing the problems of employment-related education and training deserve the highest quality of informed, inquiry-oriented leadership. The ability of institutions and individuals to move closer and closer to a realization of the conditions promised in the greatest of American constitutional documents is a crucial text of democracy. The task is enormous. The public and our students are waiting.

CHAPTER III

Vocational Education in Other Countries

BEATRICE G. REUBENS

In other countries even the definition of vocational education is not identical to the American concept. Educational forms that are regarded as part of vocational education in the United States may not be so classified in some countries. By the same token, forms such as apprenticeship, which are not usually considered part of American vocational education, actually are a mainstay of the vocational education system in certain nations.

Recognizing that there is much disagreement on definitional matters, the European Communities, through its Statistical Office, has been examining educational classifications in its nine member countries in an attempt to establish education and training categories that are acceptable to all of the member nations (Belgium, Denmark, France, Germany, Ireland, Italy, Luxembourg, the Netherlands, and the United Kingdom). The exercise is instructive. Education is divided into "general" and "vocational." A further separation is made between education associated with the ordinary school and university system, through university level, and out-of-school education. It is assumed that students in the regular educational system have not yet entered active working life, while out-of-school education applies primarily to those already in the labor force. A youth-adult division also is implied, but age as such is not a factor in the classification.

The result is that both school-based and industry-based initial vocational training, mostly in the form of apprenticeship, are counted as vocational education so long as the participants have not yet held jobs and the training "comprises any process enabling a person to acquire, keep up-to-date, and perfect the technical knowledge and skills required for the exercise of a given occupation."[1]

1. Statistical office of the European Communities, *Education and Training, 1970/71-1977/78* (Luxembourg: Statistical Office of the European Communities, 1980), pp. 59-65.

The desirability of formal initial occupational skill training for all young people, whether it be given in conventional classrooms or in workshops or offices, is far more widely accepted abroad than in the United States. Because of this attitude in other countries, vocational education, in the American sense, tends to be viewed as part of a larger system of initial skill training. As such, vocational education is utilized differently in each country, according to national traditions and circumstances. In some countries (for example, France, Belgium, and Sweden), school-based vocational education is the leading method of offering occupational skill training to young people who have not yet entered the labor market. In other countries (for example, Japan, Germany, and Switzerland), the prevailing method is industry-based initial training, although Japan's training is firm-specific, in contrast to the adherence to broad-based apprenticeship in the other countries.

A description of vocational education in foreign countries, therefore, cannot come from a single mold. Differences among the countries are substantial in matters of clientele, expectations, educational methods, organization, and administration. It is best to consider countries individually, to relate full-time vocational education in regular schools to the national system of initial occupational skill training, and to confine the discussion to young people of upper-secondary age who have not been in the labor force. While these limits immediately exclude certain important facets of the American vocational education system, such as the part-time student in the community colleges, outreach programs to disadvantaged out-of-school youth, and the adult programs, an understanding of the foreign systems is best achieved in their own terms.

Japan

Throughout the prewar and war periods, the effort to produce skills for Japan's growing industrial sector through public vocational schools was judged inadequate, due to the poor quality of vocational schools, especially their failure to keep up with technological change. Skill training of youth was located mainly in the enterprise, in keeping with the needs of each firm. The Allied Occupation in 1945 soon introduced a new educational system, featuring nine years of compulsory education from age six, a uniform pattern of six years of elementary school, and three years each of junior (middle) and senior high school. Much emphasis was placed on educational democratization, including a purge of ultranationalistic teachers.[2]

In the early postwar years, Japanese educators opposed vocational and technical education in the school system because it was considered antiegalitarian, would restore multitracking in schools, and might support totalitarian forces in the society.[3] Over the years, however, the senior high school system developed vocational courses, including specializations in industry, business, agriculture, fishery, home economics, or nursing. By 1980, 31.1 percent of all high school students were enrolled in vocational courses, but the proportion had been higher in earlier years. From 1960 to 1980 the proportion of high school students in the vocational sector dropped by over 10 percentage points, with by far the greatest decline occurring from 1970 to 1980, according to unpublished data. This decrease reflects the growing desire of Japanese youth to enter higher education after the completion of the general high school course.

Vocational education is offered in public and private schools. In 1978 over 1.5 million vocational students attended public institutions, while more than 350,000 were in private schools. Full-time students constituted the vast majority. In 1980 vocational students were highly concentrated in the business courses (mostly female) and the industrial-technical courses (overwhelmingly male); together these accounted for over two-thirds of all vocational students. Compared to 1960, the 1980 vocational registrations showed a relative decline in agriculture and home economics, while enrollments in the industrial-technical courses showed an increase in the share both of vocational students and all high school students. Regardless of which course students selected, they had to earn a minimum number of credits in required general courses. Vocational subjects, therefore, have been chosen chiefly toward the end of the three-year upper-secondary course.

2. Solomon B. Levine and Hisashi Kawada, *Human Resources in Japanese Industrial Development* (Princeton, N.J.: Princeton University Press, 1980), pp. 55, 100-104, 107-121.

3. Ibid., p. 105.

In 1979 there were 3,882 purely academic high schools out of a total of 5,135 senior high schools. Vocational courses are offered either in completely independent schools or in "attached" schools; this latter type of school operates either in a separate building located close to an academic high school or, less frequently, within an academic high school, but with no sharing of courses or staff. Vocational schools tend to specialize in one or two of the major occupational areas. Those schools that offer commercial, home economics, and nursing courses, all female-intensive, are more likely to be "attached" than independent schools, while industrial-technical and fishery courses tend to be conducted in independent vocational schools.

Despite the provision of some vocational education, Japanese senior high schools have functioned essentially as preparatory schools for the university entrance examination. A Japanese view is that graduates of upper-secondary schools usually "have not received any special vocational education and training during their school days, and know little about the occupations they have chosen. Probably vocational training is accorded the least attention in Japan's school education, compared to other major advanced nations."[4] This may be an extreme view, inasmuch as interviews in 1981 with employers revealed a division of opinion about the utility of the vocational courses for high school students. Depending on the type of business, some employers preferred vocational graduates from the commercial and technical courses over academic graduates.

A few employers have established their own senior high schools for junior high school graduates whom they intend to hire later. Such company-owned schools, if approved by the local education authorities and the Ministry of Education, can grant diplomas equivalent to those of the regular schools.[5] In addition, a group of schools called "miscellaneous," which had offered vocational education or training under private auspices for the most part,

4. Hirohide Tanaka, "Low Growth and Aging Labor Force," *Japan Quarterly* 27 (January-March 1980): 42.

5. Hidetoshi Kato, *Education and Youth Employment in Japan* (Berkeley, Calif.: Carnegie Council on Policy Studies in Higher Education, 1978), pp. 9, 11.

achieved legal status in 1976, provided that they enrolled at least forty students for one year of work (at least 800 hours). This status made them eligible for low-interest government loans. As of 1978, some 2,300 such approved schools enrolled 400,000 and gave courses in dressmaking, nursing, dental assistant, medical assistant, civil engineering and construction, information processing, hairdressing, business management, and culinary arts, among others.

These rapidly growing schools, chiefly serving graduates of academic high schools and enrolling more females than males, have their largest numbers in the paramedical and home economics fields and constitute an important new vocational alternative to junior college and university. To a lesser extent, they enroll junior high school graduates who prefer this course to senior high school education, whether in the general or vocational education line. Junior high school graduates also have the option of entering a five-year advanced course in a technical college. Completion provides a tertiary education credential and direct occupational access to technical jobs. Absorbing only a tiny fraction of junior high school graduates, overwhelmingly males, this type of institution is an alternative to vocational education in a senior high school.[6]

To provide for the fraction of school-leavers whose jobs offer no formal training or who are unemployed, government vocational training centers offer special courses that are especially suited to the requirements of the small firms, especially those unable to provide the type of training described above. In 1980, 48,595 persons, mostly young, participated in basic training in public training centers, while another 72,000 were trained on employer's premises through public subsidies. According to the official report of the Ministry of Labor, both of these totals were lower than they had been in the previous decade.

Both the criticism of vocational education in the senior high schools and the development of alternatives have spurred reform of high school vocational education, including plans to offer additional vocational and labor market preparation to academic high school students who do not proceed to higher education. As discussed in interviews with officials of the Ministry of Education in

6. Japan, Ministry of Education, Science, and Culture, Elementary and Secondary Education Bureau, *Outline of Vocational Education in Japan* (Tokyo, 1980).

1981 and presented in the report cited in footnote 6, the main changes scheduled to take effect in vocational courses in 1982 are:

1. Greater flexibility and independence in choice of curriculum by each school, with a reduction in central direction.

2. Greater attention to the needs and abilities of individual students within schools, accompanied by a reduction in the number of compulsory subjects and credits as well as the total number of course credits required for graduation. (Females will have at least four more compulsory credits than males because general home economics is a required subject only for girls).

3. Reorganization and streamlining of vocational curricula to provide a number of key courses within each major field. For example, industrial technical courses are to be subdivided into thirteen key courses, ranging from electronics to textiles, and further divided into sixty-four industry-related subjects. Individual courses are to be designed to relate to the key course and help accomplish the objective stated for each key course.

4. An emphasis on the relation between vocational and general subjects.

5. Provision of increased time and facilities for practical training in firms, workshop experience, experimental periods, and other nonclassroom settings.

Reviews of the national program for 1982 by forty-seven prefectual authorities and their advisory committees will proceed. At the same time a national advisory council continues to explore further reform of high school vocational education and will consider suggestions on how such education should relate to the special training schools, described previously, whose growth and popularity highlight the weaknesses of high school vocational education.

No discussion of vocational education for young people in Japan is complete without reference to on-the-job training. As part of the distinctive Japanese employment system, many companies offer firm-specific training to new senior and junior high school graduates. The latter are a vanishing breed, however, since only a small proportion do not proceed directly to senior high school. The hiring of inexperienced young workers straight from school is favored by most employers because they can choose the best applicants and train them in their own way, and because such young workers' wage rates, though rising more rapidly since the 1960s than those of prime age workers, still are relatively low compared to wage differentials by age in other countries. The internal training system, especially in the large Japanese firms, is based on the recruitment of a group of graduates, mostly males, before the end of the school year and the offer of a training program suited to each educational level. Females, especially women university graduates, have a more difficult time in finding jobs that offer such training.

New graduates who enter large, and some medium-sized, firms in white collar divisions receive a wide-ranging introduction to the firm's operations, particularly if they are considered promotable. They first undergo an orientation period and then they are posted to particular sections according to the company's plans rather than their own desires; such assignments are accepted as part of the system. Every two or three years satisfactory employees are rotated to different sections in a regular procedure, which usually occurs around April 1, the beginning of the business year and the end of the school year. Such coordination in timing assists in the regular recruitment and systematic training of new graduates.

As matters stand, it is unlikely that either Japanese high school vocational education, no matter how improved, or government vocational training will supplement enterprise training. Rather, these forms will provide an introduction to training within the firm, especially in the larger enterprises.

Sweden

Before 1971 Swedish upper-secondary education was divided into three separate institutions, similar to the pattern in other European countries. Select academic high schools, catering almost entirely to entrants to higher education, were supplemented by continuation schools that served a middle group and by vocational schools whose courses were closely geared to employers' needs. After an experimental period, the three school types were abolished nationally and supplanted by a single, integrated, comprehensive upper-secondary school, open in principle to all graduates of the compulsory school, which usually is completed at age sixteen.

Within the new upper-secondary school three main groupings of students were established around a common core of required courses. By far the largest part is the two-year line chiefly composed of vocational specializations. In addition, there are a three-year line that serves primarily, but not necessarily, as preparation for university entrance and a four-year technical line, which also leads mostly to technical higher education. In addition, one-year and special courses of a vocational nature are offered and these may be taken by others apart from recent graduates of the compulsory school.

In spite of the distinctions that persist in the comprehensive high school in Sweden, access to higher education has been opened to those who successfully complete a two-year upper-secondary course. As might be expected, the fraction of such graduates taking immediate advantage of this opportunity has remained smaller than among graduates of the three- and four-year lines, but many two-year graduates may make later use of this option due to official Swedish policy, which encourages a delay in proceeding directly to higher education and entrance after some years of work experience. Recent data indicate that over half of all entrants to Swedish institutions of higher education are over twenty-four years old and that most of the accepted candidates in this age group do not possess conventional academic qualifications.

The two-year line in the comprehensive high school offers specific occupational specializations. Among these specializations are clothing manufacture, building and construction, distribution and clerical, electro-communications, motor engineering, food manufacture, consumer, processing techniques, woodwork and carpentry, workshop practice, nursing, agriculture, and forestry. Students in each of these lines receive a wider general education than their predecessors in the vocational schools who specialized in even narrower occupational fields.

Prospective students in the high school apply for a number of specific vocational lines, ranking them in order of their preference. Since the number of openings in each line, both nationally and locally, are set by the Labor Market Boards after they calculate the need for workers in the occupations associated with each line, many students do not obtain the course of their first choice. In fact, in the courses where student demand most exceeds the supply of places there are relatively high academic point scores as pre-requisites for admission. Some well-qualified applicants therefore request courses where there is less competition for places in the hope of later entering the preferred university course or occupation through this route. All of the vocational lines are not available in each school, somewhat limiting the choices of young people in the less settled areas, especially in the north, unless they leave home to study.

Disappointed applicants whose assignment was not to their liking have postponed or foregone entrance to the upper-secondary school or have dropped out fairly soon. Some of the dropouts subsequently have entered one of the government adult vocational training centers where much the same training was offered as they had forsaken, but at much higher training allowances than the upper-secondary educational allowances provided. This discrepancy, and others between educational allowances and the benefits paid in various manpower training and employment programs, has been a concern to employers and government authorities, among others. Efforts are underway to rectify the disparities and make manpower training programs no more attractive financially than regular upper-secondary school, so far as the relevant age group is concerned.

All students in the vocational lines at the high school take classes in Swedish, physical education, and working-life orientation, and they also must choose among optional general subjects. The working-life orientation course, considered very important by Swedish educators and labor market specialists, provides background and orientation on conditions in the labor market and in the working environment, occupational safety, industrial democracy, trade union organization (over 70 percent of the Swedish labor force belong to trade unions), welfare programs in the firm, worker participation in management, government institutions (such as the employment service), social security, taxation, and related issues.

Each vocational course calls for a certain amount of practical experience in a workplace. In some cases it is required prior to acceptance for the course, as a test of aptitude and attitudes. Some of the practical work may be done during the school year. On a recent visit, pupils in the building and construction course were observed on a building site where they were integrated into the regular work force, but also had their own instructor and lessons on the site. For a fixed period of time they would not be in the classroom at all but would report daily to this or another construction site where they would participate directly in Sweden's highly advanced and industrialized housing construction methods.

Fully supported by the appropriate trade unions, this paid on-the-site experience appeared similar to apprenticeship in other countries, except that the program was controlled by the educational authorities and the pay was an educational allowance, such as all upper-secondary students receive.

Sweden has a limited amount of true apprenticeship; it is confined to the traditional crafts and skills and subsidized by the government. Both the trade unions and the Social Democratic Party, under whose influence the reform of the upper-secondary school occurred, have a deep-rooted distrust of employer-based initial skill training on the ground that firm-specific training tends to be offered, restricting the later occupational mobility and progress of workers as well as the growth of the economy. Therefore, the educational and labor market authorities, with full cooperation and consultation from employers' groups and trade unions, have been designated the best agency for planning and conducting the vocational lines in the upper-secondary schools. Not only is the skill training broad enough to meet the needs of many different employers, but general education and opportunities to continue in the educational cycle are directly open to vocational students.

Recently, questions have arisen about whether this model is the only acceptable one. A shortage of suitable places in employers' premises to give the practical experience and some dissatisfaction on the part of employers with the products of the existing vocational lines led the government to introduce a proposal in 1979 to utilize employers' premises as a basic site for educational programs, with greater authority for the employers than they possess under the upper-secondary school program. A national election and a new government delayed consideration of this proposal, which the Metal Workers' Union opposed strongly in keeping with its critical appraisal of the quality of employers' skill training and educational capacity. It is possible, however, that an increase in direct employer participation in educational training will occur in Sweden.

Continuous evaluation of the new upper-secondary school, especially the two-year vocational line, has been underway for some time. An evaluation was made of outcomes for students eighteen months after they had completed a vocational line.[7] Their situation as of late 1975 and their opinions of the educational program they had experienced were sought through questionnaires and interviews. If one omits the 20 percent of males in 1975 who were performing compulsory military service, 90 percent of the males and 74 percent of the females were employed, 5 percent of males and 13 percent of the females still were students, and smaller proportions were looking for work, helping with a family farm or business, were at home (6 percent of females), or were chronically ill. Including family helpers among the employed, the evaluators found that students who had pursued the vocational specializations of motor engineering, building and construction, and workshop practice, all of which are male-intensive, had the highest rates of employment. Among the female-intensive occupations, only the distribution and clerical lines had an employment rate over 80 percent. Sex of the student and the earlier choice of vocational line were related to later differential employment rates. Moreover, those who faced unsatisfactory employment opportunities were found more prone to have continued their studies; studying was identified as latent unemployment in some cases.

Of all who were employed, 70 percent were working in a job identified by the student as training-related or were trainees in such work. Some employers regard vocational education as a base on which to build additional training, usually firm-specific. Students who had studied nursing, agriculture, forestry, building construc-

---

7. Rune Axelsson, *Vocational Education in the Swedish Upper Secondary School: An Evaluation* (Uppsala: Uppsala University, Department of Educational Research, 1978), p. 68.

tion, and workshop practice were most likely to hold training related jobs, while those from the consumer, clothing manufacture, and carpentry lines showed the least correspondence. Some students claimed that in their jobs as trainees they were underpaid and that the school should supervise this period of employment, including more rigid control by the trade unions of the training given by employers. Some youth obtained their full-time jobs by accepting offers from the same employers who had given them practical experience while they were in school. In general, connections were seen between academic performance at school and the level type of jobs held eighteen months later, but the direction of causality and significance were not clear.

At this early period in the life of the new upper-secondary school, practical training was not available to all students. Not only did such students say they regretted not having had this training, but those who had experienced it for the most part wished it had been longer. Advantages attributed to such training were contact with the reality of the workplace, observation of differences between classroom instruction and actual practice, chances to become more accurate and faster in work, cooperation with other workers, and understanding the demands of the actual job.

Criticism of the lack of coordination between the school and the firms was voiced by many students. Specific points made included the following: theoretical instruction in the school did not sufficiently incorporate the practical experience, students felt inhibited in asking questions at the workplace, supervisors did not devote enough time to students at the workplace, and students were sometimes assigned to irrelevant and trivial tasks, being treated as available manpower rather than students.

As further evaluation reports are made public concerning subsequent graduating classes, it will be possible to determine whether these early conditions have been improved. Comparisons with American evaluations of cooperative education may also become feasible. Finally, if Sweden develops additional employer-based skill training programs, these will be subject to comparisons with the school-based vocational lines in the upper-secondary school, which is likely to continue as the primary form.

Denmark

Danish education has many vocational elements and recent changes are of particular interest.[8] Basic education formally ended at age fourteen until 1972 when Parliament voted nine years of compulsory general education, starting at age seven. Two-thirds now remain for an optional tenth year. Since 1976, the basic school has been organized on comprehensive lines in the first seven years. Some practice-oriented subjects are offered as options in the last years, which correspond to lower-secondary school; some pupils in these years become trainees in firms and institutions.

When they leave the basic school, mostly at sixteen and seventeen years of age, Danish youth have several choices, some of them outside the normal educational system and containing occupational components. Continuation schools for the age group fourteen to eighteen are private residential institutions with government subsidies. While not vocational schools, they usually provide an education with broad occupational aims, facilitating entry to employment. Youth schools, also for the fourteen to eighteen age group, offer basic vocational education, among other courses. These are part-time schools and are supplementary rather than alternatives to regular schools. Almost 60 percent of all pupils attend youth schools.

Continuing in the regular educational channels, academically oriented students who meet entrance requirements can proceed to the grammar school, which leads to university, or can take a course preparing for the Higher Preparatory Examination. In addition, full-time technical schools, lasting two to four years and mixing classroom and practical experience, provide diploma courses leading to such occupations as technician, engineer, technical designer, and laboratory technologist. Two-year courses in commercial schools prepare for the business world and also offer diplomas that are the equivalent of the university entrance examination, but are more vocationally oriented.

8. Denmark, Ministry of Education, *Education in Denmark* (Copenhagen, 1979), pp. 31-34; idem, *Recent Developments and Trends in the Educational System in Denmark* (Copenhagen, 1979), pp. 8-10; idem, *Vocational Education and Training in Denmark* (Copenhagen, 1979); idem, Central Council of Education, *Danish Educational Planning and Policy in a Social Context to the End of the 20th Century* (Copenhagen, 1978), ch. II-V.

Agricultural schools, which offer certificates enabling future farmers to obtain favorable government loans, provide the final years of training with the basic year offered through the farming option in the basic vocational training scheme, the new vocational education system discussed below. In addition, domestic science schools train institutional cooks, dieticians, and supervisors. Finally, vocational schools, outside the jurisdiction of the Ministry of Education, are operated for the sixteen to nineteen age group by the official agencies such as the Post Office, State Railways, Customs Administration, and in the fields of nautical affairs, health and social services, and public administration.

A majority of the sixteen to nineteen age group, however, proceeds to apprenticeship or the new form of vocational education introduced experimentally in 1969 and fully established in 1977. It is called basic vocational training or EFG. Prior to the implementation of the EFG system, which is still not fully operative, commercial schools also offered a one-year course and a final examination, which enabled graduates to take an apprenticeship, continue their education, or proceed directly to employment. Such one-year students now enter the EFG program and constitute almost half of its total enrollment. The other source of recruitment for EFG is pupils who earlier might have entered apprenticeship or employment, or would have been unemployed or out of the labor force.

Discontent with apprenticeship, the predominant form until recently, was the basis for the decision to institute EFG, a school-based vocational education system. The decline in the intake of apprenticeship in the 1960s gave evidence of the need for another alternative. EFG also is seen as a means of attracting school-weary youth, currently 20 percent of the age group, who do not proceed beyond compulsory education and who come disproportionately from the lower socioeconomic groups.

The main elements of the EFG vocational education system are:

1. About 100 individual trades are combined into eight major occupational groups: commerce and clerical work, iron and metal trades, building and construction, graphic arts, food, services, agriculture, and road transport.

2. Eligible students are accepted for one of the eight main fields and spend the first year entirely in classroom studies, emphasizing general subjects and practical and theoretical introductions to the main field.

3. In addition to the required subjects, optional subjects enable students to qualify for further education or training at the end of the EFG course.

4. During the year, group and individual guidance and counseling assist individual students to choose a more specialized occupation.

5. Instruction is organized on a modular base, permitting students to leave at appropriate times and reenter later. This provision has not yet been widely utilized.

6. At the end of the first year, students, with the assistance of the schools and other agencies, try to find employers who are willing to give them suitable practical training.

7. Practical training at the employer's establishment, with no participation in direct production, is planned and supervised by the EFG system and lasts two to three years, alternating with periods spent in the vocational school.

8. Since 1976 no wages have been paid to students in the first year, but regular student allowances are granted. During the second part of the program, wages are paid to EFG students at the same rate as similar apprentices receive.

9. A levy on employers establishes a fund from which employers are compensated in part or full for the wages and other expenses connected with offering the practical training. Employers with apprentices also receive compensation for wages paid.

10. Operating expenses are met by the Ministry of Education. Building costs are in most cases financed by local governments.

11. Successful completion of the course gives the same skilled-worker accreditation as apprentices receive on completion. If a shorter course is completed, an independent vocational qualification is obtained by EFG students.

12. Control and administration of EFG are legally vested in the national Ministries of Education and Labor, the local technical and commercial school boards, and the representatives of employers and trade unions relevant to each trade. As was observed on a

visit, in practice each curriculum appears to be set by the employers and trade unions who take a serious and professional interest in this activity and dominate the local school boards.

Recruitment to EFG has not been rapid when account is taken of the contribution made by transfer of one-year commercial students from special schools to the EFG courses. From 1976-77 to the first months of 1978, the drop in enrollments in commercial courses was from 15,200 to 3,100, while EFG recruitment rose from 9,000 to 25,800, allowing for a net increase of about 4,000 in EFG. Apprenticeship fell by 1,000 from 16,000 to 15,000, in the same period. In 1979-80, almost 28,000 were enrolled in EFG; by 1981 it is expected that over 31,000 will be enrolled in EFG, contrasted with 12,100 in apprenticeship.

This last forecast indicates that apprenticeship will not be entirely replaced, in spite of the original intentions of the legislation and the perceived advantages of EFG over apprenticeship in offering a delayed choice of specialization, possibilities of changing trades (thus avoiding a great loss of training time), more and broader education, and wider geographical training opportunities. The reasons for the strong survival of apprenticeship arise both from the trade and student sides. Apprentices receive pay in the first year, are more certain of obtaining a training place and of completing training, and they may have better access to regular jobs. During the recession, EFG students have had difficulty in finding training places, even when government provided some of the places as a special measure.

It also became clear that some industries preferred apprenticeship training to EFG. The decision has therefore been made that each trade (employers and trade unions jointly) will make its own decision on the form of training. Possibly some trades will approve both forms, side by side, at least for some time.

A study of students enrolled in EFG from 1973 to 1977 found that children of skilled workers and lower-grade salaried workers were particularly represented and that the "residual group" was not drawn in, as has been hoped. Choices of occupational fields and trades divided according to traditional sex biases, but less so than in apprenticeship. Dropout rates from EFG have been high, higher than in apprenticeship, and especially high for girls in EFG. About

50 percent of dropping out was attributed to a failure to find a practical training place. Among females who had completed training, two-thirds found skilled jobs and half of the remainder were unemployed. Since many males were doing compulsory military service, their employment records were not analyzed. While recruitment of EFG students directly from schools was found to be an asset, the program was faulted on its failure to incorporate direct provision of practical training places in the program.[9]

Danish data on annual operational costs per student in the 1977-78 school year are among the few that permit comparisons of the academic, vocational, and apprenticeship forms of education/training.[10] As is to be expected, the statistics are not perfectly comparable, inasmuch as expenditures related to capital outlays cannot always be separated from operational expenditures, expenditures are included on pupils who do not complete the year, and part-time as well as full-time students are included. Nevertheless, the differences are significant.

Costs for upper-secondary academic education, at Dkr. 18,000 per year per student, exceeded all other categories except for EFG in the graphic arts. EFG in four selected occupational groups cost two-thirds to over two and a half times as much as similar apprenticeship training. The lowest cost was Dkr. 3,000 per year for apprentices in commercial, clerical, and public administration training, rising to Dkr. 8,000 for apprentices in graphic arts. The range for EFG was from Dkr. 5,000 per year for EFG in the commercial, clerical, and public administration fields to Dkr. 21,000 in graphic arts.

The meaning of these sums may become clearer when they are placed beside annual operational costs per student in other occupations. These costs, which include research costs, are: doctors (including clinical training), Dkr. 48,400; dentists, Dkr. 79,000; pharmacist, Dkr. 42,000; veterinarian, Dkr. 74,000; Danish M. Sc. in engineering, Dkr. 72,000. Americans may be surprised at the

9. Carl Nørregaard, Inge Mærkedahl, and Bente Ørum, *Efg.: Uddannelsen og eleverne, (Basic Vocational Training: Provision and Students)*, Publication No. 98 (Copenhagen: Danish National Institute of Social Research, 1980).

10. Denmark, Ministry of Education, *Unit Costs in the Danish Education System 1976-77, 1977-78* (Copenhagen, 1979), pp. 3-7.

relatively low cost of medical training or the high cost of dental and engineering students. In any case, it is clear that thus far vocational education generally costs considerably less than academic education for the high school age group.

France

Compulsory education in France was raised from fourteen to sixteen years of age and frequent changes have occurred in the structure, organization, and nomenclature of the educational system in the postwar period. Nevertheless, certain distinctive features of the French system have persisted until the recent elections:

1. The degree of control over education exercised by the national Ministry of Education in Paris exceeds that of central governments in other countries.

2. Postcompulsory education is divided into a long cycle, mostly academic, and a short cycle. There is some advanced technical education in the long cycle while initial skilled-worker training and technician training are found in the short cycle. Each has a vertical structure through higher education level.

3. School-based vocational education has been the dominant form, with apprenticeship a smaller program mainly confined to the artisan trades.

4. Great importance is attached to the acquisition of occupational certificates and diplomas after the compulsory years for those not proceeding to higher education. Occupational certificates and diplomas are granted nationally by a complex, external examination system, which examines both the practical and theoretical knowledge of candidates from the educational system, apprenticeship, and working life.

Currently, concern is felt about the fairly large number of young people (about 140,000 out of 800,000 leaving all levels of education each year) who do not continue beyond compulsory school, another 80,000 who drop out from short-cycle vocational schools at the upper-secondary level, 30,000 others who drop out from similar long-cycle technical education, and 80,000 university students who drop out without obtaining more than a high school diploma. In France an academic high school diploma (*baccalau-*

réat) is regarded as an inadequate employment credential and preparation for work.

Recent changes in the French vocational educational system, still in process, are directed toward improving the preparation of those who complete their courses as well as to reducing the number of drop outs by making courses more relevant, useful, and attractive. Vocational education had been established as a totally in-school function in a postwar agreement between the government and industry in which the latter promised to increase industrial output and the former pledged to provide the needed skilled manpower. This arrangement did not give complete satisfaction to employers or students, but it has persisted for many years.

Vocational schools, nationally built, funded, and controlled, are separate institutions in their own buildings, which are of different age and quality. The schools have uniform curricula, teaching methods, equipment, and preparation for the specialized examinations. Some general education is given. The various schools in an area offer different occupational specializations so that each can have a large enough student body to provide the full range of training. Schools are set up much like workplaces for the practical training, but the pace of work usually is not as rapid as that in the workplace and fully skilled workers are not turned out in the initial two- and three-year courses.

Teacher training for the vocational schools is highly organized. Attached to several operating schools, the technical teacher training institutes draw from many sources and offer a full program in general education, pedagogy, and the theoretical and practical elements of the specific occupation. Practice teaching can be done right on the site of the school. A visit to such a school in the northern part of Paris revealed a modern complex of buildings and large workshops with up-to-date machinery.

Until recently the Ministry of Education expressed satisfaction with the inschool programs, which provided no time in an actual workplace. But employers and others criticized the schools' products, the failure to change curricula rapidly or adequately, the lack of real impact by employers' organizations on the program, and expressed doubts about the utility or relevance of the formal final examinations. With the recession of 1974 and mounting youth unemployment, new youth programs were launched in which employers were subsidized to expand apprenticeship and to offer training to unemployed young people, some of whom had completed a two- or three-year vocational education course and had obtained a certificate.

As reliance on employers grew, open criticism of the isolation of the schools from the work world began to appear even in the Ministry of Education. In 1979, an educational philosophy, called *alternance*, was introduced into the lower-secondary schools. Eventually all pupils may spend part of the year in school and part in a firm and more of the curriculum will concern technological education and manual skills. With these changes, entrance to the vocational schools could come earlier and an overlap between lower-secondary school and the vocational course could occur. A modular system was to be introduced to enable each pupil to complete units in vocational school at his own pace. Those completing the vocational education courses would be eligible for higher vocational courses.

These changes are too recent to judge whether the proportion of school leavers entering and completing initial vocational qualifications will rise to satisfactory levels. If the use of employer premises for the younger pupils proves successful, there may be a much greater use of cooperative education than presently exists.

Other Nations

The four countries described above do not exhaust the diversity exhibited by the industrialized market-economy countries in their efforts to provide initial occupational skills to young people emerging from compulsory education. Some countries provide vocational schools in the lower-secondary phase, rather than waiting until upper-secondary education begins. In the Netherlands, where this has been the case, it is significant that these schools have been devoting an increased share of the school year to general education and their function of preparing certain groups of youth for entrance to jobs or apprenticeship appears to be withering away.

National educational policies are only slightly affected by regional or local variation in the four countries, but in other nations with central governments much more local control of educational policy is exercised. British vocational education, called further education, not only is shaped locally for the most part, but it also is separate and distinct in administration and control from general education below the higher education level. The resulting lack of coordination has imposed hardships on some categories of students and recent efforts have provided some link courses and cooperative arrangements.

Policy on initial skill training in other federal countries has, except for Canada, generally had more elements of national government control than are found in the United States. European federal countries—Germany, Austria, Switzerland—have retained centralized supervision of the occupational portions of training, leaving general and theoretical education to the local authorities. These three countries also exemplify situations where American-style vocational education (that is, full-time courses operated by educational authorities) is less important than industry-based apprenticeship in the provisions for teenagers.

At this level of specificity, many differences in vocational education are found among countries. Instead of forming a solid group which stands in sharp contrast to American practice, the foreign countries occupy the full spectrum of possible positions and the United States simply fits in among them. From the amount of dissatisfaction and change reported in these countries, it is clear that no country currently has a model entirely satisfactory to itself, let alone suitable for replication elsewhere.

Common Trends

In presenting the diversity that characterizes initial skill training and vocational education in the industrialized market economy countries, one must not lose sight of common trends among them, some of which are less visible or absent in the United States. Among the most important trends in foreign countries are the following:

1. There is increased acceptance of the idea that all young people require initial formal occupational skill training, either in a school setting or in firms.

2. While school-based skill training continues to gain on industry-based training, especially in the more technological fields, there is growing unanimity on the need for a large part of the school-based training to occur in actual workplaces. In other words, cooperative education is becoming the universal form.

3. Active participation of representatives of employer and worker organizations in planning and operating vocational education courses is gaining in importance as a necessary factor in successful operation of such schools.

4. Following American leadership, occupational skill training, whatever its setting, begins at a later age than it previously did, due to the extension of compulsory education and the conversion of lower-secondary education to general education only.

5. Also following American initiatives, career education and general preparation for work and the transition from school to work has become important in the education of the younger age groups.

CHAPTER IV

The Structure of the Labor Market and Associated Training Patterns

MARCIA FREEDMAN

Trends in Employment Patterns

The structure of employment in the American economy has undergone two major transformations in this century. The first was the movement out of agriculture, which came earlier in the United States than in any other country except England. By 1920, the farm population had already declined, but it still constituted 30 percent of the total; by 1950, the proportion had fallen to 15 percent, by 1970, to 5 percent, and by 1978 (under a somewhat more restrictive definition), to 3 percent.[1]

The decline of agricultural employment, it should be noted, had quite different origins and consequences in the major farming areas of the nation. In the Middle West, mechanization and productivity increases were the order of the day, while in the South, the collapse of the cotton economy deepened the impoverishment *and* the depopulation of rural areas. The transfer of population from farm to factory was by no means a smooth or joyful process, but burgeoning industrial centers did provide employment for displaced farm tenants and farm laborers.

The second transformation took place more gradually. In 1947, manufacturing accounted for 35 percent of total nonagricultural employment, a proportion that has drifted downward to reach about 24 percent in the late 1970s. In the middle 1960s, when this downturn became apparent, there was some concern about the employment effects of "automation," but more frequently it was

---

1. U.S. Bureau of the Census, *Farm Population of the United States: 1978*, Current Population Reports, P-27, No. 52 (Washington, D.C.: U.S. Government Printing Office, 1979).

interpreted as the emergence of a prosperous postindustrial society that could readily support a life-enhancing shift to services. This optimistic assessment was somewhat clouded by concern for the alleged low productivity of service activities; more recently, it gave way altogether to the realization that the United States had for some time been falling behind other countries in the quality, the price, and the competitiveness of its manufactured goods. It turns out that the hegemony of American industry in the domestic market has been undermined, not only in textiles and apparel, but also in steel, automobiles, and electronics.

The slow decline in manufacturing employment, together with concomitant expansion in the service industries, has shaped the occupational requirements and rewards of the current period. The shift in industry shares of employment over the last two decades shows these effects in greater detail. In the period from 1960 to 1976, some industries grew in proportion to the total economy, but there were outstanding losers and gainers. (See table 1.)

TABLE 1

GROWTH AND DECLINE BY INDUSTRIAL SECTOR, 1960-1976

	PERCENT OF TOTAL EMPLOYMENT	
	1960	1976
Stable Growth		
Construction	6.2	5.9
Communications and utilities	2.7	2.7
Trade	17.1	17.6
Consumer services	11.7	11.2
Public administration	4.9	5.3
Lower Growth		
Agriculture	8.5	3.5
Mining	1.1	0.9
Manufacturing	26.2	22.0
Transportation	3.9	3.1
Higher Growth		
Producer and legal services	7.0	9.7
Health	4.2	7.2
Education	6.9	10.4
Total	100.0	100.0

Source: Industry-Occupation Matrices for 1960 and 1976, Bureau of Labor Statistics microdata.

A conventional interpretation of the proportionate shifts in table 1 focuses on professional and technical jobs in the services.

Such jobs, requiring high levels of education and training, did in fact increase more rapidly than the average, but so too did the poorly paid and unstable occupations at the bottom of the structure. What decreased in number were those jobs in the middle range that combined loose requirements with decent pay, such as blue-collar production jobs in large-scale manufacturing.

The underlying shifts in *industry* categories are largely responsible for profound changes in the occupational structure and the demand for labor. Table 2 shows these changes in two stages,

TABLE 2

CHANGE IN EMPLOYMENT BY OCCUPATIONAL GROUPS, 1960-1967 AND 1970-1976

OCCUPATION	EMPLOYMENT 1960 (000)	1960-1967 PERCENT CHANGE	EMPLOYMENT 1970 (000)	1970-1976 PERCENT CHANGE
Professionals	5,014	34.4	7,248	17.5
Semiprofessionals and technicians	2,860	29.3	4,597	29.6
Nonfarm managers	8,155	8.9	8,729	20.4
Office clericals	3,795	28.3	6,918	13.7
Nonoffice clericals	5,940	25.2	6,483	11.9
Sales workers	4,210	7.1	4,892	9.9
Craft workers	7,646	13.4	9,296	8.5
Operatives	11,693	16.4	13,023	0.5
Service workers	7,574	15.2	9,848	14.2
Nonfarm laborers	3,539	− 0.5	4,173	3.5
Farmers and farm workers	5,212	−31.3	2,655	− 6.0
Total	65,638	13.1	77,862	11.4

Source: Industry-Occupation Matrices for 1960, 1967, 1970, and 1976, Bureau of Labor Statistics microdata.

from 1960 to 1967 and from 1970 to 1976, as a way of highlighting the critical divergence that occurred in the late 1960s. Data from the early 1960s show an economy gaining strength in manufacturing (hence, larger than average increases in craft workers and operatives, albeit with a continuing decline among laborers); a very large decline in farm workers at all levels; and extraordinary increase in all other white-collar categories, much of it due to expansion in the health and education industries.

These trends (up to 1968) were the result of several interacting factors. The economic growth rate was relatively higher (4-5 percent annually)[2] than in the 1950s, in part because of the guns and butter strategy followed during the simultaneous prosecution of the Vietnam War and the War on Poverty. The bouyancy of manufacturing and the concomitant growth in the health and education industries are directly linked to the twin policies of the period. Expansion in education and in certain manufacturing industries was also helped along by demographic trends, the increase in school-age children, increases in college enrollment, the high rate of family formation, and the booming increases in demand for consumer durables.

In retrospect, it is clear that the 1960s encouraged expectations that the 1970s did not, and perhaps could not, fulfill. In fact, the events of the 1960s were the forerunners in both economic and political terms of many of the reversals of the 1970s. The adverse balance of payments, the creation of the Eurodollar Market, and the export of capital, all had the effect of weakening the American economy even before the surge in energy and other basic commodity prices. The prosperity of the early 1960s, and the optimism it engendered, turns out to have been the unusual rather than the usual state of affairs in this era, which now seems to be characterized by chronically high rates of inflation and unemployment.

One reflection of this turn of events is apparent in employment shifts from 1970 to 1976. First, it is apparent that the decline in farmers and farm workers had practically bottomed out. In fact, most of the decrease in this period was an artifact of a higher dollar standard for defining commercial farming, which cut off the smallest size class. On an industry basis, agricultural employment actually increased slightly, but not enough to offset the loss in those classified as farmers.

Second, compared to overall growth, the service worker share of employment was greater than in the 1960s. A 24 percent decline in private household workers (from just under 1.5 to 1.1 million) was overwhelmed by the growth in other low-paid although somewhat less menial jobs in industries like restaurants and hotels and health.

2. In contrast, the annual real growth rate of the 1950s was 3.2 percent, and between 1970 and 1976, 2.9 percent. U.S. Bureau of the Census, *Statistical Abstract of the United States: 1978* (Washington, D.C.: U.S. Government Printing Office, 1978), p. 442.

The figures for blue-collar categories reflect the basic weakness of the manufacturing sector that had been obscured by the Vietnam War. Laborers showed a slow rate of increase; craft workers grew faster, but still below the average for the period; and operatives hardly grew at all. While some of this relative loss was due to a lag in recovery from the 1975 recession trough, the long-term trend in manufacturing remains unmistakably downward.

Blue-collar workers, however, are also employed in nonmanufacturing industries, and some of these have provided offsets to employment losses in manufacturing. The recovery of coal mining in the 1970s resulted in an increase of about 92,000 jobs between 1970 and 1976. Construction, which held up fairly well in the first half of the 1970s, provided 292,000 additional craft and operative jobs, offset in turn by a loss of 90,000 laborer jobs. Mining employment will continue to grow, but the trend is toward surface operations that produce a small proportion of jobs to output. The outlook for construction is always uncertain, but it is difficult to foresee a large boom during the 1980s, given population trends, pressure on public budgets, and the gyrations of money markets.

Finally, growth patterns among white-collar workers diverged from the earlier period, in some cases even more than among blue-collar workers. The rate of increase among professionals, while still above average, slowed down considerably. Two of the largest categories, teachers (3.6 million) and engineers (1.2 million) increased only 8 and 10 percent respectively. The slow growth in engineers is part of the manufacturing story. Teachers were affected by the leveling off of school and university enrollments, which are bound to decline more sharply in the 1980s as the absolute number of school-age children turns downward.

Physicians and dentists increased 17 percent, but the big growth was among accountants (29 percent), lawyers (40 percent) and the smaller group of computer systems analysts (58 percent). The increases in accounting, legal, and computing employment are intimately related to the growth of the producer and legal services industry and to the explosion in managerial, administrative, and supervisory functions. The data show a pattern of change in the rates of increase among white-collar workers that reflects new relationships and organizational styles.

The large increase in managers and administrators is the culmination of a long-term trend, which emerged more clearly in the 1970s because of the further decline in self-employed proprietors. (By 1976, the self-employed constituted only 17 percent of all managers.) Behind the growth of salaried managers is the expansion of white-collar hierarchies, which in turn emanates from more complex functions. Examples of this phenomenon abound. When large firms, and particularly conglomerates, must coordinate activities in many locations, their administrative ranks grow larger. When increasingly complicated benefit plans are put into place, the work formerly handled by clerks expands to new departments. When regulation becomes more complex, personnel are required, not only for compliance, but also for ferreting out loopholes. For every turn in the tax laws, specialists are required for interpretation and for maximizing tax-related advantages.

These are not new circumstances. Immediately after World War II, corporations like General Motors could afford a long strike of auto workers as a write-off against an existing excess profits tax, but that particular trade-off seems simple compared to current opportunities for improving the ubiquitous "bottom line" through acquisitions, mergers, investment credits, depreciation allowances, and even speculative activities in foreign currency markets. All of these produce paper, or latterly, computerized records, and a good deal of employment expansion to go with them. The result has been a certain amount of title upgrading. Yesterday's clerk may be today's administrative assistant, transferred thereby to the category of managers, at least as far as the census takers are concerned.

Clerical workers continued to show above-average increases in this period, but growth was not as strong as in the 1960s. Among those typically found in offices, secretaries increased 20 percent, but stenographers (a smaller group to begin with) declined 28 percent. Duplicating machine operators also increased 20 percent, a change associated with the relative decline of typists, who increased only 3 percent. Computer operators almost doubled, but keypunch operators declined, an evidence of the increasing sophistication of on-line operations. The introduction of "word processing" has made it possible to rationalize communications activity by the use of computerized typing and editing machines, telephone dictation directly onto tape, and the transmission of documents over telephone lines. This type of technological innovation has already cut into clerical employment (namely stenographers and typists), but the increase in industry sectors that use large numbers of clerical workers has more than outweighed the losses.

The potential for further displacement in office clerical jobs is clear by analogy to the history of the printing industry. Almost all printing is now some version of photo offset, most often beginning with a typewriter keyboard attached to a visual display terminal, a set of new processes that have altered the occupational structure of the industry. Lithographers have increased, while compositors have declined, but for the printing crafts as a whole, the period from 1970 to 1976 showed no change in employment, a forerunner of future absolute declines.

Meanwhile, the growth in the employment of nonoffice clericals was about average, which is to say, considerably slower than in the 1960s. Some jobs were curtailed because of computerized methods for dealing with inventory; thus, stock clerks and shipping and receiving clerks showed almost no gains. Post office employment also declined because of the introduction of automated mail sorting and the decline in services. The trend to self-service in retail stores continued unabated, however, so that while cashiers increased 30 percent, retail sales workers increased only 3 percent.

The most striking feature of table 2 is the continuing rapid increase among "Semiprofessionals and Technicians" (SPT). This category is a heterogeneous mix of specialists performing widely different duties in different industries. What happened in the 1970s is that the most important of these occupations, numerically, became a larger share in their respective industries. In the 1960s, for example, a good deal of the increase in SPT (including registered nurses) was health-related. In the 1970s, health personnel continued to expand (by 41 percent) with the industry, but groups attached to other industries also grew. The second largest of these was made up of engineering and science technicians, whose numbers increased slightly above the period average (14 percent). The growth in firefighters and police (23 percent) raised the share of the SPT category in the public administration sector. The increase of airline pilots and air traffic controllers (26 percent) had a similar effect on the transportation industry. Computer programmers and other middle-level data-processing specialists increased 46 percent; here the effect was felt across industries, not so much in numerical control of production processes, but rather in the record-keeping functions common to all.

A much larger group—athletes, artists, musicians, writers, and entertainers—increased 43 percent from 1970 to 1976 to almost a million. Some of this group are engaged in mundane activities, like the roughly 117,000 public relations specialists, but 187,000 painters and 153,000 musicians are surely not employed in commercial art and revenue-producing sound. What seems to lie behind these numbers is a greatly expanded interest in the arts, and an increase in the number of young adult aspirants. Helped out by families, earnings from casual employment, and the willingness to eschew the consumption urges of the majority in the short run, a certain number of the young spend at least some of their "moratorium" time in pursuit of the arts. Taking the labor market as a whole, this demonstrates a degree of flexibility made possible by the low opportunity cost of following one's desire in a loose labor market at a time when joining the mature labor force takes longer than in the past.

At the end of the 1970s, the same loosening of organizational ties was reflected in the rise of self-employment, which after decades of steady decreases actually grew faster than wage and salary work from 1976 to 1979.[3] What was particularly striking was the growth among younger workers. Taken together with the fact that the construction industry led the increase, we can infer that some portion of young full-time entrants to the labor market have substituted blue-collar self-employment for those missing jobs in traditionally more stable and higher-paid sectors.

From the point of view of the demand for workers, the labor market can be divided into a number of occupationally distinct segments, hierarchically ordered according to pay, associated bene-fits, and job security, that is, according to the degree of shelter

3. T. Scott Fain, "Self-Employed Americans: Their Number Has In-creased," *Monthly Labor Review* 103 (November 1980): 3-8.

afforded to their incumbents.[4] The results of the industry/occupation shifts described above can then be expressed in summary form by aggregating labor market segments into three levels of annual earnings that imply relative degrees of shelter in the market: at the top, earnings average 165 percent of overall mean earnings; in the middle, they approximate overall mean earnings; and at the bottom they are 60 percent of overall mean earnings. (See table 3.) The occupations at the top are heavily weighted toward professional and managerial pursuits. The bottom includes semiskilled and unskilled blue-collar jobs in low-wage industries, and white-collar and service jobs in retail trade, hospitals, restaurants, and other industries where employment is most likely to be unstable, wages low, and promotion unlikely.

TABLE 3

CHANGES IN EMPLOYMENT AND EARNINGS, 1970-76

| | 1976 EARNINGS CLASSES | | | |
	Top Third	Middle Third	Lowest Third	Total
Employment (000)	19,508	26,965	40,230	86,703
Percent change in employment 1970–76	16.9	6.1	12.5	11.4
Ratio to 1976 mean earnings	1.65	1.13	.60	1.00
Percent change in earnings, 1970–76	30.0	38.6	25.8	32.4

Source: 1970 Census and U.S. Bureau of the Census, *Survey of Income and Education,* 1976.

Table 3 shows the turn away from the experience of the 1960s in a different form. From 1970 to 1976, the number of jobs in both the high and the low earnings segments increased more than average at the expense of the middle segments; conversely, earnings improvements were smaller, on balance, in the top and bottom clusters, but greater in the middle. This reversal of conventional expectations does not signify the abrogation of the law of supply and demand. It does, however, show how labor market institutions stretch out any tendency toward equilibrium.

4. For the origins of the segmentation scheme used here, see Marcia Freedman, *Labor Markets: Segments and Shelters* (Montclair, N.J.: Allan-held, Osmun, and Co., 1976).

Given the slow buildup of structures that protect the status and earnings of workers, it is not surprising that imbalances can persist for some time before these arrangements are undermined. Furthermore, the earnings prospects of an aggregated group depend on what is happening to subgroups. Among the highest paid occupations, for example, physicians, who still have unparalleled power to protect and increase their earnings through entry restrictions and service pricing practices, increased less than other professionals. Lawyers, on the other hand, have increased more and flourished less. Given the recent crowding in this field, it is easy to anticipate a further decline in relative earnings since lawyers have nothing like the market power of doctors. Even the most litigious society in history can hardly be expected to absorb all the lawyers being turned out under present conditions. Market signals may result in slower growth of this profession, but in any case, legal training seems to be on the way to becoming a more general form of preparation, especially for administrators who find its language useful for exegesis. As they move into such occupations, lawyers, like college graduates in general, illustrate the case of a too large supply that can be absorbed in the labor market but with diminishing rates of return.

Included in the top third are other professionals, technicians, and craftworkers in government whose employment shelter derives from civil service status. At the federal level, they benefited from the Salary Reform Act of 1962, which mandated the principle of "prevailing wages," in effect establishing parity with the private sector. At the local level, wages increased rapidly as the result of informal political pressures in the wage-setting process, the spread of unionization, and the growing militancy of such groups as police and firefighters.[5]

The middle of the earnings distribution had the largest dollar gains overall and the smallest numerical increases. Most of the occupations represented here have strong sheltering arrangements, mainly through collective bargaining coverage, but also through civil service status and employment in large firms. In the public

5. Police and firefighters are classified here as "technicians in public administration." For an analysis of public sector wage determination, see David Lewin, "Aspects of Wage Determination in Local Government Employment," *Public Administration Review* 34 (March/April 1974): 149-55.

sector, teachers' earnings went up 47 percent, with postal workers not far behind. Construction craftworkers fell somewhat behind their previous level, with a 22 percent earnings gain, a harbinger of weakened effectiveness of union control. Meanwhile, a diminishing number of semiskilled and unskilled workers in sheltered industries shared a 43 percent earnings increase.

Those workers at the bottom of the structure increased in numbers at somewhat above the average rate but enjoyed less than average increases in earnings. Among them were operatives in low-wage manufacturing industries, like textiles and apparel; retail sales clerks; health service workers; and the lowest-paid occupations in the economy—service jobs in restaurants and hotels, consumer and repair services, and education; and nonoffice clericals in retailing (cashiers, stock clerks, and so forth).

Trends in Labor Supply

While these shifts in the occupational structure have profoundly affected opportunity, complementary changes have also occurred in labor supply. It is not necessary to assign cause and effect to see how new patterns of labor force participation fit into the new structure of employment. The most dramatic change has been in the number of working women. By 1978, 57 percent of all women sixteen years of age and over worked sometime during the year. While two-thirds of the increase over the previous decade was among women who worked all year, less than half of all female workers (44 percent) were employed both full-time and full-year in 1978, compared to about two-thirds of all male workers.[6] Women have increased their share of nontraditional jobs, but in absolute numbers not enough to affect their overall earnings position; they continue to earn about 60 percent as much as men, largely due to their disproportionate representation in the lower-paid, less stable, and part-time occupations, especially in those at the bottom of the earnings distribution that constitute about 40 percent of all jobs.

A few examples suffice to show their overall disadvantage. Among professional occupations, women outnumber men only in

6. The data on work experience in this section come from Anne McDougall Young, "Work Experience of the Population in 1978," *Special Labor Force Report 236* (Washington, D.C.: U.S. Department of Labor, 1980).

noncollege teaching, by a little more than 2.5 to 1; in contrast, there are only about 20,000 women engineers out of a total of 1.4 million. In sales work, women dominate in retail trade where pay is low, while men dominate in wholesale trade, where pay is higher. The same division is clear in manufacturing, where female operatives are an absolute majority in such nondurable manufacturing industries as textiles and apparel, while men are a majority in the basic, durable goods industries. Furthermore, women predominate in all the low-paid service categories—in health, education, food service, and personal services.

Black workers are also disproportionately represented in low-paid jobs. Overall, they constituted 10 percent, or 1 in 10, of those with work experience in 1978; while they were 1 in 7 of service workers, among professionals, they were only 1 in 16, and among managers, 1 in 22. These figures have to be viewed in the context of the proportion who worked during the year, a figure that was significantly lower for black men (73 percent) than for white men (82 percent) and Hispanic men (83 percent). Meanwhile, there was a sharp decline in year-round work among black men under age twenty-five, continuing the deterioration of the past twenty-five years, even in times of general economic improvement.

All young workers encounter more difficulty now than in the past in becoming established in the labor market. Those who can spend their teenage and some of their young adult years in school gain a double advantage; they not only acquire important credentials for working, but they also achieve a postponement of the search for a first full-time job. For most occupations outside of the (now traditional) youth labor market where the archetypical job is at a fast-food counter, we have a kind of age rationing. The stretching out of full-time entry has obvious consequences for training, but what is often overlooked is that the fragmented training patterns characteristic of the American scene also influence the prospects of young workers who are not college graduates. It is hardly overstating the case to say that in Japan, *only* young entry workers are attractive to employers who train them in anticipation of long tenure on the job, while in the United States, the better the job or its prospects, the less likely a young worker is to be hired.

What matters, then, are not only the formally stated requirements for job performance, but two other factors of overriding importance: the institutional patterns for acquiring these credentials and the differential access to entry jobs with prospects for skill acquisition and promotion.

Education and Training Requirements

Even though general education and specific vocational preparation may take place in the same institutional setting, it is useful to maintain the distinction between them, if only because the basic literacy acquired in school is logically prior to the acquisition of occupationally related skills. The question of how much schooling is required for adequate performance in a given job category cannot be definitively answered by looking at data on incumbents because the standard for entry rises with the educational achievements of the population. There is nothing mysterious about this phenomenon; quite simply, if the majority of new entrants to the labor force are high school graduates, and some have an additional one to three years of schooling, the jobs they fill are naturally transformed into "high-school-required" occupations.

The serious mismatch occurs at both ends of the structure. Jobs for dropouts have diminished faster than the dropout population, while jobs for college graduates have increased more slowly than the college graduate population. Since education confers benefits apart from returns in the labor market, it is more appropriate to speak of "underutilization" rather than "overeducation," but such semantic niceties aside, it is likely that formal schooling will continue to outpace opportunity in an evolving occupational structure.[7]

The trends described earlier in this chapter will not neatly accommodate projected increases in schooling (see table 4). The brief period from 1972 to 1978 shows the rapidity of the increase; the projection for 1980 anticipates further strengthening of the

7. There is a large literature on this subject. For a review of major work in the 1970s, see Ivar Berg and Marcia Freedman, "The American Workplace: Illusions and Realities," Change 9 (November 1977): 24-30 ff.

trend.[8] The quality of schooling remains an issue, and it should be clear that for those who never achieve basic literacy, employment prospects are by so much the worse as the general educational level is raised.

TABLE 4

EDUCATIONAL ATTAINMENT OF THE CIVILIAN LABOR FORCE

16 YEARS AND OVER, 1972, 1978, AND 1990 (PROJECTED)

YEARS OF SCHOOLING COMPLETED	PERCENT COMPLETING		
	1972	1978	1990 (projected)
11 or less	34.1	26.5	19.9
12–15	52.3	56.6	58.5
16 or more	13.6	16.9	21.7

Source: U.S. Department of Labor and U.S. Department of Health, Education, and Welfare, *Employment and Training Report of the President, 1979* (Washington, D.C.: U.S. Government Printing Office, 1979), p. 363, Table E-12.

TRAINING REQUIREMENTS

The question of training is, if anything, more vexed than the question of schooling. The variation in patterns of skill acquisition, not only for different occupations, but often for the same occupation, probably accounts for the approach to categorization adopted some time ago by the job analysts who produce the *Dictionary of Occupational Titles*. In their measurement scheme, time is the common denominator. Thus, "specific vocational preparation" (SVP) is divided into nine levels and defined as:

The amount of time required to learn the techniques, acquire information, and develop the facility needed for average performance in a specific job-worker situation. This training may be acquired in a school, work, military, institutional, or avocational environment. It does not include orientation training required of even every fully qualified worker to become accustomed to the special conditions of any new job. Specific vocational training includes training given in any of the following circumstances.

What follows is a list of possible sources of training, including

8. The figures overstate the proportion without high school diplomas because they include: (a) sixteen-to-nineteen-year-olds who accounted for about a third of the "dropout" population; and (b) an unknown number of adults who earn high school equivalency diplomas at some point after leaving school.

vocational education, apprenticeship, in-plant training, on-the-job training, and essential experience in other jobs.[9]

The interaction of shifts in the occupational structure with the complexities of training becomes somewhat clearer if we divide jobs into clusters that reflect both the level of training and the presence or absence of preemployment training. Table 5 represents a crude attempt to delineate such clusters and estimate their relative proportions.

TABLE 5

Occupations Clustered by Training Requirements

Training Pattern	Estimated Percent of Civilian Labor Force
Diverse in time and source	
Artists and performers	0.5
Managers, administrators, and supervisors	12.4
Preemployment training required	
Professionals (two years or more of preparation in college and graduate and professional schools)	10.5
Technical, clerical, and service workers (three months to two years of specific vocational preparation)	13.5
Preemployment training not required	
Skilled and semiskilled occupations	
High-skill, white-collar occupations (new entrants increasingly recruited from colleges and trained on the job)	2.9
High-skill, blue-collar occupations (two or more years of training after employment)	10.7
Other skilled and semiskilled occupations (three months to two years of training after employment)	12.2
Low-skill occupations (training less than three months and entirely on the job)	
Clerical	9.9
Blue collar	18.4
Service	9.0
Total	100.0

Source: Marcia Freedman and Anna Dutka, *Training Information for Policy Guidance,* U.S. Department of Labor, Employment and Training Administration, R and D Monograph 76 (Washington, D.C.: U.S. Government Printing Office, 1980), Table 1, p. 5.

Diverse training patterns. At least two major occupational groupings have training patterns so diverse as to defy classification.

9. U.S. Department of Labor, *Dictionary of Occupational Titles,* 4th ed. (Washington, D.C.: U.S. Government Printing Office, 1977).

Wherever artistic talent is involved, there has never been a simple sequence of mastery. But here, as in more prosaic pursuits, the growth of school-based training is evident in conservatories, ballet companies, art schools, and in university curricula for athletes, writers, and artists of all kinds.

Among managers, training is split three ways: the self-employed tend to be self-taught in the sense of acquiring their skills through experience, complete with error-filled trials. At the other extreme, growing numbers of MBAs in diverse specialties are hired to fill the ranks of managers and administrators in large firms. The third stream is recruited from college graduates—engineers and a fair number of humanities and social science majors—who become fellow-trainees of MBAs. The obvious trend in response to the increase in demand for administrative personnel is the "professionalization" of their training.

Professional training. The move toward more formal preparation among managers follows the pattern among traditionally defined professionals—physicians, dentists, lawyers, teachers, and the like—whose training was formalized early in the century. These occupations now have the most rigidly defined requirements, including not only standardized degrees, but also professional examinations and state licenses. Taken as a whole, the earnings advantage of this cluster has diminished somewhat, in line with the tendency to crowding evidenced among lawyers and aspirants for academic posts.

Other preemployment training. Besides professionals, only one additional cluster of occupations typically requires preemployment training as a condition of entry. About 60 percent of the cluster is accounted for by office clerical jobs—typists, secretaries, bookkeepers, and the like. These were and are jobs dominated by female high school graduates. Two countertrends are now diluting the homogeneity of the group. First is the transformation of a relatively small number of secretaries into administrative assistants. The other, and more significant, is the deskilling of certain job elements. Stenography, for example, is dying out, as more and more use is made of dictating and word processing equipment, which minimizes correction time and produces copies at will.

The remainder of this cluster includes allied health occupations

(15 percent of the total) and other engineering and science technicians (9 percent). Both of these are the stock in trade of the two-year technical and community colleges where the bulk of training takes place. Their success in the health industry is a good illustration of how exogenous factors can come together to shift the locus of training. The big demand for health personnel in the past two decades was largely due to the spread of third-party payment schemes, both public and private, but these rising reimbursements did not cover the cost of training, which more and more has been moved out of the hospital-based classroom and into the community.

Training for the remainder of the occupations in this cluster takes place in diverse institutional settings—from pilots trained by the military services to barbers, hairdressers, and cosmetologists who qualify for licensure in both public high schools and proprietary schools.

The lowest skilled jobs. The clusters discussed to this point account for about 37 percent of all jobs. At the other end of the spectrum is an equal proportion with minimal *occupational* skills learned entirely on the job in a relatively short time (less than three months). White-collar, blue-collar, and service jobs are all represented. The white-collar group consists of low-skilled office clericals—file clerks and duplicating machine operators, for example—together with a large number of nonoffice clericals—bank tellers, telephone operators, mail carriers, and cashiers and almost 2.5 million retail sales clerks.

Among low-skill blue-collar workers, the typical occupations are machine operatives, assemblers, and truck drivers. The service occupations include food-service workers, janitors and cleaners of all kinds, and the bottom rung of the allied health jobs—aides and orderlies.

Taken together, these jobs offer the lowest paid and least stable employment in the labor market. They are the province of young workers, minorities, women, and new immigrants—everyone, that is, except mature white males. Since many of these jobs are part-time (some can only be described as casual), putting their share of the labor market at over one-third somewhat overstates their importance; in the white-collar and service occupations, growth in demand nevertheless has corresponded with the rise in female participation in the labor force, as well as the demographic bulge in the youth population.

On-the-job skill acquisition. Skill acquisition for the approximately 25 percent of the remaining jobs also occurs in the workplace, but the levels involve significant training time, ranging from three months to several years. A significant proportion of these jobs, which typically employ mature men, are affected by declining demand. At the top are high-skill white-collar jobs that have been transformed over the years from "high-school" to "college" jobs. That is to say, they are filled by college graduates who learn their skills after employment. A typical occupational group consists of insurance specialists—agents, brokers, and underwriters—employed in an industry that provides a graded set of curriculum materials and examinations for skill acquisition.

While these occupations have increased in number, high-skill blue-collar occupations have leveled off or declined, in line with the diminished importance of manufacturing in the economy. It is in this context that contradictions arise with respect to training. Apprenticeship, the classical training modality, has never been strong in the United States, and while it is allegedly preferred, most craft workers have gained their skills in a less structured, even haphazard, set of experiences. The training problem, which remains unresolved, becomes critical from time to time in key occupations like machinists and tool and die makers. Here too, several circumstances combine: most shops in the critical machine tool industry are small, and they experience large and sudden shifts in demand. When business is brisk, there is no time for training; when it is slow, there is no money. The long-range effect is to undermine the capacity of American metal manufacturing to meet the competition from abroad. In this and other crafts, it is likely that fully trained immigrants are becoming a more significant source of supply than native-born trainees.

Finally, there is a melange of intermediate jobs where training time ranges from three months to two years—sewers and stitchers, deliverymen, painters, and the telephone crafts are included here, together with postal clerks and stock clerks. None of these jobs involves occupational skill acquisition before employment. Like the others described above, to get the job is to get the training, whether informally through experience or in structured, company-based programs.

Implications

The trends in the demand for workers at various skill levels and in the patterns of their training interact with such demographic factors as the age distribution of the population, labor force participation rates, levels of achieved schooling, and the special position of minority groups in such a way as to produce some general, if speculative, implications.

1. As long as years of schooling continue to increase, educational credentials for employment will rise. Questions about the *quality* of schooling, while they are important in their own right, have little bearing on this phenomenon. Presumably, individuals will continue to make investments in education for defensive reasons—that is, while the return is not guaranteed, diplomas and degrees remain a necessary condition for employment in most well-paying occupations.

2. Demand in the labor market has been strongest at the top and at the bottom of the skill hierarchy. At the top, training credentials are added to educational ones; at the bottom, training has little effect in improving opportunity.

3. Expansion of the more casual employment at the bottom of the skill hierarchy has meant more workers, each of whom earns less income. When these workers are the only earners in the family, the income produced is generally insufficient to live at acceptable standards of health and decency.

4. The increase in classroom training prior to full-time entry into the labor market has the same delaying effect as the lengthening of education, with which it is sometimes joined. Employers are willing to hire graduates of certain programs as a cost-cutting measure, but the growth of this kind of training in both public and proprietary schools has not yet made a significant contribution to the systematization of training in the middle-skill ranges.

5. The confusion attendant on training paths and skill acquisition contributes to the uncertainty of returns to education. Perhaps the single most telling critique of human capital theory is that it

fails to provide a coherent account of occupational choice.[10] Part of the reason is that while education credentials may be standardized, training is so diverse and so bound up with access to particular occupations as to increase the riskiness of prior educational investments.

6. In a labor market with excess supply, information about specific job opportunities and access (in the form of sponsorship or advance information) becomes critical for competing aspirants. It is here that minority groups are at the greatest disadvantage. The fact that more formal training also provides more formal channels of access is helpful to the disadvantaged, but it is important to emphasize that access is the prerequisite. It is only if employers agree beforehand to hire graduates that the opportunity opened up by training can be realized rather than remaining implicit.

10. Mark Blaug, "The Empirical Status of Human Capital Theory: A Slightly Jaundiced Survey," *Journal of Economic Literature* 14 (September 1976): 827-55.

CHAPTER V

Licensure and Certification

BENJAMIN SHIMBERG

Licensure has many faces. To the average consumer it is seen as a mechanism for quality assurance, a way to protect the unwary or uninformed against incompetent, dishonest, or unethical practitioners. To members of regulated occupations and professions, it is viewed as a way of upholding standards and enforcing professional discipline. To manpower officials, it is perceived as a means by which occupational groups may, on occasion, limit entry into a field or restrict mobility of skilled workers and professionals. To antitrust officials, it is often viewed as a method by which members of an occupational group may restrict competition.

How do vocational educators view licensing? Nobody knows for sure, but it is unlikely that there is any single point of view. Former practitioners who now prepare students for entry into licensed occupations are likely to favor licensure along with those already licensed. After all, their own jobs as teachers are made more secure by the existence of licensing requirements. Their students may receive higher pay and enjoy greater job security because of licensure. Even vocational educators who are not presently involved with a licensed occupation may see licensure as a way of enhancing the image as well as improving the social and economic status of their own occupational groups. Others may feel ambivalent, recognizing some possible benefits but also sensing drawbacks such as the loss of flexibility in what they can teach or in their methods of instruction.

This chapter will attempt to place licensing into perspective for the vocational educator. It will explain the differences between licensing and certification, how the licensing system works, requirements for licensure, the social consequences of licensure, and implications of licensure and certification for vocational education.

Some Terminology: Licensing and Certification Defined

The terms licensing and certification are often used interchangeably. While both are terms concerned with the credentialing of individuals, they are not synonymous.

LICENSING (PRACTICE CONTROL)

The underlying theory of licensure is that the state has an interest in regulating certain occupations because failure to do so might result in harm to the public health, safety, or welfare. Thus, the state exercises its police power to make it illegal for individuals to engage in activities or practices associated with a given occupation unless they first receive permission to engage in those activities from an appropriate governmental agency. The granting of licenses is usually based on the satisfaction of certain prerequisites, such as education, training, experience, and/or passing an examination. Licenses may be suspended or revoked for cause, such as being found guilty of negligence, incompetence, or unprofessional conduct. Typical examples of licensed practitioners are: doctors, dentists, pharmacists, nurses, plumbers, electricians, barbers, cosmetologists, real estate salespersons, and funeral directors.

CERTIFICATION (TITLE CONTROL)

The concept underlying certification is that it should be possible for the public to be able to differentiate between practitioners of an occupation who have met some predetermined standard (education, training, experience, passing an examination) and those who have not met that standard. When an occupation is certified (either by statute or through voluntary action of a professional or trade association), noncertified individuals are *not* prohibited from practicing. However, only those who have met the standard are permitted to use a designated title. For example, in most states anyone may call himself an auto mechanic and repair cars. However, only those mechanics who have met the standards of the National Institute of Automotive Service Excellence (NIASE), a nongovernmental certifying agency, may wear the insignia which identifies them as NIASE "certified mechanics." Typical examples of other certified workers are: respiratory therapists, dental assistants, medical technologists, and travel agents.

The confusion of terminology is compounded by historical usage of labels that no longer apply. For example, nurses are licensed, but they are still called "Registered Nurse" because at one time the names of qualified nurses were placed on an official register. In the life insurance field, those who meet the standards of the American College of Life Underwriters, the certification agency, are entitled to use the title "Chartered Life Underwriter" (CLU). Physicians who meet the standards of various medical specialty (certification) boards are called "Diplomates."

This chapter will deal primarily with licensure, although references will be made to certification where appropriate.

Historical Perspective

While licensure resembles the guild system of the middle ages as a method of regulating entry into various crafts, its development in the United States had little to do with apprenticeship training. Rather, it was the professions that provided the impetus for licensure in this country. During the latter part of the nineteenth century there were no laws governing who could practice medicine, dentistry, pharmacy, or various other professions. As a result, many untrained or poorly trained individuals were practicing on a hapless public. In an effort to set themselves apart from the quacks and charlatans, the better trained practitioners formed professional societies and restricted entry to those who could meet certain training and experience requirements. They also adopted codes of ethical practice.

These early professional societies may have helped improve the image of their professions, but they were totally ineffective in keeping unqualified individuals from practicing. Leaders of such groups eventually called on state legislators to use the police power of the state to prevent unqualified individuals from practicing. That is how the first modern licensing laws were passed. Responsibility for administering these early licensing laws was lodged with boards made up of leaders of the professional societies. Thus began the tradition of self-regulation. Boards were given authority to set standards, promulgate rules, prepare and administer examinations, and oversee the conduct of licensees. By 1900 there were provisions for licensure of the older professions in practically every state.

As other groups recognized the potential benefits of self-regulation, they too asked legislatures to pass laws similar to those licensing the older professions. From only a handful of occupations licensed at the turn of the century, the number has grown to more than 800.[1] During the past few years, in response to allegations of abuse, there has been an effort on the part of legislators in many states to slow the growth of licensure. A publication of the Council of State Governments, *Occupational Licensing: Questions a Legislator Should Ask*,[2] is part of a growing movement to persuade legislators to reexamine the need for so much regulation and to urge consideration of less restrictive regulatory techniques, such as certification.

Occupational licensing has also received more intense scrutiny than ever before as a result of the passage of "sunset" legislation by more than thirty states. The purpose of sunset laws is to identify agencies or programs that may have outlived their usefulness or which are not doing a satisfactory job. The result hoped for is that unnecessary or nonfunctioning agencies would either be terminated or reorganized. Rather than inaugurate the sunset process by reviewing the large, complex agencies, such as education, corrections, or social welfare, most states have focused their initial attention on occupational regulatory agencies. These are usually much smaller in size and seemed to many legislators like a promising arena in which to evaluate the usefulness of the sunset process. As a result, a massive amount of data has been collected about the activities, strengths, and shortcomings of licensing boards. Although relatively few boards have been abolished, a number of boards have been consolidated and a number of operating reforms have been introduced.

How the Licensing System Works

LICENSING BOARDS

The licensing system in the United States revolves around the

1. Karen Greene and R. Gay, *Occupational Regulation in the U.S.* (Washington, D.C.: Employment and Training Administration, U.S. Department of Labor, 1980).

2. Benjamin Shimberg and Doug Roederer, *Occupational Licensing: Questions a Legislator Should Ask* (Lexington, Ky.: Council of State Governments, 1978).

existence of licensing boards. Until recently, most boards were made up exclusively of members of the occupational group. When exceptions occurred, it was because the legislature may have seen fit to include a representative of some appropriate governmental agency or from a related occupational group on the board. For example, a health department sanitarian is often found on the plumbing board, a code enforcement official on the electrical board, or a physician on the nursing board.

During the past decade there has been a movement to add consumer representatives to licensing boards. Initially these "public members" were few in number, but as the consumer movement has become more powerful, their number has increased. A 1980 survey by the Council of State Governments (CSG) of public members on health-related boards, showed that public members are found in every state except Louisiana.[3] The number of boards requiring public members varied from one or two to as many as sixteen (Nevada); fifteen (Maine); fourteen (New York, Arizona, and Michigan); and thirteen (West Virginia, Wisconsin). The CSG tabulation showed a total of 587 public members on health related boards.

Because of the complexity of most occupational fields, legislators usually set forth general regulatory policies and standards in a licensing law and give boards the responsibility for working out details. These boards have the power, pursuant to the legislation that created them, to adopt regulations that have the force of law. They can set forth standards of good practice as well as standards of good conduct. They also have the power to investigate complaints against licensees, conduct hearings, and take disciplinary action, including the suspension of licenses and revocation of a licensee's right to practice.

As licensing boards were created, they were usually left to stand alone, unattached to any department or agency of government. This meant that they could operate with virtually no oversight. They hired their own staffs, processed their own paper work, prepared and administered their own tests, and conducted their own investigations. Their feeling of independence was heightened

3. Doug Roederer, *Public Members on Health Licensure Boards* (Lexington, Ken.: Council on State Governments, 1980).

by the fact that most boards were supported out of income from licensing fees. Unlike other agencies of government, they usually did not have to appear before the legislature to ask for funds or justify their expenditures.

Efforts to curb the power of boards by establishing "umbrella" agencies go back to 1892, when all professional boards in New York State were placed under the Board of Regents. Similar agencies were established in Illinois (1917), Washington (1932), Pennsylvania (1923), and California (1929). In 1969, sixteen states had centralized licensing agencies. By 1980, that number had increased to thirty-one.[4]

In a 1980 survey, Roederer and Shimberg queried legislative staff members, board members, and central agency personnel regarding their reasons for favoring or opposing the centralization of state licensure functions.[5] Of the 133 respondents, drawn from all fifty states, 25 percent favored autonomy for licensing boards, 32.6 percent favored centralization, and 42.4 percent were neutral and their position could not be determined. Among the reasons often cited for favoring autonomous boards were: peer control over standards and conduct, avoidance of unnecessary layers of bureaucracy, and insulation of boards from political pressures. By contrast, critics of autonomous boards argued that centralized agencies could operate more efficiently by sharing staff and facilities, promoting greater coordination among boards, providing greater oversight of board activities, and making boards more accountable to the public. In the absence of adequate oversight, said some critics, boards have sometimes used their powers to promote the interests of the occupational group rather than those of the public.

THE MECHANICS OF LICENSURE

Applicants for licensure must file an application and pay a fee. The qualifications of applicants are then reviewed either by the staff of the central agency or by the staff of the individual board. Those who meet a board's stated qualifications are usually required

4. Doug Roederer and Benjamin Shimberg, *Centralizing State Licensure Functions* (Lexington, Ky.: Council of State Governments, 1980).

5. Ibid., p. 5.

to take an examination. Those who pass are almost certain to be licensed.

Once individuals have been licensed, they may usually renew their licenses simply by paying a fee. Certain occupations require that licensees submit evidence that they have met stipulated continuing education requirements.[6] At the present time, no licensed occupation requires that its licensees be reexamined or provide evidence of continued competence as a condition of relicensure. However, a number of certification agencies, such as the National Board of Family Practice, do require periodic reassessment as a condition of relicensure.

Licensing agencies often use inspectors to make sure that board regulations are being observed and investigations are made to follow up on complaints. When a complaint against a licensee appears to have merit, the licensee is ordered to appear before the board for a hearing. Some boards conduct their own hearings, but there is a growing tendency for boards to utilize attorneys experienced in administrative law to function as hearing officers. A hearing officer may present the board with findings of fact, conclusions of law, and with recommendations regarding appropriate disciplinary action. However, the final decision regarding disciplinary action usually rests with the board, subject, in some instances, to review by the director of the umbrella agency.[7]

Requirements for Licensure or Certification

In order to be licensed or certified, individuals must meet the standards set by the agency authorized to grant the credential. Where licensing or certification is controlled by a state law, the requirements may be set forth in the law or they may be found in regulations adopted by a board. Certification agencies, which do not have any basis in law, are often created by members of the occupational group with assistance from their trade or professional associations. Enforcement of the standards of voluntary certifica-

6. L. Phillips, "Status of Mandatory Continuing Education for Selected Professions," in *Higher Education Desk Book 1980-81* (Washington, D.C.: Editorial Projects in Education, Inc., 1980), pp. 212-13.

7. Committee of the Office of Attorney General, *Disciplinary Action Manual for Occupational Licensing Boards* (Lexington, Ky.: Council of State Governments, 1978).

tion usually rests on peer pressure rather than on legal sanctions. Credentialing, whether by a licensing or certification agency, is usually based on evidence that the individual has met specified education, training, and experience requirements and has passed an examination. These requirements will be discussed briefly.

EDUCATION

Some minimum level of traditional education, such as completion of high school, is often included as a requirement for licensure for jobs in the skilled trades and service occupations. In the field of cosmetology, for example, some states, like Pennsylvania, will license an applicant who has completed the tenth grade. Others, such as New Jersey, insist on a high school diploma. What happens when a person with a tenth-grade education licensed in Pennsylvania wishes to relocate to New Jersey? The existence of an educational requirement in New Jersey makes licensure very difficult. The law says that one must have a high school diploma in order to be licensed. The board has no discretion. The fact that the individual may have practiced successfully for years in another state makes no difference. When such situations arise, people ask "What has a high school diploma to do with being a competent hairdresser?"

Nobody is sure of the historical basis for having an educational requirement in the first place, but it probably stemmed from a desire to encourage people to finish high school; or it may have arisen because of a belief that a high school education was needed to complete the training program successfully. In the author's view, neither reason is relevant to the purpose of licensing (that is, to protect the public). If completion of high school is considered socially desirable, it should be made mandatory for all students, not dealt with in an indirect way. If high school graduation is considered necessary for success in a training program, it should be made a requirement for admission to the program. Once a person has successfully completed training, however, it makes little sense to make formal education a requirement for licensure.

TRAINING

In professions such as medicine and dentistry, licensing boards require completion of specialized training in an accredited institution. Accreditation is usually bestowed by regional or specialty accreditation associations. In some fields such as nursing and cosmetology, however, the licensing board often assumes responsibility for setting educational and training facility standards, approving schools, and even certifying the instructors who do the teaching.

The requirement that applicants must have completed an approved program of study creates problems for individuals who may have acquired the requisite skills in other ways. For example, army or navy "medics" with excellent training in service schools and years of experience in military hospitals, were often denied the opportunity even to take the examination for licensed practical nurse because they had not completed a program of training in an approved school of practical nursing as required by law.

Such incidents have led to increased demands for greater flexibility in satisfying training requirements. Critics of the existing system, with its rigid training and experience requirements, say that it does not matter how people acquired their skills. What matters is the ability to perform the job in a safe and effective manner. While the concept of "alternate pathways" may not be applicable to all fields, there can be little doubt that it is applicable to many fields. Thus far, there has been relatively little progress in the licensure field toward the development of measures to assess competence that may have been acquired in nontraditional ways or the acceptance of "alternate pathways" as a legitimate method of satisfying training requirements.

EXPERIENCE

Like the training requirement, the experience requirement is usually accepted uncritically because it is clearly job-related and it seems to make sense that an individual should have had some experience under supervision before being allowed to practice independently.

Many training programs provide for a considerable amount of such hands-on experience. Nurses, dentists, physical therapists, cosmetologists, and plumbers all spend some time performing the job under supervision prior to graduation from training. But many training programs for licensed occupations emphasize theory and expect the practitioner to get supervised experience after completion of formal training. Professional programs for engineers and architects usually fall into this category.

One would anticipate that the experience requirement would apply to the latter category, but not the former. Yet in practice one finds little uniformity. Cathcart and Graff made a study of the experience requirements in California licensing laws.[8] They found that dispensing opticians who fit and sell eyeglasses only upon prescription of an optometrist or ophthalmologist are required to have five years of experience prior to licensure. Yet a hearing aid dispenser who diagnoses hearing disorders and fits and sells hearing aids need not have any experience.

Using a rating system that took into account (a) seriousness of impact on the consumer, (b) need for discretion on the part of the licensee and (c) need for additional practical training beyond formal education courses, Cathcart and Graff were able to assign index values (o to 10.5) to various occupations. It seemed reasonable to them that occupations with similar index values would require similar amounts of experience. "If some amount of experience might be justified," they concluded, "it would be in those occupations scoring at the high end of the rating continuum."

They found that dentists, registered nurses, veterinarians, chiropractors, hearing aid dispensers, podiatrists, and registered social workers all had index values of 5.5 to 6.0. Since none of these is required to meet an experience requirement beyond the educational requirement, it would seem that pharmacists, speech pathologists and audiologists, and dispensing opticians (also 5.5 to 6.0) should be similarly treated. But in fact, the experience requirement for the latter group, varies from 1500 hours to five years! Among nonhealth occupations, construction inspectors, funeral directors, insurance adjusters, pest control field representatives, and geologists all have ratings of 5.5. This suggests that they should have roughly comparable experience requirements. In reality, the amount of experience for these fields ranges from zero to seven

8. James A. Cathcart and Gil Graff, "Occupational Licensing: Factoring It Out," *Pacific Law Journal* 9 (January 1978): 147-63.

years. The authors could find no discernable rationale for the randomness of the requirements.

Despite the confusion and contradictions in their findings, Cathcart and Graff do not advocate abolishing the experience requirement. Rather, they suggest that more refined procedures be developed for determining when such a requirement is necessary and how long it should be.

EXAMINATIONS

Most boards give only written examinations, but some, such as dentistry and cosmetology, may also require applicants to pass a "practical" or "hands on" examination. Responsibility for examining applicants rests with the licensing board. In a number of occupations, mainly the skilled trades, board members often assume responsibility for deciding what is to be covered, what kinds of questions to ask, what constitutes a satisfactory answer to each question, and what score is needed to pass. There has been a growing tendency of boards, especially in the professions, to rely on central testing agencies to prepare, administer, and score their licensing examinations. Among the leading national testing agencies are the American College Testing Program, Educational Testing Service, National Evaluation Systems, the Professional Examination Service, and the Psychological Corporation. The National Board of Medical Examiners also prepares licensing examinations for physicians and certification examinations for a number of medical specialty groups.

In a 1972 study, Shimberg called attention to shortcomings of some licensure examinations, especially those prepared by state boards without the assistance of qualified testing specialists.[9] He noted an extensive use of essay examinations with highly subjective grading standards. He also found that examinations were often prepared without the benefit of an up-to-date job analysis or specifications to assure that various topics received their proper weight in the test questions. Multiple-choice questions were often poorly constructed without adequate review or consideration of their psychometric properties. Practical or performance examinations

9. Benjamin Shimberg, Daniel H. Kruger, and Barbara F. Esser, *Occupational Licensing: Practices and Policies* (Washington, D.C.: Public Affairs Press, 1972).

were also faulted for lack of standardization, lack of clear grading standards, and for the unreliability of judgments by those who rated the applicants.

Title VII of the Civil Rights Act of 1964 prohibited private employers from using tests or other employment procedures that discriminated unfairly against members of minority groups and women. However, employees of state and local government were not covered by the law. In March 1972, Congress amended the 1964 law to include government employees.

To implement the intent of Congress, several federal agencies began work in 1972 to develop guidelines covering employment selection procedures. The task was not completed until December 1978, when "Uniform Guidelines on Employee Selection Procedures" were published.[10] While there is some controversy as to whether or not the uniform guidelines apply to tests used for licensing and certification, they nevertheless provide technical validation standards which boards may wish to consider in evaluating the relationship between their tests and the occupational and professional competencies they are designed to assess.

The major thrust of the guidelines is toward insuring that tests are job-related and valid. Three types of validity are recognized in the guidelines, but only content validity and criterion-related validity will be discussed here.

Content validity. The content validity of a test depends on the degree to which the questions (or other tasks) may be accepted as representative of performance within a specifically defined content domain of which the test is a sample. If a test is to be used for making a licensure decision, the relevant content may be a performance sample (such as requiring an auto mechanic to adjust a set of brakes) or it may be a set of questions which sample the knowledge, skills, or abilities judged necessary by the licensing board for that level of competence which adequately protects the public's health, safety, and welfare. The content validity of a test can be established through several means, most effectively by demonstrating that the job in question was subjected to a careful

10. "Uniform Guidelines on Employee Selection Procedures adopted by U.S. Equal Employment Opportunity Commission, U.S. Civil Service Commission, U.S. Department of Labor, and U.S. Department of Justice," *Federal Register,* August 25, 1978, Part IV.

job analysis, that the test specifications are closely linked to the findings of the job analysis, and that the questions or problems on the examination are based on the test specifications. Under certain circumstances the pooled judgment of experts may be used instead of a formal job analysis in developing test specifications.

Criterion-related validity. One measure of a good test is its ability to identify those who will do well or poorly with respect to some measure of performance, such as productivity or a supervisor's rating of job performance. The performance measure, whatever its nature, is referred to as a "criterion." When those scoring high on a test also do well with respect to the criterion, the test is said to have criterion-related validity. Criterion-related validity can be established in two ways: by comparing test scores with the performance ratings of current employees (concurrent validity) or by comparing test scores of newly hired employees with subsequent performance on the job (predictive validity).

One of the major uses of tests in the business world is to help in employee selection. The purpose of the test is to permit a ranking of applicants by test score, so that the employer may hire those with the highest scores. If the test has predictive validity, those with high scores are likely to do better on the job than those with low scores.

In licensing and certification, users of tests have a different purpose in mind. They are not faced with the problem of selecting from among many applicants those best qualified to fill a limited number of job openings. Rather, their goal is to determine, from among all those who apply for licensure or certification, which ones meet a predetermined standard. For licensure, that standard is usually defined as "minimum competence" because the stated purpose of licensure is to protect public health, safety, and welfare. One way of protecting the public is by denying licensure to those who fail to meet minimum competence standards. If everyone who applies meets the standard, all should be licensed.

Certification agencies, in contrast, frequently set a higher standard because they want their credential to signify something more than minimum competence. Indeed, some groups say that their certification award is indicative of "excellence."

The differences in purpose between selection tests and licensing/certification tests raises questions about the appropriate validation techniques. For the criterion-related validation strategy to be feasible, it is necessary to have a common performance criterion. Such a criterion is usually available in the business setting because the employees who were tested usually work for a common employer who determines the standards of performance for the job. Licensees, on the other hand, may be employed in a diversity of work settings. While the license is an authorization to practice, it usually does not specify the practice locale. Not only are licensees likely to do different tasks under different conditions, but the expectations of their supervisors and supervisory evaluation standards may vary enormously. For example, all physicians may take the same examination for licensure. Some will go into solo practice, while others will work in clinics or hospitals. Some will conduct research and some may work for insurance or pharmaceutical companies. Their duties will vary greatly. Hence the likelihood of being able to evaluate their performance in terms of a common criterion is slim. That is why content validity, rather than criterion-related validity, would appear to be the preferred strategy for evaluating licensing and certification tests.

REQUIREMENTS UNRELATED TO COMPETENCE

Licensure laws sometimes contain requirements that bear little or no relationship to the competence of the applicant. These will be mentioned briefly so that readers will be aware of them, but no attempt will be made to discuss these requirements in detail.[11]

Citizenship. The United States Supreme Court has on several occasions ruled that citizenship is not a valid requirement for licensure,[12] yet it is still found in many state licensure laws. Legal aliens may be deterred from applying for licensure in the mistaken belief that they would be rejected because they are not citizens.

Residency. This requirement has also been declared invalid by

11. For a more detailed discussion of licensure requirements see Benjamin Shimberg, *Occupational Licensing: A Public Perspective* (Princeton, N.J.: Educational Testing Service, 1980), pp. 55–105.

12. See *Graham v. Richardson,* 403 U.S. 365 (1971).

the Supreme Court,[13] but it is still found in licensure statutes in a number of states. Some qualified applicants may not seek licensure in the belief that they are ineligible because they have not lived in the state for a sufficient period of time.

Good moral character. This requirement often works a hardship on those who have at some time in the past run afoul of the law. The American Bar Association (ABA) has recommended that only arrests followed by conviction be considered and that denial of a license be based only on conviction for serious crimes that bear a direct relationship to the occupation for which licensure is sought.[14] For example, conviction for manslaughter or murder should not necessarily disqualify applicants seeking licensure in skilled trades or professions, since these crimes bear no relationship to the occupations in question. However, conviction for embezzlement might disqualify a person seeking to be licensed as an accountant or a real estate broker because both involve fiduciary responsibilities. The ABA also urges that the following factors be taken into consideration: (a) age of the individual and surrounding circumstances at the time of the offense, (b) length of time that has elapsed since the unlawful activity, (c) evidence of successful rehabilitation.

Social Consequences of Licensure

Among the frequently cited benefits of licensure are: in-depth screening of those seeking to enter an occupation; higher practice and conduct standards; a mechanism for investigating and taking disciplinary action against incompetents and wrongdoers; and a method by which the public can identify practitioners who are at least minimally qualified.

Critics say that there is altogether too much licensing and that some of the by-products of licensing are detrimental to the public.

---

13. See *Shapiro v. Thompson*, 394 U.S. 618 (1969); *Keenan v. Board of Law Examiners*, 317 F Supp. 1350 (EDNC 1970); *Hindin v. Orbeck*, H37 U.S. 518 (1978); and *Matter v. Gordon* (No. 482) as reported in *National Law Journal*, November 20, 1979.

14. James W. Hunt, James E. Bowers, and Neal Miller, *Laws, Licenses. and the Offenders' Right to Work: A Study of Laws Restricting the Occupational Licensing of Former Defenders* (Washington, D.C.: American Bar Association, National Clearinghouse on Offender Employment Restrictions, 1973).

Following are a number of points on which licensure has been criticized. Not everyone agrees on the validity of these allegations, but they are presented here so that readers will be aware of the issues currently being debated.

RESTRICTED ENTRY TO JOBS

Licensing laws are enacted to keep out incompetents, yet new licensing laws often provide that those currently practicing in an occupation will be automatically granted licensure under a so-called "grandfather clause." In other words, the higher standards usually apply only to those seeking entry subsequent to enactment of the law. Certification programs, by contrast, seldom include a grandfather provision.

It has been alleged that boards have, on occasion, sought to restrict entry of newcomers by giving exceptionally difficult tests or raising the score required to pass. Such allegations are difficult to prove, but some evidence to support them may be found in a study by Rayack, an economist at the University of Rhode Island. He studied pass/fail rates on licensing examinations for twelve occupations (plumber, barber, hairdresser, electrician, funeral director, embalmer, electrologist, real estate salesperson, real estate broker, dental hygienist, physical therapist, and optician) in three New England states. He used records going back to the creation of most boards—in some instances spanning a period of nearly sixty years. In every occupation studied, he found that in periods of prosperity, when employment was high, passing rates for these occupations also tended to be high. When there was widespread unemployment and job opportunities were scarce, however, the passing rates tended to be low. In ten of the twelve occupations, the differences in passing rates were statistically significant. Only hairdressers in Connecticut and funeral directors in Rhode Island failed to yield statistically significant differences, but even these two occupations showed failure rates on examinations positively correlated with unemployment.[15]

Since Rayack's study covered only a limited number of occupa-

15. Elton Rayack, *An Economic Analysis of Occupational Licensure* (Washington, D.C.: Employment and Training Administration, U.S. Department of Labor, 1976), p. 146.

tions, it is not safe to generalize too broadly from his data. More studies are needed to determine the extent to which boards may have used tests to restrict entry in the past and to ascertain whether or not such practices continue at the present time.

Another means by which the supply of practitioners is limited is found in apprenticeship programs. By agreement between the union and employers, the number of apprentices accepted for training is often set as a proportion of employed journeymen. Thus, during periods of low employment, those seeking training will find few openings. Since completion of an approved apprenticeship program is a requirement for licensure in certain skilled trades, those individuals who cannot gain entry into the program have no hope of becoming licensed.

The duration of apprenticeship training is another area of concern. Many people feel that apprenticeship programs are often made longer than necessary so as to limit the number of individuals who can qualify. When apprenticeship is made a formal requirement for licensure, graduates of vocational programs will find themselves unable to obtain a license no matter how competent they may be. If they want to qualify, they must seek admittance to an apprenticeship program. In all likelihood, they would probably be given some credit for time spent in the vocational program, but they would still be required to put in several years of apprenticeship regardless of the level or skill they possessed at entry into the program.

INCREASED COST TO THE PUBLIC

When an occupational group achieves licensed status, newcomers seeking to enter the field may be turned away because they are unable to meet the new, higher standards or to pass the examination. Thus, the group in control may artificially limit the number of practitioners. As when any commodity or service is in short supply, its price is likely to rise without necessarily providing higher quality to consumers.

Another charge to the public may come in the form of higher costs for school-based vocational programs. For example, owners of proprietary cosmetology schools may seek to persuade the licensing board that it would be desirable to increase the number of training hours required for licensure. They could then charge higher tuition and also derive additional income from fees paid by patrons of the school salon at which students provide services without compensation. Thus, an increase in the number of hours required could provide economic benefits to school owners. However, vocational educators in the public sector would also have to increase the number of instructional hours if they wanted their students to qualify for licensure, but they could not pass on the cost of those extra hours to their students since their students paid no tuition for their training. The increased cost of providing training in cosmetology would have to come out of the vocational program budget, which is ultimately paid by the public.

LIMITED SCOPES OF PRACTICE

Licensing laws are often called "practice acts" because they set forth the "scope of practice" for the occupational group. When groups sought licensure, they have usually argued that it is necessary to have their scopes of practice defined broadly in order to prevent unqualified persons from engaging in *any* aspect of the occupation. However, as technology has expanded and as new occupational categories have emerged, members of these newly emerging groups have often found themselves in conflict with already licensed groups. The established groups are likely to want to protect their "turf" and to take legal action to prevent "illegal" practice by the newcomers. The response of some emerging groups has been to seek licensed status. The result has often been the creation of new licensed categories and the further fragmentation of service.

Conflicts also arise when an already licensed group seeks to expand its functions. Suppose, for example, nursing educators are convinced that they can train students to assume responsibilities for functions that go beyond those permitted under existing law and that permitting nurses to carry out such functions would be in the public interest. To bring about a change in the law to permit expanded practice, they would have to convince the legislature that the change was both safe and socially desirable. At hearings on the proposed change, legislators would in all likelihood hear a great deal of conflicting testimony about the proposal. Their decision would have to be made on the basis of expert opinion rather than on the basis of objective evidence, because under existing law there would be no way to collect such evidence. It would be illegal for licensees to perform acts outside of their scopes of practice; hence no data bearing on the practicality or safety of the proposed change could be collected.

To break out of this impasse, the California legislature enacted a Health Manpower Pilot Projects Act (HMPP) in 1973.[16] The law authorizes the Office of Statewide Planning and Development within the State Health Department to approve projects which would provide training for new or expanded roles for health workers and subsequently to evaluate the performance of these health workers in their new roles. The goal of the legislation is to determine whether health care personnel can be utilized in new roles and whether health tasks can be reallocated to better meet the health needs of the community. The act permits scopes of practice of existing licensees to be expanded beyond current legal definitions for limited periods. The applicant group must specify the tasks trainees would perform, training facilities, faculty resources, and how the performance of trainees is to be evaluated. Since 1973, more than 140 pilot projects have been approved and a number of them have resulted in the expansion of functions performed by nurses, dental hygienists, physician's assistants, and pharmacists.[17]

LIMITED INTERSTATE MOBILITY

Americans live in a highly mobile society. Corporations frequently transfer executives from one state to another. Skilled workers and professionals often relocate to other parts of the country as new job opportunities open up.

Those in licensed occupations often do not have as much freedom to relocate as do other citizens. Many states jealously guard their right to grant licenses. Each state insists on being sole judge of who it will allow to practice an occupation within its borders.

16. See Article 18 of the *California Health and Safety Code,* commencing with Section 429.70.

17. For additional information about the HMPP program, contact Jean Ann Harlow, Chief, Health Professions Development Section, Division of Health Professions Development, Office of Statewide Health Planning and Development, 714 P Street, Sacramento, Calif., 95814.

Some refuse to recognize the licenses of other states for certain occupations, no matter how high the standards of these other states may be. Others will honor the license of another state only if a formal reciprocity agreement has been negotiated. Under such an agreement, persons licensed in a reciprocating state are not required to take an examination or to prove that they have met training and experience requirements of the state where they are seeking licensure. All that is necessary is a valid license from the reciprocating state.

Reciprocity agreements are usually considered "beneficial" and "fair" by those who are covered by them, but may be viewed as "discriminatory" and "exclusionary" by those who are not. This difference in perception stems from the favored position enjoyed by those who are fortunate enough to be covered. These individuals are able to practice in any state with which their home state has a reciprocity agreement. They may move at will and are not required to pass the current examination or to meet current licensure requirements. They are also protected against economic competition from practitioners from nonreciprocating states who may wish to set up practice in their states. The latter may have had excellent training, passed licensure exams, and practiced successfully for many years in their own states. However, when they seek to become licensed in a state with which their home state does not have a reciprocity agreement, they are likely to find that their licenses will not be honored. In the absence of such an agreement, these out-of-state licensees are required to meet all current licensing requirements and pass the current licensing examination. The fact that they may hold licenses in other states where requirements may be as high or higher than the state to which they wish to migrate is of no consequence. In the absence of a formal reciprocity agreement, they must meet all current entry requirements.

On the surface this may seem fair enough, but in practice it is often very difficult for practitioners who have been out of school for a number of years to pass the current licensing examinations. Such examinations are usually tailored to the current curriculum so that even well qualified practitioners who have been practicing for many years may find them difficult to pass. Indeed, critics of reciprocity have questioned whether many in-state practitioners

with comparable years of experience would be able to pass the
current examination. But neither in-state licensees nor those from
reciprocating states need to worry about passing since the requirement applies only to applicants of nonreciprocating states.

In order for these out-of-state applicants to prepare for the
current licensing examination, it is often necessary for them to cease
practice for a period of time in order to return to school. Even
then, they may have difficulty passing because the examination may
contain material unique to or emphasized by in-state training programs although not necessarily based on any unique conditions
within the state. For example, at one time the dental examination in
California continued to give heavy weight to a seldom used procedure (gold foil inlay) which was taught in California dental
schools, but given only scant attention in schools elsewhere. Graduates of California training institutions had no difficulty passing
this part of the examination because they had practiced doing gold
foil inlays, but out-of-state applicants frequently failed because
they had not been taught to perform the procedure, since newer
materials and techniques had displaced it in contemporary dental
practice.

Many people feel that a fairer approach is licensure by "endorsement." Under the endorsement approach, a state decides that it
will honor the license of any other state once it has determined
that the standards of the other state are comparable, although not
necessarily equivalent, to its own. In some instances where significant differences exist, a state may require applicants to meet
certain additional requirements. For example, if the applicants have
not previously passed a performance examination, and if such an
examination is required of all in-state applicants, they are required
to pass one before their licenses are endorsed.

Prospects for Voluntary Certification

As legislators and leaders of consumer groups have become
aware of the limitations and social costs of licensure there has been
a growing reluctance to license new groups. At the same time
there remain what some feel are compelling reasons for developing
credible mechanisms for credentialing individuals, especially in the
rapidly expanding health field. A variety of auxiliary groups are

seeking credentials as a way to gain identity and status. Medicare, Medicaid, and the large health insurance companies need some way of determining which health service providers are eligible for reimbursement. Licensing is seen as a useful mechanism for making such determinations. Finally, employers of health service personnel need ways to evaluate the technical qualifications of job applicants without resorting to costly testing procedures. In situations were licensure is not available, certification may be viewed as an acceptable alternative.

The fly in the certification ointment has been the lack of any type of quality control over certifying agencies. Since such agencies are subject to no regulation, any group that wished to do so could establish its own certification program. Agencies that have established high standards or a good reputation over a period of years might find themselves competing with newly formed certification bodies that have similar sounding names, but apply lower standards. Faced with a bewildering array of certification agencies, all purporting to be the "official" certifiers of practitioners in a given field, potential users of credentials have no convenient way to investigate competing claims so that they can honor legitimate credentials and ignore questionable ones.

In an effort to bring some semblance of order to the voluntary health certification field, the Department of Health, Education, and Welfare (now Health and Human Services) supported a feasibility study and provided start-up funds for the creation of an independent nongovernmental agency to perform an accreditation function for health certifying agencies. The National Commission for Health Certifying Agencies (NCHCA) does not certify individuals. Rather, it grants recognition by admitting to membership certifying groups that meet certain standards. The standards relate to the certifying agency's structure, examination processes, dissemination of information, and efforts to keep pace with latest developments in occupational credentialing. According to a 1980 report issued by the Commission:

Certifying agencies must be nongovernmental and non-profit-making, administratively independent and broadly based with governing board representation from members of the certified profession, interested employers, and consumers. The agencies must at least have access to trained knowledgeable authorities in psychometrics and must be financially secure. Job-relatedness, periodic review, adequate security, appropriately established pass/fail levels and reliability as well as validity are all required of certification examinations.

In addition, the criteria require member certifying agencies to make available to the public descriptive materials about their activities and examination structure. Applicants for certification must be furnished with extensive information about the nature of the certification process and qualifications for certification. Discrimination according to age, sex, race, religion, national origin, disability, or marital status is prohibited. Significantly, agencies are further required to establish alternate pathways where appropriate, as an option to strictly educational qualifications, by the beginning of 1982. Confidentiality of results, prompt reporting of decisions, and feedback on areas of deficiency and confidentiality all are considered essential components of Commission-sanctioned certification procedures. And, even the attainment of all these criteria is insufficient, if the applicant agency has not developed or is not developing a program for recertification or continuing competence.[18]

In the three years since its formation in 1977 only six certification agencies that have applied have met all of the membership requirements and been accorded full membership status. They are the Board of Registry of the American Society of Clinical Pathologists, the Commission on National Dental Examinations of the American Dental Association, the Dental Assisting National Board, the National Board of Chiropractic Examiners, the National Board for Respiratory Therapy, and the National Commission on Certification of Physician's Assistants.

Nine other certification agencies were accorded "conditional membership," which signifies that the group has met most but not all basic requirements. Once the deficiencies have been eliminated, the groups will be considered for full membership. As of January 1981, conditional members of the NCHCA were the Certifying American Association of Medical Assistants; the American Board for Certification in Orthotics and Prosthetics; the American College of Nursing Home Administrators, the American Dietetic Association, the American Medical Record Association, the American

18. National Commission for Health Certifying Agencies, *Perspectives on Health Occupational Credentialing*, Publication No. (HRA) 80-39 (Washington, D.C.: Public Health Service, Division of Associated Health Professions, U.S. Department of Health and Human Services, 1980), pp. 95-96.

Medical Technologists, the National Registry of Microbiologists of the American Society for Microbiology, the National Certification Agency for Medical Laboratory Personnel, and the Nuclear Medicine Technology Certification Board. It should be noted that many certification boards, such as those for the various medical specialties, have elected not to participate in the NCHCA program.

Leaders of NCHCA point out that the organization represents an opportunity for groups involved in the delivery of health services to take an active role in determining their own futures. They note that voluntary certification avoids most of the artificial restrictions imposed by state licensure laws. Instead of setting minimum standards as in licensing, the certification agency can set standards that stress excellence. The inability of certain individuals to meet certification standards does not necessarily deprive them of the opportunity to work, but may prevent them from obtaining the best jobs. Thus, certification can provide an incentive for practitioners to seek additional training and experience in order to meet certification requirements.

There seems to be little likelihood that the amount of health personnel credentialing will diminish significantly in the future. In all likelihood it will increase as new groups emerge and clamor for status and recognition. As these emerging groups—and even some well established groups—find the licensure route closed, they are likely to turn to certification as the best available alternative. Thus, the future growth of credentialing, at least in the health field but probably in other fields as well, will probably be in the certification area rather than in licensing.

Implications for Vocational Educators

Vocational educators have probably failed in the past to pay sufficient attention to the implications of licensing and certification for their own activities. They have too often remained aloof while policy decisions affecting them or their students were made by others. Vocational educators in administrative positions should begin to play a more active role in the decision-making process. For example, when new licensure laws are being proposed or existing laws modified, comments are usually invited from interested parties and opportunities are afforded for testifying at hearings before legislative committees. Such hearings provide vocational educators with opportunities to raise pertinent questions: Is regulation needed? Could the need be satisfied by some less restrictive method, such as certification? Are the proposed entry qualifications job related and fair? During sunset hearings, vocational educators also have an opportunity to urge repeal of regulatory laws that serve no useful purpose or which may be doing harm to their students and the public, and to suggest changes that will make the regulatory process more effective or more equitable. For example, they may wish to stress the need for competency based examinations instead of rigid training and experience requirements.

Recognizing that their own students often migrate to states where better opportunities exist, vocational educators may wish to support efforts to facilitate interstate mobility of licensees. They may also wish to support efforts to provide continuing education for practitioners in order to help them keep abreast of new developments.

Another way vocational educators can contribute is by offering to serve on licensing boards or certifying agencies. In some instances, it may be appropriate for vocational educators to serve as occupational members of boards that regulate the field in which they teach. At other times, they may serve as public members of boards that have no direct relationship to their own fields of specialization. Vocational educators can bring to such board service backgrounds and perspectives that are likely to differ from those of full-time practitioners in the field. They may be able to raise questions and provide input from an educator's perspective that could enrich the decision-making process.

Winning an appointment to a regulatory board may not be easy because the limited number of vacancies are usually filled by those recommended by leaders of trade and professional groups. However, governors and others who handle licensing board appointments are becoming increasingly aware of the need to provide viewpoints that may not necessarily agree with those of the associations. In a number of states, governors have made an effort to find qualified professionals who will bring a public interest viewpoint, rather than a narrow occupational viewpoint, to board deliberations. One governor told a "blue ribbon" committee, which he had appointed to help him screen prospective licensing board members, that he wanted professionals who were not afraid to explore innovative methods of delivering services and who had open minds about expanding the roles of health auxiliaries.[19]

By making the governor's office in their state aware of their interest in licensing and of their willingness to serve, some vocational educators may find themselves in positions where they may be able to influence licensing policies and procedures. By becoming actively involved in licensure and/or certification, educators may be in a position to address some of the problems and issues that have been discussed in this chapter. They may thus be able to help bring about improvements that will insure that these institutions will be better equipped to serve the needs of society and of the vocational education community than they have been in the past.

19. Informal remarks by Governor Robert Graham of Florida at an orientation meeting of a "blue ribbon" committee he had appointed to assist in screening prospective board members, Tallahassee, Florida, April 11, 1979.

CHAPTER VI

Career Development and Vocational Guidance

EDWIN L. HERR

Since the beginning of the 1960s manpower policy in the United States has taken on an affective quality reflecting concern for a work force which has not only occupation-specific skills but also personal commitment to work, positive self-concepts as effective workers, and employability skills, including skill in searching for work and in adjusting to a new job. As Tennyson has reported,[1] emphases in legislation and in program development during this period shifted from a primary concern about developing competent persons as defined by the needs of specific occupations to a much broader perspective that emphasizes the development of personal competence as defined by individual needs and the emerging perspectives provided by research and theory in career development. Such goals have contributed substantially to reconceptualizations of both vocational guidance and vocational education and their interaction.

The Legacies of the 1960s: Career Development, Vocational Guidance, and Vocational Education

When John F. Kennedy became President of the United States in 1961, unemployment and poverty were both major national issues. The nation was in its third post-Korean war recession with unemployment in excess of 8.1 million in February of 1961.[2] Influenced by such books as Harrington's *The Other America*,[3] which

1. W. Wesley Tennyson, "The Psychology of Developing Competent Personnel," *American Vocational Journal* 42 (February 1967): 27-29.

2. Advisory Council on Vocational Education, *Vocational Education: The Bridge between Man and His Work* (Washington, D.C.: Advisory Council on Vocational Education, 1968), p. 3.

3. Michael Harrington, *The Other America: Poverty in the United States* (New York: MacMillan Company, 1962).

poignantly depicted the plight of the very poor in the midst of an affluent America, Kennedy initiated a series of legislative acts that were "antipoverty" in their focus. In addition, he directed the Secretary of Health, Education, and Welfare to appoint a panel of consultants to examine the role of vocational education in alleviating the levels of unemployment being experienced in many parts of the nation.

From 1961 through the end of the Johnson presidency in 1968, the nation fell heir to an unprecedented outpouring of federal legislation designed to improve the quality of life, reduce unemployment, help persons to cope with the onrush of automation and change, and create other modifications in the traditional policies regarding the development of human capital as well as individual fulfillment.

A legislative capstone of this period was the Vocational Education Act of 1963. Among its several provisions, this legislation specifically stated that vocational guidance and counseling were to be provided to students enrolled (or planning to enroll) in vocational courses. Although vocational guidance and counseling had been permissive expenditures and were occasionally mentioned in virtually all vocational education legislation from the Smith-Hughes Act of 1916 forward, the Vocational Education Act of 1963 explicitly integrated vocational guidance and counseling with vocational education. By doing so the Vocational Education Act bridged a schism between vocational guidance and vocational education that had begun in 1917. Until that time vocational guidance and vocational education were seen as a partnership—mutually required to launch youth into the work world. In 1917, however, the National Education Association caused each of these processes to go its independent way when it defined guidance in the schools as educational, not vocational.[4]

In addition to reestablishing the importance of an interaction between vocational guidance and vocational education, the Vocational Education Act of 1963 asserted the importance of tailoring the offerings of vocational education to "special needs" populations, that is, to persons whose academic, socioeconomic, physical,

4. William R. Stephens, *Social Reform and the Origins of Vocational Guidance* (Washington, D.C.: National Vocational Guidance Association, 1970), pp. 81-92.

or other handicaps prevented them from succeeding in the regular vocational education program. The emphasis in this legislation upon guidance and special individual needs prompted a national education task force to observe that "the most important change between 1917 and 1963 was the conceptual shift of emphasis from the needs of employers for skilled labor (the Smith-Hughes Act) to skills needed by people to assure their own welfare (the Vocational Education Act of 1963)."[5]

The Vocational Education Act of 1963 was not implemented until 1965. In 1967 a prestigious panel of consultants was asked to examine the current status of vocational education and, in particular, the impact of the 1963 act to that time. Among the many conclusions of the panel were continuing concerns that vocational education was not yet serving those who needed it most (for example, women, out-of-school youth, students in inner-city schools); that counseling and guidance needed to place greater emphasis on the world of work and its requirements; and that the school program needed to be modified to include instruction designed to orient all students to the world of work. In particular, the panel recommended that occupational preparation should not be confined to the senior high school but should begin in the elementary schools with a realistic picture of the world of work, with more complex concepts about economics and occupational preparation being introduced to the junior high school curriculum.[6]

These recommendations were translated into legislation in the Vocational Education Act Amendments of 1968. This legislation extended the provisions of the 1963 legislation for special needs groups, particularly the disadvantaged and the physically handicapped. It also included an expanded concept of guidance and counseling to include services that facilitate job choices and job placement. These emphases included prevocational activity beginning in the elementary schools. Much of the impetus for such legislative perspectives came from the emerging influence of theory and research pertaining to career development. The influence of

5. Vocational Education Review Task Force, U.S. Department of Health, Education, and Welfare, *Report of the Analysis Group* (Washington, D.C.: U.S. Government Printing Office, September 1970).

6. Advisory Council on Vocational Education, *Vocational Education.*

career development theory upon conceptions of vocational education is supported in a U.S. Office of Education discussion paper which, in addressing vocational education for the 1970s, indicated that:

> Vocational education in this decade must be conceptualized as lifelong career education for every person who can profit from such a program. . . . Vocational education must now provide the framework for a career education system that will: (1) introduce the elementary school child to the world of careers; (2) provide exploration, guidance, and counseling for career choices throughout elementary and secondary education; (3) provide specific skills training, job clusters skills, or pretechnical education at the secondary level.[7]

Further, the Exemplary Programs and Services Branch, Division of Vocational and Technical Education, Office of Education, stated in an internal memorandum that the Exemplary Programs and Projects funded by Part D of the 1968 Amendments to the Vocational Education Act were "early attempts to structure operating models of what is now coming to be referred to as a K through 12 career education system. The roots for such a system go back into many years of basic research on career development theory."[8]

Given such perspectives as those cited, it seems reasonable to assert that the legacy of the 1960s was the creation of a conceptual base and an incentive system for an interactive network of career development, vocational guidance, and vocational education which is yet to be fully articulated. From this base the 1970s have moved and the 1980s are moving inexorably toward the implementation of such schema.

Career Development: An Overview

In order to understand the relationships between career development and either vocational guidance and counseling or vocational education, it is important to see the former as the target of

7. Division of Vocational and Technical Education, U.S. Office of Education, "Vocational Education for the 1970s" (Conference discussion paper, Washington, D.C., 1971).

8. Exemplary Programs and Services Branch, Division of Vocational and Technical Education, U.S. Office of Education, "Background on the Design, Development, and Implementation of Vocational Exemplary Projects Funded under Part D, Section 142(C) of the Vocational Education Amendments of 1968" (Washington, D.C.: U.S. Office of Education, 1971).

the latter. Both vocational guidance and vocational education are intervention strategies with potential for directly modifying the career development processes of children, youth, and adults.

Career development theory is concerned about both the structural dimensions of work-related behavior and about the changes that occur in these dimensions across time. Career development describes the lifelong behavioral processes and the influences upon them that lead to or interrelate with one's work values, choice of occupation(s), decision-making style, role integration, self and career identity, understanding of educational opportunities, work adjustment, and related phenomena. Thus, all persons engage in career development whether jaggedly, smoothly, positively, or negatively. Career development, like sexual or emotional development, proceeds whether or not there is formal intervention in it.

The conceptual and research insights that are subsumed by career development theory comprise descriptions of the behavioral domains—including the psychological, cultural, and economic influences upon them—which intervention strategies might modify in order to facilitate more positive and purposeful individual behavior. While the term "theory" has been used in its singular form in this overview, there are in fact several different theories of career development or of aspects of such processes. As a result, theorists tend to vary in their conceptual emphases, and the range of variables included in career development theory is large.

In summarizing the major current perspectives on career development theory, Herr and Cramer have suggested the following notions,[9] which appear here in paraphrased and abbreviated form:

1. The degree and nature of personal career maturity is a function of complex learning processes that begin in early childhood and continue throughout life.

2. Choices related to the establishment of a career pattern occur not at a point in time but continuously. Specific choices relate both to antecedent experiences and perceptions of future alternatives.

3. Choice making tends to be continuous, tentative, and often more psychological than logical.

4. Because of the importance to adult career behavior of early childhood experiences in the family, the school, and the community,

9. Edwin L. Herr and Stanley H. Cramer, *Career Guidance through the Life Span: Systematic Approaches* (Boston: Little, Brown and Co., 1979), pp. 100-1.

intervention strategies designed to facilitate positive career development need to begin during the first decade of life.

5. The career development tasks with which persons must cope vary from one life stage to another and many of these tasks are culturally defined and imposed upon individuals by the institutions through which they pass (for example, schools).

6. Value systems, both individual and cultural, are important in shaping the career development of groups and of individuals.

7. Effective information about occupations or career paths must include emphases not only on objective factors such as earnings potential, performance requirements, or number of positions available but also on the sociological and psychological aspects of work, occupations, or careers.

8. As much as possible, career information should be provided in contexts, actual or simulated (for example, gaming, field trips, career-sensitive curricula, work study, role playing, computer-mediated information retrieval), by which individuals can project themselves into possible occupational, educational, or career roles, act them out, and test their meaning.

9. Since educational, occupational, and career choices are methods of implementing an individual's self-concept, information about self-characteristics—attitudes, aptitudes, interests, values—is as necessary as the information about the alternatives to be chosen. Unless individuals know what personal resources they have to commit to choice and the outcomes sought, they have no guidelines by which to evaluate whether anything is of value to them.

10. Career development concepts provide the substance for program goals in vocational guidance, career education, and some aspects of vocational education. Career development concepts can be translated into behavioral expectations for students which can guide the creation of instructional and experiential opportunities designed to facilitate such behaviors.

11. Career development theory indicates that decision making involves action. Therefore, within the contexts of vocational guidance and vocational education ways need to be found to help persons take responsibility for their own learning and for their own direction. Persons need to be helped to develop planning skills and the courage to execute their plans.

12. Persons need to be helped to develop a conscious awareness that they do have choices, to determine at any given time what kind of decision is involved and the factors inherent in the decision that make a personal difference.

13. Career development is not independent of individual development in physical, emotional, psychomotor, and mental areas.

14. Opportunities for choice for most persons are so complex that

vocational guidance in the family or neighborhood is likely to be inadequate to today's realities.

15. Occupational choices and career patterns are basic to one's lifestyle and reflect development experiences, personality, and goals.

16. Career choice can be an essentially rational process if the person knows how to select and obtain appropriate information and then apply the decision-making process to it.

PREDICTORS OF CAREER DEVELOPMENT PATTERNS

The synthesis of theory and research perspectives just cited suggests that a large number of predictor variables are involved in career related behavior. Each of the following has shown a significant relationship to educational achievement, to success in particular types of vocational education curricula, to choice of particular occupations or vocational curricula, to realistic decision making, or to job satisfaction: abilities (scholastic achievement, spatial relations, abstract reasoning, clerical speed and accuracy, eye-hand coordination, fine or gross manual dexterity); needs and interests; stereotypes and expectations; work values; influences of significant others; size of community; childrearing patterns; socioeconomic background; general psychological adjustment; risk taking; level of aspiration; level and type of occupational information possessed; career maturity (vocational choice attitudes and competencies); sex differences; racial differences; personality characteristics (acceptance of responsibility, honesty, and so forth); curriculum.

The large number of these variables suggests the validity of a rather simple point: given sufficient ability to perform a particular work activity, the choice of, satisfaction with, or advancement in that work activity is dependent upon a complex range of psychological, personality, and possibility factors. These factors make up the content of such rubrics as employability, adjustment, industrial discipline, or job satisfaction. They also represent the content of vocational guidance as well as the bases for curricular modification in vocational education.

CAREER DEVELOPMENT PERSPECTIVES ON PROGRAM DEVELOPMENT

A major conceptual outcome of most contemporary views of career development theory and research is that much, if not most, career behavior is learned. For example, differences in choices of occupations or commitments to work or stability in work are frequently related to what types of initial information one has about jobs or work expectations. Such decisions are also related to the types of encouragement, modeling, or experience one acquires in the family or the community in which one resides. Thus, many of the differences in career patterns among people are related to information or its lack, experiential differences, and family influences, all of which may have little to do with one's multipotentiality or ability to perform at particular skill levels.

If much of career behavior is learned, then it can also be relearned or unlearned. Education can neutralize a lack of information as well as a lack of encouragement to explore, to plan, to choose. Indeed, most career development theorists now advocate the systematic development of programs that can be organized to facilitate positive career behavior for young people. Often these become a responsibility of vocational guidance; sometimes they reflect curriculum modifications in vocational education; frequently they become much of the substance of career education. Ordinarily such programs are built around the career development tasks found to be of particular importance at the elementary, junior high, or senior high school level.

Many such models exist. A particularly comprehensive model is that developed by the University of Minnesota and the Minnesota Department of Education.[10] This model is comprised of "career management tasks" that persons need to master in order to achieve career maturity at different educational levels. Each of these tasks can be considered a program goal around which vocational guidance or other educational efforts might be implemented. In relation to each of these tasks are behavioral indicators which research suggests underlie the task identified. Each of the career management tasks is broken down into performance objectives and enabling objectives.

The Minnesota model is similar to many of the current models underlying career education. Specific tasks, particularly those at the senior high school level, can readily be incorporated into var-

10. W. Wesley Tennyson, L. Sunny Hansen, Mary K. Klaurens, and Mary B. Antholz, *Education for Career Development* (St. Paul: Minnesota Department of Education, 1975), p. 75.

ious aspects of vocational education or vocational guidance programs as well.

A related but different perspective has been provided by Kazanas.[11] His research has focused on the importance of affective work competencies (work attitudes, values, and habits) as these are manifested in the work behaviors of individuals in the workplace. He argues that to prepare today's vocational education graduates for successful employment, curricula should be provided that will facilitate acquisition of desirable affective work competencies as well as specific job skills and knowledge. After an extensive review of pertinent research studies in industry, among employees and supervisors as well as among vocational educators, Kazanas identified sixty-three work competencies that could serve as the basis for curriculum development in vocational education. While not all of the competencies listed are affective in their substance (for example, intelligence), the vast majority are. They include such behaviors as punctuality, cooperativeness, emotional stability, honesty, dependability, loyalty, judgment, and many others which in some other nations have been combined under such terms as "industrial discipline."

To summarize the relationship of career development to vocational guidance and/or vocational education is to say that such perspectives represent the substance of programmatic efforts designed to help students acquire knowledge and skills associated with mastering the work context and being self-directed. Each of these emphases can be discussed separately, although they also have an interactive quality.

Work-context skills. Work-context skills include those psychological aspects of the situation in which work activity is carried on but which can be viewed separately from technical skills. Included might be knowledge and outcomes associated with employer-employee relations, supervisor-worker relations, interpersonal skills in relation to coworkers, willingness to follow rules, adaptability, punctuality and regularity of attendance, understanding of life in an organization, loyalty, accuracy, dependability, pride in work,

11. Hercules C. Kazanas, *Affective Work Competencies for Vocational Education* (Columbus, Ohio: ERIC Clearinghouse on Adult, Career, and Vocational Education, 1978), p. 70.

self-discipline, and efficiency. Such work-context skills tend to be those that research studies and surveys of employer preference have shown repeatedly to be at the heart of work adjustment, job satisfaction, and worker satisfactoriness. The lack of them is at the core of reasons for workers being discharged. While more subjective and psychological than occupation- or task-specific skills, they are nevertheless capable of being analyzed and taught. Just as behavioral objectives and incremental hurdles can be built into vocational education curricula to teach persons occupation- or task-specific skills, a similar organization of knowledge and experiences can be formulated to emphasize the importance of teaching work-context skills.

Guidance learnings. In many ways, however, the teaching of work-context skills is incomplete without attention to individual learning described as guidance in nature. Indeed, it is conceivable that many of the problems now associated with the work context (for example, worker alienation, mid-career crisis) are really problems of self-learning or deficits in other guidance related skills. Such learnings, like work-context skills, are more psychological than technical and they can be taught. Guidance skills are typically those now described under the rubric of career development. They concentrate on assisting persons to become aware of their self-characteristics (for example, aptitude, values, interests), their career opportunities (for example, occupational alternatives, educational options, the relationship between subject matter and jobs), as well as the bringing together of self and career opportunities into a plan for action. In essence, guidance learnings are designed to help persons become more purposeful, goal directed, and capable of self-management. They include attention to decision-making skills, job search and interview strategies, and general planfulness. They also include concern for such emphases as the ability to use exploratory resources to make reality tests of choices, constructive use of leisure, personal economics skills, and other pertinent areas of behavior by which one is helped to get and keep a job. In general, they argue that forging a career requires two types of knowledge: self-knowledge and job knowledge.

With respect to self-knowledge, guidance specialists would contend that persons need to be assisted to come to terms with who they are; what kinds of commitments they are willing to make; the nature of their aptitudes, interests, values, and goals; their feelings of competence and confidence. In essence, the provision and consideration of self-information provides a base to which anything else can be related. Knowing one's strengths and weaknesses, preferences, and goals defines an evaluative foundation to which any option or action can be referred to determine its relevance. This base of information also helps one determine what information one has, what one needs, and what should be secured.

In the second case, job knowledge, persons need to know about and consider the range of environmental options available to them and how these might be accessed. This requires having knowledge about and considering the personal relevance of such matters as the characteristics of curricular majors available, their prerequisites and content; the relationship between subject matter and occupations in which that subject matter is required; the outcomes of pursuing various curricula (What is the placement record? Into what kinds of jobs are people placed?); the matching of personal characteristics with those required in preferred curricula or occupations.

In addition, considerations of occupational and other opportunities will likely require information about methods of access. Are the preferred occupations available locally? If not, where are they available? How are potential employers identified? What is the best procedure to use to make contact with an employer? What information or procedures are pertinent to the completion of letters of inquiry, resumés, applications? What types of questions or other conditions are likely to prevail in an interview situation? How does one follow up a contact with an employer?

Decision-making skills. The third area of needed information is likely to deal with the decision-making process itself. Here the emphasis is not so much on acquiring and incorporating information about personal characteristics or educational, occupational, and other environmental alternatives but applying this information within a decision-making process. The assumption is that once such a process is learned, it can be used repeatedly as a logical or systematic approach by which to process information and to weigh alternatives.

Current Approaches to Vocational Guidance

It is important to acknowledge that while vocational guidance and vocational education have important relationships, vocational guidance can also be viewed independently of vocational education. Indeed, during the past two decades vocational guidance has undergone a major evolution that was stimulated largely by forces other than vocational education. Before turning to the contributions of vocational guidance to vocational education, a broader perspective on current approaches to vocational guidance is worth considering.

VOCATIONAL GUIDANCE → CAREER GUIDANCE

While "vocational guidance" is the term used as the subject of this chapter, professional literature and professional organizations have increasingly substituted the term "career guidance." The matter is more than semantic, as it reflects shifts both in the content and the processes traditionally associated with vocational guidance.

For most of the first fifty years of this century, vocational guidance has been concerned primarily with one point in the life of the individual, either entry to the labor market or readjustment through an immediate choice after occupational dislocation. It has been heavily dependent on one-to-one counseling as the primary process in which the intent was to match persons and jobs in a trait and factor format. The dominant unit of concern was occupational differences or difference in work activity across settings. Thus, the intent was to profile the individual through test scores, usually of aptitudes and interests, and previous achievements and match these as closely as possible to the requirements of available job options as various types of occupational information could reveal them.

In his presidential address to the National Vocational Guidance Association in 1950, Hoppock indicated that such a traditional view of vocational guidance was "crumbling."[12] Indeed, in 1951, Super recommended revision of the official National Vocational Guidance Association definition of vocational guidance, which had stood since 1937 as "the process of assisting the individual to choose an

12. Robert Hoppock, "Presidential Address, 1950," *Occupations* 28 (May 1950): 497-99.

occupation, prepare for it, enter upon it, and progress in it." The 1951 revision defined vocational guidance as "the process of helping a person to develop and accept an integrated and adequate picture of himself and of his role in the world of work, to test this concept against reality, and to convert it into a reality, with satisfaction to himself and to society."[13]

The 1951 definition of vocational guidance emphasized the psychological nature of vocational choice rather than the relatively simple matching of person and job. The resulting base for vocational guidance moved the locus of fundamental concern from the occupation to be chosen to the self-concept of the chooser. This definition focused primarily on self-understanding and self-acceptance as the evaluative bases to which can be related the occupational and educational alternatives available to the individual.

Following Super's redefinition of vocational guidance in 1951 there has been a subtle but important shifting from occupational to career models in the professional literature and in theory development.

By definition, career embraces a longer time frame than does occupational choice. It is concerned with prevocational activity such as that which occurs in the family and the school as well as with postvocational activity such as that of the retiree engaging in voluntary community activities. Prime considerations in a career model are not only the differences among occupations but the factors related to the continuity or discontinuity in the career development of persons across time and settings.

McDaniels has recently contended that career means more than one's job or occupation.[14] It is a life-style concept that also involves a sequence of work or leisure activities in which one engages throughout a lifetime. Super has indicated that career is comprised of "the sequence of occupations and other life roles which combine to express the person's commitment to work in his or her total pattern of self-development."[15] He also adds the

13. Donald E. Super, "Vocational Adjustment: Implementing a Self-Concept," *Occupations* 30 (November 1951): 88-92.

14. Carl McDaniels, "The Practice of Career Guidance and Counseling," *INFORM* 7 (August 1978): 1-8.

15. Donald E. Super, *Career Education and the Meanings of Work* (Washington, D.C.: Office of Career Education, U.S. Office of Education, 1976).

notion that "careers exist only as people pursue them; they are person-centered." Unlike occupations that exist as classifications of work activity, careers reflect the unique types of decisions each individual makes.

Career models introduce several aspects into the conception of vocational guidance which are not apparent in the occupational model. One of these is the idea of developmental career guidance. In such an emphasis the vocational guidance practitioner is not concerned only with immediate choice of training or job but also with the students' intermediate and long-range goals and how immediate choices relate to such goals. Thus personal values, the clarity of the self-concept, personal planfulness, and exploratory behavior vis à vis choice options become important variables to be considered in career guidance.

Career models also emphasize the role of vocational or career guidance in systematically educating students or adults to the knowledge, attitudes, and skills that will be required of them at future choice points, in planning their educational program, in selecting and preparing for work. This education would begin in the elementary school and spiral in complexity throughout the secondary school. This approach stands in contrast to intervening only after it has been clearly established that particular persons have not acquired such skills and behaviors and are experiencing problems because of these deficits in their behavioral repertoire.

Career guidance as just described tends to view all students, not just a few, as the recipients of such developmental services. Therefore, it is likely to be concerned not only with vocational counseling as a one-to-one process but with group work, computer-assisted vocational guidance, career shadowing, cooperative vocational education, community volunteer projects, work simulations, gaming, role playing, self-directed assessment, values clarification, and other processes by which students can be exposed to information and reality testing of self and environmental characteristics. Whether entitled vocational or career guidance, it is with this larger conceptualization that this chapter is primarily concerned.

RELATIONSHIP OF VOCATIONAL GUIDANCE TO VOCATIONAL EDUCATION

In general, the literature on vocational guidance or vocational counseling *in* vocational education is not large. Rather, the literature speaks primarily to vocational guidance in secondary schools, sometimes differentiating the needs and treatment of vocational education students and sometimes not. There are, however, studies which suggest that, as compared to other students, vocational students may be disadvantaged in the degree to which they receive vocational guidance. Examples of some of these studies follow.

In 1966, Campbell and his colleagues undertook a national study of the status of guidance and counseling in secondary schools by comparing the viewpoints of school administrators, counselors, teachers, and students on guidance issues. Some 353 high schools and 7,000 respondents were included in the study. Among other findings it was reported that in most schools no one assumed the primary responsibility for assisting students to decide on and enter into vocational programs.[16]

In two major studies of vocational education Kauffman and his colleagues found that over half the vocational students, but less than one-third of those who followed an academic or general program, reported that they had never discussed their course choices with a counselor; of those students who reported that they had had some formal guidance, three-quarters had a favorable estimate, but vocational students were less likely to report favorably than students in other curricular options.[17]

Palmo and DeVantier studied the counseling needs of vocational students over the course of an academic year in one vocational-technical school. A similarity of concerns and problems existed among the students. The majority expressed difficulties with teachers, failure in school, peer relationships, home problems, and vocational/career plans. In particular, although vocational students have tentatively chosen a vocational path to follow by enrolling in a vocational curriculum, approximately 30 percent of the students in this study were dissatisfied or confused by their choices

16. Robert E. Campbell, *Vocational Guidance in Secondary Education: A National Survey* (Columbus, Ohio: Center for Vocational Education, 1968).

17. Joseph Kauffman et al., *The Role of the Secondary School in the Preparation of Youth for Employment* (University Park, Penn.: Institute for Human Resources, Pennsylvania State University, 1967). See also, Terrence N. Davidson and Joseph A. Johnston, "High School Boys in Vocational Education Programs: Facts vs. Fallacies," *Vocational Guidance Quarterly* 25 (December 1976): 106-111.

and were not really aware of the alternatives available to them. The vocational students expressed a need "for more vocational counseling and additional materials that might help them with impending decisions."[18]

Stern has summarized other studies of vocational students or graduates which reflect, however indirectly, upon their needs for vocational guidance. Such findings are that vocational students are no more knowledgeable about the world of work than nonvocational students; they are as likely to drop out as other students; they are no more satisfied with their jobs than graduates of the general track, and somewhat less satisfied than commercial and college preparatory graduates.[19]

VOCATIONAL GUIDANCE IN VOCATIONAL EDUCATION

Vocational guidance *in* vocational education is typically seen as a support to the latter. Although there is a historical rhetoric as well as more recent legislative support for vocational guidance and vocational education as a partnership, that view does not always predominate in practice.

Support services can be defined in many ways. By tradition those aspects of education tend to be included which facilitate the central role of instruction but are not themselves instructional in their primary processes or content. Guidance and counseling generally meet these criteria and can play important support roles prior to and after the conduct of vocational education instruction. For example, vocational guidance has a significant role to play in attracting, recruiting, and/or selecting students for vocational education options. Given the large array of educational choices from which youth can choose, attracting appropriately motivated and talented students becomes a major concern to vocational educators in any setting. Guidance and counseling function in such a support role by conveying the image and possibilities of vocational educa-

18. J. Artis Palmo and Joseph DeVantier, "An Examination of Counseling Needs of Vo-Tech Students," *Vocational Guidance Quarterly* 25 (December 1976): 170-76.

19. Barry E. Stern, *Toward a Federal Policy on Education and Work* (Washington, D.C.: U.S. Department of Health, Education, and Welfare, 1977), p. xix.

tion to potential enrollees, parents, sending schools, and other sources of input to vocational education programs.

A second role for vocational guidance in vocational education is that of assisting in the selection of students for admission to various vocational education programs. Such a role involves individual assessment of aptitudes and preferences which, in turn, must be considered in relation to probabilities of success and satisfaction as these derive from research about differences in vocational education curricula and the characteristics of those who are successful in them. When individual desires and the realities of course availability come into conflict, school counselors assist potential enrollees in considering the alternatives available to them in as nonarbitrary a manner as possible. Whether or not such conflict exists, school counselors have a major role in insuring that students are properly motivated and equipped to take advantage of the vocational instruction chosen. Where such a condition does not occur, vocational guidance personnel need to assist students in choosing a different option in vocational education or to exit from it into another option that holds promise of meeting their current needs.

A third role that vocational guidance plays in vocational education is directly related to instruction itself. As suggested previously, recent emphases in subject matter in vocational education have been entitled work-context skills and guidance or career development skills. Since these skills are composed of attitudes, emotions, psychological factors, as well as cognitive and informational aspects, school counselors can and often do become very involved in helping students acquire such skills. Counselors may work with vocational teachers as collaborators or consultants as such learnings are infused into curricula. Or, in some instances, school counselors may take direct responsibility for providing such instruction. Through separate group courses, seminars, interactive computer-assisted instruction, gaming, role playing, and other techniques students can be provided opportunities to gain work-context and personal guidance learnings. As this occurs, vocational guidance as a support service tends to blur into vocational guidance as subject matter.

A fourth contribution to vocational education is the role of vocational guidance in the placement of students. Conceived in traditional terms, placement of vocational education graduates into suitable employment or postsecondary education has been seen as an event, not a process. The assumption has been that when students are about to complete the vocational education program, they would be brought into direct contact with employer(s) seeking persons with such training. The rationale for such an assumption is that the student is employable (that is, possesses the appropriate attitudes, marketable skills, job search and interview behaviors) and only needs assistance to obtain a suitable employer. The role of vocational guidance was conceived as that of matchmaker at the point when the student exited the vocational education system.

Increasingly, placement is being conceived as a process rather than an event. As such, it is seen as a stream of career development and guidance learnings which go on concurrently with occupation-specific task learnings throughout the student's vocational education experience, not just when the student is about to enter work full-time. In this sense, assisting vocational education students to focus on their learning and performance capabilities to gain decision-making capacity to formulate an awareness of their options and of how to prepare for them and gain access to them, and to acquire job search and job interview behavior is seen as preparing these persons for the school-to-work transition or for placement as a natural extension of all vocational education, not something abrupt and different from it.

The Outcomes of Vocational Guidance

The term vocational guidance does not describe a singular process nor does it describe a singular outcome. Vocational guidance, provided either in vocational education or in a comprehensive sending school serving vocational students, includes a range of processes. These processes have different outcomes associated with them and thus can contribute to more than one outcome.

No single study is sufficiently comprehensive to assess the effects of vocational guidance. Rather one must consider studies of different processes and outcomes to capture the real or potential contributions of vocational guidance to vocational education. The following are examples of findings of studies on the effects of vocational guidance.

SELF-ESTEEM AND SELF-CONCEPT

Students who have been helped by counselors to evaluate their problems, to break them into components, and to master these components one at a time gain self-confidence.[20]

Minority students who are assisted to decide upon vocational objectives are typically found to have more positive self-concepts and higher ideal selves than those who do not have such objectives.[21]

The degree of self-esteem possessed by students relates to the appropriateness of vocational choice and to high school achievement.[22]

DECISION MAKING

Guidance processes help students to become competent decision-makers and to select high school courses and to make high school plans more congruent with their abilities than is true of students not exposed to such processes.[23]

Decision-making processes can be taught to junior high school and senior high school students using a variety of modeling techniques, sequential learning exercises, and activity packages.[24]

20. Edward C. Bennett, "Operation C.O.D.: A Program Designed to Improve Pupil Self-Esteem, Thereby Reducing Future School Dropouts" (Doct. diss., Nova University, 1975), ED 136 091; Edwin L. Herr, "Does Counseling Work?" (Paper presented at the Seventh International Round Table for the Advancement of Counseling, University of Wurzburg, Germany, April 9, 1976).

21. P. S. Higgins, *The Desegregation Counselor Aide Program of the 1974-75 Minneapolis Emergency School Aid Project* (Minneapolis, Minn.: Minneapolis Public Schools, 1976); Robert L. Williams and Harry Byars, "Negro Self-Esteem in a Transitional Society," *Personnel and Guidance Journal* 47 (October 1968): 120-25.

22. Robert P. O'Hara, "Vocational Self-Concepts and High School Achievement," *Vocational Guidance Quarterly* 15 (December 1966): 106-12; Norman W. Sievart, "The Role of the Self-Concept in Determining an Adolescent's Occupational Choice," *Journal of Industrial Teacher Education* 9 (1972): 47-53.

23. Leona E. Tyler, *The Work of the Counselor*, 3d ed. (New York: Appleton-Century-Crofts, 1969), p. 236.

24. Bruce W. Bergland, Louis A. Quatrano, and Gerald W. Lundquist, "Group Social Models and Structured Interaction in Teaching Decision Making," *Vocational Guidance Quarterly* 24 (September 1975): 28-36; Edwin L. Herr, *Research in Career Education: The State of the Art* (Columbus, Ohio: ERIC Clearinghouse for Adult, Career, and Vocational Education, 1978); J. B. Meyer, Wray Strowig, and Raymond E. Hosford, "Behavioral-Reinforcement Counseling with Rural High School Youth," *Journal of Counseling Psychology* 17 (March 1970): 127-32.

Directed learning of decision-making processes is more effective than nondirected practice. Such directed learning aids in the transfer of decision-making skills to real-life circumstances outside of guidance and counseling settings.[25]

Through group problem-solving methods, students can be helped to understand the relationship between educational and vocational development, to clarify goals, and to acquire skill in identifying and using relevant information for their decision-making needs.[26]

CAREER PLANNING AND CAREER MATURITY

Students, including inner-city disadvantaged youth, who are exposed to systematically planned career guidance classes dealing with such topics as values clarification, decision making, job satisfaction, sources of occupational information, work power projections, and career planning, make greater gains in self-knowledge and in relating self-knowledge to occupations and engage in more career planning activities than students who have not participated in such classes.[27]

Student users of computer-based career guidance systems make larger gains than nonusers in such characteristics as degree of planfulness, knowledge and use of resources for career exploration, awareness of career options open to them, and the risks associated with these options.[28]

25. John R. Evans and John J. Cody, "Transfer of Decision-making Skills Learned in a Counseling-Like Setting to Similar and Dissimilar Situations," *Journal of Counseling Psychology* 16 (September 1969): 427-32.

26. Robert J. Babcock and Marilyn A. Kauffman, "Effectiveness of a Career Course," *Vocational Guidance Quarterly* 24 (March 1976): 261-66; John D. Krumboltz and Carl E. Thoresen, "The Effect of Behavioral Counseling in Group and Individual Settings on Information-Seeking Behavior," *Journal of Counseling Psychology* 11 (Winter 1964): 324-33.

27. Clayton V. Omvig, R. W. Tollocy, and E. G. Thomas, "The Effect of Career Education on Career Maturity," *Journal of Vocational Behavior* 7 (1975): 265-73; Asma Hamdani, "Facilitating Vocational Development among Disadvantaged Inner-City Adolescents," *Vocational Guidance Quarterly* 26 (September 1977): 60-68.

28. Roger Myers, Richard Lindeman, and Albert Thompson, "Effects of the Educational and Career Exploration System on Vocational Maturity," *Journal of Vocational Behavior* 6 (1975): 245-54; Herr, *Research in Career Education*. See also, K. Richard Pyle and Robert O. Stripling, "The Counselor, the Computer, and Career Development," *Vocational Guidance Quarterly* 25 (September 1976): 71-75.

Individual and group counseling that involves specific skill training in self-assessment, gathering pertinent career information, and planning can enhance student career planning.[29]

If students learn about themselves before they are exposed to occupational information, or if they request such information as they are ready, their career planning is significantly facilitated.[30]

Short-term counseling (three sessions) with high school students has been found to facilitate the career maturity of these students with regard to such emphases as orientation to decision making, planfulness, and independence of choice.[31]

Guidance films (for example, *Careers in the 70s*) have been found to affect high school students' attitudes positively, to motivate them to seek additional information, and to assist them to make career choices. These outcomes are strengthened when such films are used as part of a planned guidance program.[32]

High school students exposed to model reinforcement and reinforcement counseling participate more intensely in external information-seeking behavior than students not so exposed.[33]

The use of simulated occupational experience in guidance and counseling programs has positive effects upon occupational knowledge of secondary school students.[34]

Games and other simulations permit various types of information to be assimilated by students while they are engaged in

29. Norman R. Stewart and Carl E. Thoresen, "Behavioral Group Counseling for Career Development" (Symposium presented at the Annual Convention of the American Personnel and Guidance Association, Detroit, 1968).

30. Franklin D. Westbrook, "A Comparison of Three Methods of Group Vocational Counseling," *Journal of Counseling Psychology* 21 (November 1974): 502-6.

31. Muriel H. Flake, Arthur J. Roach, and Walter F. Stenning, "Effects of Short-term Counseling on Career Maturity of Tenth-Grade Students," *Journal of Vocational Behavior* 6 (1975): 73-80.

32. Anita Mitchell, *An Evaluation of Career Guidance Films* (Santa Ana, Calif.: Culver City Unified School District, Orange County Department of Education, 1971).

33. Krumboltz and Thoresen, "The Effect of Behavioral Counseling in Groups and Individual Settings on Information-Seeking Behavior"; Jack A. Hamilton and Bruce W. Bergland, "A Strategy for Creating Peer Social Models," *Vocational Guidance Quarterly* 20 (June 1972): 271-78.

34. Stewart and Thoresen, "Behavioral Group Counseling for Career Development."

activity. For students with reading difficulties, such activity diminishes problems of information-seeking associated with books and directories as the primary resources.[35]

Group counseling can effectively facilitate student understanding of the relationship between educational and vocational development, goal clarification, and the acquisition of skill in identifying and using relevant information for their decision-making needs. Particularly important elements in such group contexts are cueing participants as to appropriate responses and selectively reinforcing goal-relevant statements.[36]

A ten-week group counseling intervention, combined with teaching materials designed to aid students in improving their career maturity and decision-making skills, was found to yield the following outcomes for both academic and nonacademic high school students: more knowledge about occupational choices, knowing how to get information, recognizing values and using them in making decisions, considering and ranking alternatives, making career decisions, and reassessing previous occupational choices.[37]

TRANSITION TO WORK AND WORK ADJUSTMENT

Guidance and counseling processes can help the young worker to sort out available work choices, consider personal commitments to work, and develop feelings of psychological competence in the work place.[38]

Young workers who have been trained in job search and inter-

35. Herr, *Research in Career Education.*

36. Bergland, Quatrano, and Lundquist, "Group Social Models and Structured Interaction in Teaching Decision-making"; Westbrook, "A Comparison of Three Methods of Group Vocational Counseling."

37. Joan R. Egner and Dorothy J. Jackson, "Effectiveness of a Counseling Intervention Program for Teaching Career Decision-making Skills," *Journal of Counseling Psychology* 25 (January 1978): 45-52.

38. W. C. Aiken et al., "Meeting the Training, Counseling, and Placement Needs of Unemployed Youth and Adults" (Paper presented at the First Southern Regional Vocational Education Leadership Development Conference, Atlanta, Georgia, April 1976); Edwin L. Herr, *The Relationship of Guidance and Counseling to National Educational, Occupational, and Social Priorities* (Washington, D.C.: American Personnel and Guidance Association, December 1977).

view skills, communication, and human relations at work are more likely to make an effective transition to work than those who have not had such training.[39]

Behavior rehearsal in which young workers can act out or role play with a counselor specific work-related social and interpersonal problems is more effective in resolving such problems than direct advice.[40]

From these and other studies it seems appropriate to conclude that there is an expanding body of empirical findings which, in general, supports the capability of vocational guidance processes to achieve outcomes that are compatible with the goals of vocational education.

Summary

This chapter has reviewed the historical and the current partnership between vocational guidance and vocational education. It has implied that there is validity to the perspective that every aspect of vocational education carries implications for vocational guidance. This truism applies whether the issue is attracting students to vocational education, assisting them to choose an occupation or a curriculum, helping them to acquire affective work competencies, or providing them job search and interview skills requisite to placement in the work force.

Vocational guidance has been portrayed as a dynamic concept encompassing multiple processes and outcomes. Its relationship to career development theory and research as conceptual frames of reference has been examined.

In sum, this chapter has suggested that both career-related behavior and the intervention strategies—vocational education and vocational guidance—focused on it are complex, interactive, and still evolving into a maturity of conceptualization and practice.

39. Aiken et al., "Meeting the Training, Counseling, and Placement Needs of Unemployed Youth and Adults"; A. P. Garbin et al., *Worker Adjustment Problems of Youth in Transition from High School to Work* (Columbus, Ohio; Center for Vocational and Technical Education, Ohio State University, 1968).

40. Arnold A. Lazurus, "Behavioral Rehearsal versus Nondirective Therapy versus Advice in Effecting Behavior Change," *Behavior Research and Therapy* 4 (1966); 209-12.

CHAPTER VII

Employment-Related Basic Skills

LOIS-ELLIN DATTA

The problem of youth unemployment has long been a major concern. Blame for the situation has been placed on schools that do not adequately prepare youth for employment; on employers who are prejudiced against youth, particularly low-income minority youth; on inadequate linkages among youth, schools, and jobs; on a tough labor market in which there are few job opportunities; and on the youth themselves. There is considerable agreement, even among writers of varying political views, that there is some connection between basic skills and employability. As Corman has noted, "underlying the Youth Act of 1980 is the belief that lack of basic communication, comprehension, and computational skills is the most serious barrier between low-income and minority youth and successful entry into the labor market,"[1] a sentiment echoed by the Reagan administration. Another underlying belief is that schools can do something about these skills for youth who lack them.

This belief implies that schools have a special responsibility for developing basic skills and that skills associated with employability can be differentiated from skills required for further schooling. Such assumptions are hardly revolutionary. Employers seem to expect schools and training programs to deliver the basics, if nothing else, and general and academic educators long have claimed that instilling basic skills is among the things they do best. What may be worthy of attention is that these claims may be tested

---

Opinions expressed in this chapter are the author's in her private capacity. Endorsement by the National Institute of Education should not be inferred. Glen Boerrighter, Ann Drennan, Monte Penny, Ed Esty, Tom Carroll, and Louise Corman commented helpfully on earlier drafts of the chapter.

1. Louise Corman, *Basic Skills Proficiencies of Secondary Vocational Students* (Washington, D.C.: National Institute of Education, 1980), p. 1.

thoroughly through such stimuli as the youth initiatives. As programs emphasizing training (the realm of labor) and those emphasizing education (the domain of schools) gear up, more than usual interest may arise in what is known about teaching youth the basic skills for employability.

This chapter examines literacy acquisition in vocational programs. Three conclusions are reached. First, the literacy needed for employability probably differs from the literacy needed for further education. Second, current vocational and occupational training programs, while concerned with the acquisition of basic skills, have yet to demonstrate substantial attention in actual instructional practices or much success in improving basic skills. Third, recent research on effective instruction, motivation for learning, and the nature of skilled reading offers new ideas that could be applied to improving literacy for employability among youth. The last section of this chapter explores the question of responsibility, pointing out that if vocational educators were to take primary responsibility for the improvement of basic skills among youth who currently lack such skills, fairly substantial changes in staff training, curriculum responsibilities, and time allocations would be needed.

The focus here is on literacy, particularly reading comprehension. This is not because speaking, listening, writing, or computation are unimportant, but because at present information about these areas with regard to employability, instruction, or program achievements is scant in comparison to what is known about comprehension.

What Is Taught

LITERACY IN GENERAL

Literacy denotes the use of written language skills at levels of competence needed for effective functioning. Literacy seems inherently to be a moving target, with its definition differing according to the function referred to and as demands vary over time.[2] The literacy required of a journalist differs from that re-

2. Irwin Kirsch and John T. Guthrie, "The Concept and Measurement of Functional Literacy," *Reading Research Quarterly* 13, no. 4 (1977-78): 485-507; Ramsay Selden, "Literacy: Current Problems and Current Research," in *Fifth Report of the National Council on Educational Research* (Washington, D.C.: National Institute of Education, 1980), pp. 30-40.

quired by an electrician; that required by a carpenter of 1776 differs from that required by one of today. Resnick and Resnick have compared social expectations for literacy (a) by the complexity of skills required for a reasonably good life, and (b) by the proportion of people expected to have these skills. In Europe of 1400, almost no one was expected to read and write beyond a simple personal mark. In contrast, postindustrial Western societies expect most people to comprehend and produce quite complex text. As Resnick and Resnick comment:

This high literacy standard (at a minimum the reading of new material and the gleaning of new information from that material) is a relatively recent one as applied to the population at large (and) much of our present difficulty in meeting the literacy standards we are setting for ourselves can be attributed to the relatively rapid extension to large populations of educational criteria that were once applied only to a limited elite.[3]

Such analyses imply that schools are not doing worse than they used to in transmitting literacy, but that society is demanding more literacy for more people, and will continue to do so. Demands on schools for high standards of literacy among their graduates thus are likely to increase rather than to diminish over coming years.

It is fair to point out that some predict continued need for literacy skills, while others say there will be less need for those skills in the future. Societies may adjust over time to the skills of their citizens. Already efforts to simplify public documents are underway.[4] Training manuals for quite responsible jobs may be written at levels approximating the skills of a typical sixth-grade student. Even the minimum competency requirements for high school graduation can seem quite minimal, and technological devices to compensate for lack of basic skills may be close at hand.

3. Daniel P. Resnick and Lauren B. Resnick, "The Nature of Literacy: An Historical Exploration," *Harvard Educational Review* 47 (August 1977): 371.

4. Larry Mikulecky has observed (personal communication, 1981) that "most research conducted in the military on the efficacy of rewriting documents to lower readability levels has proven to be ineffective. Recruits still do not seem to know how to glean needed information from the simple documents." Some success was reported by the Document Design Project in a civilian experiment in rewriting guides for marine radio operators, but a general caution is that the effectiveness of working primarily on simplifying texts is imperfectly known.

Voice synthesizers may replace written text in instructional manuals. Television substitutes the ability to comprehend enacted and spoken information for ability to comprehend some kinds of written information. The spelling and editing capacities of word processors may reduce the importance of spelling and grammar as basic writing skills. The computation capacities of hand-held calculators have made number estimation more important than great speed or accuracy in arithmetic. Kaplan and McNeill observe:

The rapid arrival of sophisticated but easily conquered technology . . . has been both a boon and a source of confusion. Almost any employee, literate or not, can learn to use calculators and basic computers. Whole work aids in many industrial processes have become so intelligible and sensibly illustrated that possession of basic skills becomes less important than it was even a decade ago.[5]

Predicting the intersect of efforts to reduce the literacy needed and the trend to expect even more of it from even more people is difficult. Absent great assurance, however, that lack of basic skills will not be as much of a problem in the future as it is in the present, continued attention to literacy and particularly to the relationship between literacy and employability seems justified.

LITERACY AND EMPLOYABILITY

Current estimates of the relationship between literacy and employability are based on three general types of indicators: years of school completed, performance on standardized tests of achievement, and performance on competency-based tests. In addition, there are two other approaches which, though promising, are at present more on the drawing boards than usable in practice.

Years of school completed. Completion of the fifth grade and self-reported ability to write one's name are the criteria for literacy used by the U.S. Census Bureau. The relation of years of schooling to employment seems fairly well established as a step-wise rather than as a linear effect. Completion of a generally recognized end point, such as graduation from high school, from a community

5. George Kaplan and Ian McNeill, "Basic Skills and Employability: Conference Overview with Policy and Program Perspectives," in National Institute of Education, *Proceedings of a Conference on Basic Skills for Productivity and Participation* (Washington, D.C.: National Institute of Education, forthcoming).

college or technical school, or from college, increases employment rates and earnings. For example, the Vice President's Task Force on Youth Employment reported in 1980 that completing high school or a four-year college are each associated with an increase in earnings of as much as 40 to 50 percent. For high school graduates in 1979, chances of being employed were about 91 percent, and for dropouts only 79 percent. Completion of intermediate years (for example, the difference between completing the tenth and eleventh grades of high school or between completing the sophomore and junior years of college) has little effect on employment or earnings.

The explanation for this relationship is debated.[6] Fisher argues that we can identify with considerable certainty which youth will have greatest employment problems: they are a year or more behind in achievement at all grades in school and are very likely to drop out before completing high school. He urges that highest priority be given to early identification of such youth, and to the provision of effective remedial programs so they can handle more advanced school work, receive their high school diplomas, and be more valuable to employers, in part because of their greater skills.[7]

While agreeing that diplomas make a difference, Thurow concludes that the difference is a credentialling effect. The diploma, in his view, stands for personal qualities such as good work habits, perseverance, and capacity to learn that employers value rather than an increment in specific skills of use in most entry-level jobs.[8]

This difference in interpretation makes a difference for educational policy. The one focuses on the achievement of skills; the

6. John T. Grasso and J. R. Shea, *Vocational Education and Training: Impact on Youth* (Berkeley, Calif.: Carnegie Council on Policy Studies in Higher Education, 1979).

7. David L. Fisher, *Functional Literacy and the Schools* (Washington, D.C.: National Institute of Education, 1978). See also, Theodore Schultz, "Investment in Human Capital," *American Economic Review* 51 (March 1961): 1-17.

8. Lester C. Thurow, "Vocational Education as a Strategy for Eliminating Poverty," in *Planning Papers for the Vocational Education Study* (Washington, D.C.: U.S. Government Printing Office, 1979); idem, *Generating Inequality* (New York: Basic Books, 1975). See also, William Sewell and Robert Hauser, *Education, Occupation, and Earnings: Achievement in the Early Career* (New York: Academic Press, 1975).

other on work habits and attitudes. Lacking some clarification of the ambiguity, the years-of-schooling indicator gives little assistance in program design, particularly with regard to whether the literacy skills needed for employability are the same as or different from those needed for further education or, more generally, for everyday life.

Performance on standardized tests. Most standardized tests assess fairly global skills: vocabulary, spelling and grammar, text comprehension, computation speed and accuracy, ability to use mathematics to solve abstract and some applied problems. They are designed primarily for within-group comparisons: half of the general population will fall above the 50th percentile and half below; and half the population will read at grade level or above, and half at grade level or below. The content of these tests reflects general school objectives, and, not surprisingly, achievement tests are best at predicting how well people will do in more schooling. Such tests often have been used for selection into further schooling, and into employment in the military. In both uses, they have been challenged because black, Hispanic, and Native American applicants typically have lower scores than do Anglo and Asian-American groups. Defended in part because the scores have about the same predictive power across groups, the tests have proven of only modest use in the development of vocational programs because of the weakness of their predictive power for employment and the questionable relation of what is tested to the basic skills demonstrably required for effective job performance. Standardized reading tests and functional job reading task tests, for example, show moderately high correlations (.65 to .80), suggesting that these types of test measure much the same thing.[9] The relation between reading tests and job proficiency is weak, however, with correlations of .30 to .40 between reading scores and practical performance tests, and few notable relationships between reading scores and supervisory ratings.

Competency-based tests. More recently, measures of literacy have been developed by expert judgment of the skills required for practical life tasks, such as reading the provisions of health

9. Thomas G. Sticht, *Reading for Working: A Functional Literacy Anthology* (Alexandria, Va.: Human Resources Research Organization, 1975).

insurance contracts or prudent management of a grocery budget. Most have been intended for general use, rather than use with specific reference to employability. The relationships among years of schooling completed, performance on achievement tests, performance on competency-based tests, and youth employment are not known. To the extent that the skills of everyday life and those required for employment are similar, the measures could provide useful guides for instructional programs.

Also, schools throughout the country are considering or have adopted competency-based tests to assess student progress and, in some cases, as criteria for promotion to later grades or graduation from high school. Little is known about the extent to which performance on these tests predicts employment or on-the-job performance. The measures gain their legitimacy from their relation to curriculum objectives or to expert judgment on generally needed skills.

In some instances competency-based literacy tests have been used for employment selection. The Professional and Career Examination (PACE) for U.S. government employment is one instance and similar measures have been used in industry as well as in the military. These uses have been challenged in the courts, however, because some minority groups have success rates substantially lower than the proportion of minorities taking the tests, and the predictive validity for on-the-job success has not been established in many instances.

Data on functional literacy from the National Assessment of Educational Progress (NAEP) provide some estimates of need. (See table 1.) These data include only seventeen-year-old youth who are in school and thus probably overestimate the literacy skills of the older age group. Most students whose parents had a high school diploma were well prepared for the literacy demands of postschool life; only 71 percent of youth whose parents had less than a high school education had scores high enough to be considered well prepared. Many Anglo students (88 percent) are well prepared; far fewer black seventeen-year-old students (74 percent) are this skilled. (Gender differences in functional literacy estimated by these NAEP indicators are negligible.) Despite the encouraging overall picture, too many students, by this indicator, are leaving schools only marginally literate or less.

TABLE 1

PERCENT OF SEVENTEEN-YEAR-OLDS REACHING DESIRED PERFORMANCE LEVELS ON THE NAEP FUNCTIONAL LITERACY TEST (1975), BY GENDER, PARENTAL EDUCATION, AND RACE

	Ideal Level * Mean Success Percentages
Gender	
Male	87
Female	88
Parental Education	
No high school	71
Some high school	79
Graduated high school	86
Post high school	91
Race	
Black	74
White	88

Source: Charles J. Gadway and H. A. Wilson, *Functional Literacy, Basic Reading Performance: A Brief Summary and Highlights of an Assessment of Seventeen-Year-Old Students in 1974 and 1975* (Denver, Colo.: National Assessment of Educational Progress, 1976). ED 133-704

* The "ideal" level is an almost perfect score.

With regard to cross-sectional data, scores on the subtests measuring highly skilled reading, writing, and mathematics have increased for the nine-year-olds but have decreased for seventeen-year-olds during the fifteen-year period over which National Assessment data have been collected. Encouragingly, the gap between races in test performance is closing for the younger students. Concern has focused on the apparent decline in higher-order comprehension skills among even the more talented high school students, although this may be a self-correcting problem as the 1978-80 cohort of nine-year-olds becomes the 1986-88 cohort of seventeen-year-olds. The instructional implications of these data include the need to sustain development of the more complex skills after elementary school among youth who enter high school well prepared and to help the approximately 15 percent of all youth who enter high school not well prepared in the basics.

Job literacy assessments. At least two approaches to estimating literacy for employment are on the horizon. The first, and most extensively developed, is based on fine-grained analyses of tasks performed by persons in different occupations. Working backward from these analyses, instructional programs integrating job content with literacy are developed, along with tests to assess the literacy skills. The most widely known of such programs may be those developed for the military by Sticht and his colleagues, using occupations such as cook.[10]

In reporting the results of programs that integrate training for a technical job with training for literacy skills, Sticht observes:

Job reading gains were much larger than general reading. This is important because it indicates that people are learning what they are being taught. Clearly the present results show that reading is not altogether a generic skill assessable by any test of general reading. The job reading task test results show that specific literacy skills can be developed and assessed for generalizability within the domain area that corresponds to what was taught. . . . Job related literacy training is more effective in improving job reading skills and is most cost-effective because it is no more costly than general literacy programs.[11]

One advantage of such an approach is the assurance that the skills are needed for a real job and that little superfluous material is being taught, a feature of considerable value when training time should be as brief as possible to maximize the returns to the employer. It may be more appropriate, however, to training for a specific occupation than for general education,[12] and the costs of job analysis, measurement development, and tailored instructional programs can be prohibitively high for most schools. While the relation between literacy as measured by these job-related tests and that assessed by achievement or general competency-based measures is moderate, Mikulecky notes that employees perform better on job-related material than on general reading material of

10. Sticht, *Reading for Working;* idem, "Developing Literacy and Learning Strategies in Organizational Settings," in *Cognitive and Affective Learning Strategies,* ed. Harold F. O'Neil and Charles D. Spielberg (New York: Academic Press, 1979), pp. 275-307; Thomas G. Sticht and W. D. Zapf, eds., *Reading and Readability Research in the Armed Forces* (Alexandria, Va.: Human Resources Research Organization, 1976).

11. Thomas G. Sticht, *Literacy and Vocational Competence,* Report 2.12 (Washington, D.C.: U.S. Department of Labor, 1980), pp. 303-4.

12. Louise Corman has noted that this may not be true if advancement or job changes are of concern. Personal communication, 1981.

comparable difficulty, suggesting that something different seems to be meant by literacy for employability for specific occupations.[13]

One of the more promising developments is a theoretical framework for thinking about domains that differentiate literacy for employability from literacy for other functions. Mikulecky and his colleagues, for example, applied the distinctions among "reading to learn," "reading to assess," and "reading to do" to analyses of skills required in a variety of blue-collar, technical, and semiskilled occupations. They compared the distribution of these skills to what was taught in a senior high school. They found that 90 percent or more of the on-the-job reading was reading to assess or to do, but only 10 percent of the reading instruction provided in high school used these skills. Sticht interviewed students in Navy training programs, on-the-job personnel, and training school instructors to find out what they were doing when they performed tasks involving reading. He was interested in their effort and how they went about it. He found that 71 percent of on-the-job reading was "reading to do," that is, looking up information that can be applied and then forgotten. Such reading involved using tables and figures, finding facts, and following directions. Only 37 percent of reading done on the job was "reading to learn," in which information must be retained for later use. Most of the students' training, however, had focused on reading to learn.[14] The implication is that there may be domains of basic skills that differentiate skilled from less able employees and that these domains differ substantially from what schools usually teach. The insights from these frameworks, like those of the next approach to be described, have yet to be translated into widely useful measures or instructional programs, but they seem to offer considerable promise for the design of instructional programs.

Ethnographic observations. Ethnographic observations are revealing two significant differences between the basic skills assessed in tests and those used in nonschool settings. The first is the im-

13. Larry Mikulecky, *Job Literacy: The Relationship between School Participation and Workplace Actuality*, Final Report, NIE G-79-0168 (Bloomington, Ind.: Indiana University, 1981).

14. Sticht, *Literacy and Vocational Competence.*

portance of context in influencing performance. Perhaps the most dramatic illustrations are those of Ulibarri in the assessment of language proficiency in English and Spanish.[15] His analysis of the results on proficiency tests revealed that Hispanic students whose English language proficiency (and English "dominance") was greater than their proficiency in Spanish showed high levels of fluency and Spanish dominance in nonschool settings. Ulibarri found that English was the language of the school for these children, while Spanish was the language spoken almost everywhere else. To what extent school estimates of literacy for groups and for individuals similarly underestimate proficiency in other settings is unknown. We may be planning for more remedial instruction than is needed and substantially underestimating skills of individual youth.

The second difference is in understanding the transfer of school-taught skills to the solution of problems in real life. Early studies suggest that the transfer from what is taught in school to what is used in life may be low. Lave, for example, observed how well-educated and less-well-educated adults went about grocery shopping. The mathematics heuristics used by both groups (for example, estimating the cumulative totals by rounding off to the nearest units of ten) were similar and were equally effective for keeping the grocery totals within what they had wanted to spend. The better educated shoppers did not apply other approaches that might have been simpler or more precise and which could have been derived from the mathematics they were likely to have learned in school.[16] Similarly, Scribner and Jacobs have found that mathematics as taught in high school is not applied in a variety of jobs in a dairy business: the workers were more likely to create their own fairly efficient ways of handling the numbers they had to use (for example, route delivery records) than to use the tech-

15. Daniel Ulibarri, Mary Spencer, and Guillermo Rivas, "Language Proficiency and Academic Achievement: A Study of Language Proficiency Tests and Their Relationship to School Ratings as Predictors of Academic Achievement," *Journal of the National Association for Bilingual Education* 5 (Spring 1981): 47-80.

16. Jean Lave, Olivia de la Rocha, and Michael Murtaugh, "A Conceptual Framework for Locating Cognitive Processes in Everyday Life" (Paper presented at the meeting of the Society for Research in Child Development, March 1981).

niques taught in school.[17] These findings, if generalizable, again suggest that the basic skills needed for employability may be understood best through analyses of how workers use writing, reading, and mathematics, with the data then being fed back to the planning of the school curriculum. The differences also may account for some of the reasons why the achievement of basic skills, as tested by measures reflecting how these skills are taught in school, seems to predict so poorly to work performance. The skills, these studies suggest, *are* needed, but they differ from what and how they are taught in many schools.

In summary, then, the evidence for a relation between literacy and employability is strongest in inferences from the frequently reported relationship between years of schooling completed and employment and in task analyses such as Sticht's. From the theoretical work of Mikulecky and the ethnographic studies of Lave and Scribner, one would predict only modest relations between literacy as measured by standardized tests of reading, writing, and mathematics and the functions observed on-the-job, but such studies may be among our best clues to better needs assessment and better instruction. These studies also suggest that the literacy needed for employability *is* different (at least for work not presently requiring a college degree or advanced professional training) from the literacy needed for further schooling, a finding which, if verified, would indicate that some restructuring of literacy-related curricula may be urgently needed.

Current Practice in Teaching Literacy

Vocational educators have argued that in almost all programs good work habits and basic skills as well as occupational knowledge are being taught.[18] The following quotations are examples of these views:

Vocational education is a form of education which frequently combines vocational training with the teaching of nonvocational, fundamental skills. . . . [The National Planning Association] concludes that most of the programs [they surveyed] attempted to supply students

17. Sylvia Scribner and Evelyn Jacobs, personal communication, 1981.

18. M. K. Klaurens, "The Goals of Education," in *Developing the Nation's Work Force*, ed. Merle E. Strong (Washington, D.C.: American Vocational Association, 1975).

with a marketable skill while at the same time providing them with a basic knowledge of English, arithmetic, and social studies. . . . This lack of a sharp line between vocational and nonvocational education has contributed to a controversy over the role and adequacy of vocational education.[19]

Vocational educators do not wish to dismember the mathematics curriculum or reduce its value for the comprehensive development of an individual's talent. They have no desire to dichotomize mathematics content into useful versus useless, and applied versus intellectual categories. Vocational educators must, however, search for and specify the mathematical applications that underlie vocational emphasis—those irreducible elements of computing competence needed for success in the specialties they teach.[20]

The emphasis on basic skills education exists in vocational education. . . . Basic skills education has been a national priority theme in vocational education during the past year, and promises to be of continuing concern in the future. For vocational educators, however, the term "basic" suggests basic to an occupation. The focus of basic skills for vocational educators therefore is on those competencies required for success in an occupation.[21]

And Darcy, in examining criteria for assessing vocational education outcomes, focussed on improving basic education skills, developing useful occupational skills, reducing risk of unemployment, and level of postschool earnings.[22]

Such views lead to expectations that (a) the theory and practice of combining instruction in basic and technical skills would be a prominent feature of vocational education and (b) students would improve demonstrably in such skills at rates as great as or

19. Anthony J. Polemeni and Michael H. Kean, "Evaluation Politics in Large City School Districts," in *Handbook of Vocational Education Evaluation*, ed. Theodore Abramson, Carol Kehr Tittle, and Lee Cohen (Beverly Hills, Calif.: Sage Publications, 1979), p. 554.

20. Thomas E. Long, *Basic Mathematics Skills and Vocational Education*, Information Series, no. 199 (Columbus, Ohio: National Center for Research in Vocational Education, 1980), p. 12.

21. Robert E. Taylor, "Foreword," in L. Jay Thornton, *Basic Reading Skills and Vocational Education* (Columbus, Ohio: National Center for Research in Vocational Education, 1980), p. v.

22. Robert Darcy, *Vocational Education Outcomes: Perspectives for Evaluation* (Columbus, Ohio: National Center for Research in Vocational Education, 1980).

greater than comparable students who did not participate in vocational education.

PROGRAMS

Three sources of information were used to estimate the attention given to basic skills improvement in vocational education: the ERIC Clearinghouse on Adult and Vocational Education, the convention programs of the American Vocational Association, and course listings in colleges that train vocational teachers. In all of these sources there was some evidence of concern for integrating basic skills and specific occupational knowledge, but in none was there evidence of abundant guidance.

In ERIC there are scores of references that describe objective-based and skill-oriented curriculum development and give examples for specific occupations.[23] One series on literacy and vocational education includes curriculum materials such as "Individualized Math Problems in Agriculture," "Individualized Math Problems in Marketing," and "Reading Right: Nursing Aide." These materials provide examples of how literacy and technical curricula could be integrated. The ERIC references did not yield much data on the use of these materials or their effectiveness, but the series could be considered at least to represent one approach to accomplishing the integration.

A recent American Vocational Association conference had two

23. For example, see Theodore Abramson and Adrienne Vogrin, "Instructional Support Systems: Curriculum Development and Evaluation by Occupational Education Teachers," in *Handbook of Vocational Education Evaluation,* ed. Abramson, Tittle, and Cohen, pp. 353-82; J. G. Bennet and M. C. Muncrief, eds., *Instructional Materials for Distributive Education* (Ithaca, N.Y.: Cornell Institute for Research and Development in Occupational Education, 1975); Frances A. Karnes and Clyde N. Ginn, "Vocational Reading Development Program: Comparison of the Reading Comprehension Levels of Postsecondary Vocational/Technical Students with the Readability Levels of the Textbooks Utilized in the Vocational/Technical Complexes in Mississippi" (Hattiesburg, Miss.: University of Southern Mississippi, 1976), ED 137-543; Thomas E. Long, *Employment Supervisors' Perceptions of the Basic Mathematics Competencies Needed in Vocational Education* (University Park, Penn.: Pennsylvania State University, 1979); Dale L. Morrell, "The Development of Vocational Modules and an Evaluative Instrument at Readability Levels Which Are Comprehensible by All Students in the High School Vocational Program," Final Report (Bristol, Va.: Bristol Public Schools, 1977), ED 146-400; Veronica Muzic, "A Writing Program for Secondary Vocational Technical Students," *PCTE Bulletin* 36 (1977): 3-14; Pamela P. Williams, "Determining the Reading Difficulty of Vocational Materials," *Florida Vocational Journal* 4, no. 5 (1979): 16-19.

sessions on literacy and employability, with high speaker overlap for the two sessions and high title overlap. The sessions primarily reported work underway at Cornell on basic skills instruction in vocational education. There were over 500 sessions and over 1,000 speakers. Literacy and employability thus received less than 1 percent of the time in formal sessions, a pattern that seems typical of recent national meetings and which might be true, to be sure, for any single topic that might seem as specialized as basic skills and employment.

A review of course listings did not locate any courses appearing to help vocational educators learn how to improve their students' basic knowledge of English or arithmetic through vocational education courses or how to set requirements for academic and general education to produce persons who have the basic skills needed to benefit from vocational offerings. Such information may be embedded within available courses, or might be offered in some colleges through cooperating departments. Insofar as offerings within training programs for vocational education teachers can be judged by their titles, there is not wide access to focused "how to" training for teachers.

Informal discussions with some vocational educators suggested a belief that because reading skills, some writing, and much arithmetic were required to do the vocational coursework, students would improve in these skills through practice. Most believed that instructors would help students who appeared to have significant difficulty in basic skills and that the vocational education teachers would know about other resources available in the school for students in difficulty. There is little systematic information, however, supporting this sensible belief. For example, how many vocational education students are actually referred by instructors to remedial programs as compared to independent estimates of the number of students needing such help?

STUDENT PERFORMANCE

There are few reports of the changes in basic skills for participants and nonparticipants in vocational education programs.[24]

24. Long, *Employment Supervisors' Perceptions of the Basic Mathematics Competencies Needed in Vocational Education;* idem, *Basic Mathematics Skills and Vocational Education;* Louise Corman, *Effects of Vocational Education on Participants* (Washington, D.C.: National Institute of Education, 1980); Thornton, *Basic Reading Skills and Vocational Education.*

National reviews of the effectiveness of programs of vocational education have concentrated on the performance of graduates in the labor market. In these analyses, employment rates and hourly wages are predominant outcome measures.[25] Except for Corman's review, there seem to have been no recent national reviews of the impact of vocational education on improvement in basic skills.

Several recent studies permit comparison of the basic skills of vocational and nonvocational students. The National Longitudinal Study of the Class of 1972, for example, shows that the reading achievement of students enrolled in academic programs is highest, general program students are in the middle, and students in the vocational education programs are lowest. Similar data are found in the Mathematics Study of the National Assessment of Educational Progress and in data from the Scholastic Aptitude Test. In these samples, the number of students is not large enough to permit reliable disaggregations of student achievement by parental socioeconomic status. Also, it is likely that there is some selection by students of academic, general, and vocational programs based on students' initial levels of skills and abilities and their interest in further schooling. None of the national studies provides information at point of entry and none provides data on rate of improvement during high school. It is not possible, therefore, to estimate whether students in vocational education programs are improving in the basic skills as much as or more than comparable students in academic or general programs. One might expect at least equal, and hope for enhanced, rates of achievement.

Monographs by Long and by Thornton confirm the stress on basic skills in vocational education and in the reports of panels, commissions, and committees.[26] Both Long and Thornton cite analyses of the levels of difficulty of the mathematics and reading content found in vocational education textbooks, assessments of the reading and mathematical skills of vocational education students, research on the nature of reading and mathematical skills, and studies of requirements for occupational skills. They report that many programs are using tests of basic skills at entry as ways

25. See, for example, Corman, *Effects of Vocational Education on Participants* and Grasso and Shea, *Vocational Education and Training.*

26. Long, *Basic Mathematics Skills and Vocational Education;* Thornton, *Basic Reading Skills and Vocational Education.*

of increasing completion rates. In neither monograph, however, is there much empirical information on what vocational educators are now doing, and with what success, to improve their students' competencies. Thornton observes:

For the most part, the reading difficulties of vocational students have been considered to be academic difficulties. That consideration strongly supports the position that reading skills should have been mastered as a prerequisite to entry into a vocational program. The solutions have traditionally been either referral for remediation or internal or external reading course work.[27]

PROCESS AND PRODUCT IN OTHER OCCUPATIONALLY ORIENTED PROGRAMS

At least two other approaches to improving basic skills for youth in the context of occupational preparation have been tried in the recent past. One is career education; the other is job training. Career education programs are offered primarily in school settings, as are vocational education programs, but usually are open to all students as part of general education rather than only to students interested in vocational preparation. In the national statement of career education goals, improving basic skills is named first, the rationale being that when students see the relation of what is being learned in school to occupational possibilities, they will be better motivated to acquire fundamental skills. Career education does not add another course to the curriculum so much as it hopes to arouse motivation to learn what already is being taught.[28]

At least one review of the evidence from demonstration programs in career education gives career education a good score on the "as good as or better than" criterion.[29] A few of the career education projects reported that students' gains in basic skills were lower than those of students in comparison programs, but the majority reported increases as large as those made by students not in career education programs and some reported gains large

27. Thornton, *Basic Reading Skills and Vocational Education*, pp. 7-8.

28. Allen B. Moore, *Relating Literacy Development to Career Education* (Washington, D.C.: U.S. Department of Health, Education, and Welfare, 1979).

29. Robert Bhaerman, *Career Education and Basic Academic Achievement: A Descriptive Analysis of the Results* (Washington, D.C.: U.S. Government Printing Office, 1977).

enough to be consistent with the national goal for career education. None of the analyses presented disaggregated data by socioeconomic status, gender, ethnic or linguistic minority status. Most career education programs had been in operation less than three years when Bhaerman's study was prepared. The findings might be considered promising enough to leave open the validity of career education's claims to basic skills improvement.

The second approach involves programs supported by the Department of Labor for out-of-school youth or youth who are high risks for dropping out. Most programs expect to create surges of motivation to learn through the promise of a job at the end of the tunnel. In addition, many offer direct remedial instruction in basic skills, often using prepackaged curricula. One subgroup of programs for out-of-school youth, including the Job Corps (operated since 1964) and other projects such as the Work Incentive Program (WIN), combines emphasis on work habits, basic skills, and development of occupational skills. Many of these projects provide direct literacy training, often by specially developed materials and by using instructors with training in basic education for adults. Some of the evaluations of Job Corps and WIN-type projects have included analyses of basic skills acquisition. The reports indicate that attrition is high but that the basic skills courses have had significant effects on reading and mathematics skills for the 30 percent or so of the participants who complete training. Only for those reading at less than the fifth-grade level were intensive remedial programs effective. Other participants apparently attached a stigma to being removed from the classroom for remedial work. These programs, while imperfect in both retention and in enabling long-term employment in the private sector, are still good enough to be cost-effective, compared to long-term welfare or unemployment.[30]

In summarizing over a decade of experience under the Manpower Development and Training Act, Mikulecky observes that

30. Robert Taggart, *Youth Employment: Policies and Programs for the 1980s,* Youth Knowledge Development Report 2.12 (Washington, D.C.: Department of Labor, 1980). Ernst W. Stromsdorfer, *Review and Synthesis of Cost-Effectiveness Studies of Vocational and Technical Education* (Columbus, Ohio: Center for Vocational and Technical Education, Ohio State University, 1972).

literacy training is most successful when teachers are well trained and sympathetic to the trainees, when trainees enter with reading skills at the seventh- to tenth-grade levels, and when training does not involve classes meeting in high schools.[31]

A second subgroup of programs focuses on in-school youth and emphasizes various approaches to both school retention and achievement. Among the best known are the Youthwork projects, all of which have a basic skills improvement requirement; the programs intended to increase private sector involvement in job creation and placement, such as the Work-Education Councils and the Corporation for Public/Private Ventures, which do not have basic skills requirements; and the projects aimed at guaranteed later employment for youth who remain in school, which are intended to have a basic skills improvement component. Added to these should be the large national study on partial subsidies to employers for hiring persons in four groups with high unemployment rates: teenage youth, women receiving aid for dependent children, released offenders, and drug addicts. Here the emphasis was on job opportunities—on fixing the demand side rather than the supply side. Mangum and Walsh observe:

Several CETA sponsors have initiated special programs of remediation and alternative education which, on the basis of early evidence, appear to be promising. In Baltimore, for example, the CETA Youth Strategy has been built around a program (Harbor City Learning) which provides alternating two-week cycles of work and educational development. It is too early to judge the results of these programs, but their very existence is evidence that employment and training administrators are using new methods in attempting to solve an old and particularly difficult problem.[32]

31. Larry Mikulecky, *Literacy Competencies and Youth Employment*, Final Report, NIE P-80-0078 (Bloomington, Ind.: Indiana University, 1980). See also, United States, Department of Labor, *Basic Education in Manpower Programs: The R and D Experience*, Manpower Research Monograph no. 38 (Washington, D.C.: U.S. Government Printing Office, 1975); Joseph Hines and Brian Linder, "Job Corps Vocational Offerings: An Analysis of Performance Indicators by Training Area and Center Performance," in *Assessments of the Job Corps: Performance and Impacts*, vol. 2 (Washington, D.C.: Office of Youth Programs, U.S. Department of Labor, 1979).

32. Garth Mangum and John Walsh, *Employment and Training Programs for Youth: What Works Best for Whom?*, Youth Knowledge Development Report 2.2 (Washington, D.C.: Department of Labor, 1980), pp. 105-6.

After less than two full years of operation, reports indicated that for low-income, high-risk youth, services as well as subsidized employment seem essential for a successful transition to work. In the most recent report, only the women receiving aid for dependent children were shown to have made notable progress in employment. The youth, if anything, regressed.

In the immediate future, attention may focus on the results of a large comparative study of different approaches to basic skills instruction for youth enrolled in employment training programs.[33] The research design involves random assignments of youth to experimental and control treatments, and replications of all treatments across several sites. The approaches include a program designed especially for these youth as a third generation curriculum originally developed for Job Corps; a peer tutoring approach; approaches that are an extension upward of highly structured, building-block designs that have proven successful in elementary school settings; and an approach using computer-assisted instruction. The study seeks to provide definitive information on the extent to which the best available programs, according to the Department of Labor, improve basic skills in a training program. The programs being compared are:

The Adkins Employability Skills series with ten problem-centered units focussed on selecting, finding, and keeping a job.

The American Preparatory Institute program, a competency-based, open entry/exit system built on self-paced instructional modules in basic skills. The nationwide Adult Performance Level competencies are used as the curriculum objectives.

The Adult Performance Level program aimed at teaching students coping skills, claiming that through performance of the functional literacy tasks, students will also learn basic reading, language, and computational skills.

Bilingual English as a Second Language, a program prepared by the Defense Language Institute, in which the enrollee is completely immersed in the new language and no translated material is presented.

33. Barry J. Argento et al., *Alternative Education Models: The Preliminary Findings of the Job Corps Educational Improvement Effort,* Youth Knowledge Development Report 5.2 (Washington, D.C.: U.S. Government Printing Office, 1980).

The computer-assisted instruction PLATO project of the University of Illinois, which provides two hours daily for reading and two for mathematics plus participation in the PLATO laboratory.

A computer-assisted and computer-managed instruction combination, providing an individual reading prescription based on a criterion referenced diagnostic pretest.

A modification of a computer-assisted, computer-managed instructional program, including PLATO programs in reading mathematics, GED, and world of work, using also a diagnostic/prescriptive approach.

A computer-assisted mathematics program of the drill and practice variety.

The Cambridge GED program, which is a multimedia alternative to the regular Job Corps curriculum.

The learning disabilities model involving diagnostic/prescriptive training.

The New Reading Program, which is a redesign of the Sullivan Associates Programmed Reading System used for years by the Job Corps.

The picture from current information on basic skills instruction for employment is mixed. Some interesting studies are underway. There are some new curricular materials and evidence of attention to ways of meeting literacy needs of youth enrolled in vocational education and employment training programs. The findings are few, however, with regard to impact, and there may be some reasons to believe that the better designed studies may not show effects as substantial as needed. These reasons derive from research on basic skills instruction, which shows what *is* important for effective instruction, at least at elementary levels, and, by extrapolation, offers some promising new ideas for literacy training for employment.

RESEARCH AND DEVELOPMENT ON LITERACY AND BASIC SKILLS

The past ten years have seen considerable convergence of findings on basic skills development that can be applied both to predicting the outcomes of evaluations of present programs and to new program development. These areas are (a) research on academic learning time, (b) investigation of motivational factors in instruction, and (c) research on the nature of skilled reading.

Academic learning time. A large number of studies on the characteristics of instructionally effective classes have converged on two findings. The first is that very little time in many schools is "on task" for learners and the second is that time on task powerfully predicts improvement in basic skills.[34] By "time on task" is meant how many minutes students spend daily working on instructional tasks. A student getting out notebooks is "off-task" for basic skills instruction; a student reading aloud, or writing an essay, or working on mathematical problems would be "on task" for basic skills. As examples of the variation in allocated time and academic engaged time, Rosenshine reports a study in which allocated time in fifth-grade reading ranged from two hours and ten minutes daily (with students on task 80 percent of the time) to one hour and twenty-five minutes (with students on task 63 percent of the time.) In the area of mathematics, the highest average was fifty-three minutes of allocated time, with 86 percent on-task time, and the lowest average was thirty-eight minutes of daily allocated time, with 63 percent on-task time.[35]

The studies indicate fairly consistently that the greater the engaged learning time for the individual student on the skills measured later, the greater the gains. Important as a supportive classroom atmosphere or variations in text content may be, instructional time on task accounts for the greatest impact. Where the program director, the instructors, and the students all are clear on the purpose of the activities and engage in instruction related to the desired outcomes, students gain more, and students with the initially greatest problems gain most. Students in less directed classes, in more open learning or discovery learning settings, which may have as many extra resources, perform less well on measures of basic skills achievement. While many of these studies have

34. David C. Berliner and Barak Rosenshine, "The Acquisition of Knowledge in the Classroom," in *Schooling and the Acquisition of Knowledge,* ed. Richard C. Anderson, Rand J. Spiro, and William E. Montague (Hillsdale, N.J.: Lawrence Erlbaum Associates, 1977); Carolyn Denham and Ann Lieberman, eds., *Time to Learn: A Review of the Beginning Teacher Evaluation Study* (Washington, D.C.: National Institute of Education, 1980).

35. Barak V. Rosenshine, "How Time Is Spent in Elementary Classrooms," in *Time to Learn,* ed. Denham and Lieberman, pp. 107-26.

examined the instructional processes only in elementary schools, at least one well-controlled study has shown that by providing senior high school teachers serving hard-to-reach youth with training on how they can increase effective instructional time, students in the upper grades can show the same marked improvements in reading achievement as those in elementary schools. These findings underscore the significance of Mikulecky's report that workers on most jobs, including blue-collar jobs, spend more time reading (about 155 minutes daily) than do high school students (about 98 minutes daily). Comparing 48 high school juniors, 51 technical school students, and 150 workers in a cross section of occupations, Mikulecky's trained interviewers found that the high school students also read less competently and faced easier material, which they read thoroughly, than did the workers.[36]

Motivational factors in instruction. The most recent studies have *not* been examining the fairly well accepted relations among student interest in a topic, student effort, and student achievement. Rather the emphasis has been on the instructional message sent by uses of positive and negative feedback on performance, and the tone set in the classroom. One study found that students of teachers who were lavish with their praise achieved less academic growth than students of teachers who informed them where the work was unacceptable. Lavish praise, the researchers concluded, had two negative effects on achievement. The first was setting of standards of excellence that were far too low for the reality measured by independent tests. The second was loss of information when praise actually was merited: if work that students knew was the fruit of little effort received lavish encouragement, truly merited praise had less meaning.

Tomlinson has recently called for reestablishing a sense of balance between viewing schools as places whose business is learning and viewing them as places to help students who seem unable to benefit from what now may be almost equal opportunities to "learn how to learn."[37] Similar views have been expressed by Taggart:

36. Mikulecky, *Job Literacy.*

37. Tommy M. Tomlinson, "Effective Schools: Mirror or Mirage?" *Today's Education* 70 (April-May 1981): 60-61.

The requirement for performance and the risk of failure are a necessary part of any opportunity. As the opportunities are equalized for positive experiences, as disadvantaged minority youth come to have the same chances of employment in school and out . . . then application of labor market standards of success or failure, with rewards and punishments, becomes more feasible because the option for the youth who fails is not so bleak and the cause of this cannot be blamed as much on previously limited opportunities.[38]

Research on the nature of skilled reading. Many reading programs for youth and adults try to concentrate exclusively upon what have been thought to be the building blocks of fluent reading: ability to recognize and pronounce letter sounds, to merge letter sounds into words, to recognize the parts of sentences and to know their functions in conveying meaning. These programs assume that what differentiates skilled readers from less skilled readers is little more than the rapidity with which the elements are brought together.

More recent findings indicate that this is not the case. According to schema theory, reading is a constructive process.[39] The skilled reader is formulating hypotheses about the content of what is read and using text to confirm or reject these hypotheses. Using specially constructed materials that are open to misleading interpretations, researchers have shown that skilled readers quickly pick up clues to the misinterpretation, are efficient in locating the ambiguous word or phase, and swiftly reformulate their interpretation. Less skilled readers take longer to recognize the error, and have less efficient strategies for search of textual materials. The difference is in cognitive strategies for dealing with text and in

38. Taggart, *Youth Employment*, p. 47.

39. Marilyn F. Adams and Allan Collins, "A Schema-Theoretic View of Reading," in *New Directions in Discourse Processing*, ed. Roy Freedle (Norwood, N.J.: ABLEX Publishing Corp., 1979); D. C. Bobrow and Allan Collins, *Representation and Understanding* (New York: Academic Press, 1975); Ann L. Brown, "Knowing When, Where, and How to Remember: A Problem of Metacognition," in *Advances in Instructional Psychology*, vol. 1, ed. Robert Glaser (Hillsdale, N.J.: Lawrence Erlbaum Associates, 1978); Jill H. Larkin, "Information Processing Models and Science Instruction," in *Cognitive Process Instruction*, ed. Jack Lochhead and John Clement (Philadelphia: Franklin Institute Press, 1979); Rand Spiro, B. C. Bruce, and W. Brewer, eds., *Theoretical Issues in Reading Comprehension: Perspectives from Cognitive Psychology, Linguistics, Artificial Intelligence, and Education* (Hillsdale, N.J.: Lawrence Erlbaum Associates, 1980).

the richness and extent of information the reader brings to the act of reading. A reader with considerable knowledge of the text content and efficient strategies usually will comprehend quickly and fluently; readers who have little of either seem to bog down no matter how well they can decode letter and syllable sounds. Collins and Smith comment:

There are two aspects of comprehension processes that we think are important to teach: (1) comprehension monitoring and (2) hypothesis formation and evaluation. . . . Comprehension monitoring concerns the student's ability both to evaluate his or her ongoing comprehension processes while reading through a text and to take some sort of remedial action when these bog down. . . . Students also need to be able to use clues in the text to make hypotheses about what is happening or is likely to happen next, to evaluate these hypotheses as new evidence comes in, and to revise them should evidence accumulate to indicate that they are wrong.[40]

The generalizability of these findings to writing and mathematics is uncertain. Studies of differences between skilled and less skilled problem solvers show skilled persons are not necessarily better at arithmetic computations, useful as these may be. Rather, the fluent user of mathematics has acquired other skills, such as estimation of what the correct answer probably is, which provide hypotheses against which operations are checked.[41]

These findings have not yet been incorporated directly into new curricula for teaching reading and mathematics, either to youth or to children, although it is plausible that techniques based on schema theory will be more effective in improving basic skills than those that only recapitulate the building-block notion with

40. Allan Collins and Edward E. Smith, *Teaching the Process of Reading Comprehension,* Final Report, NIE C-400-76-0116 (Urbana, Ill.: Center for the Study of Reading, University of Illinois, 1980), pp. 3-4.

41. J. S. Brown and R. R. Burton, "Diagnostic Models for Procedural Bugs in Basic Mathematical Skills," *Cognitive Science* 2 (1978): 155-92; Rochel Gelman and C. R. Gallistel, *The Child's Understanding of Number* (Cambridge, Mass.: Harvard University Press, 1978); Robert Glaser, "Trends and Research Questions in Psychological Research on Learning and Schooling," *Educational Researcher* 8 (November 1979): 6-13; J. G. Greeno, "Cognitive Objectives of Instruction: Knowledge for Solving Problems and Answering Questions," in *Cognition and Instruction,* ed. David Klahr (Hillsdale, N.J.: Lawrence Erlbaum Associates, 1976).

more sophisticated materials than primers.[42] Further evidence may be found in Mikulecky's report that high school students frequently use reading comprehension strategies such as rereading or rehearsing that are less effective than those used by workers, who more often apply such approaches to on-the-job reading as relating new information to old. Mikulecky observes: "Their (students') strategies deny what we know about effective cognitive processing and use of schema."[43]

Overall, these studies argue (a) for greater attention to increasing the time directed to basic skills improvement and helping teachers develop strategies for increasing engaged learning time, (b) for techniques providing prompt, accurate information to students on their levels of performance, coupled with instruction aimed at improving this performance in a work-oriented atmosphere, and (c) for instructional materials which apply findings from cognitive and schema theory as well as the building-block approaches. Simple as these ideas may sound, there seem to be no programs at present that incorporate all three.

Who Is Responsible?

Research suggests a conclusion that can be difficult to square with current promises and practices: improvement in basic skills is not likely to be an easy by-product of such interesting content as automotive repair, home economics, or carpentry, at least not for students whose skills initially are low. If we are convinced that literacy is important for employability, and that employment-related literacy needs to be taught intensively in the schools and in a manner sensitive to findings from research and practice on what skills are needed, someone needs to be responsible for doing this.

There are at least three possibilities for vocational education: improve skills before high school, consider it someone else's job, or take it on directly, at least in part.

42. R. J. Tierney, J. E. Readance, and E. K. Dishner, *Reading Strategies and Practices: A Guide for Improving Instruction* (Boston, Mass.: Allyn and Bacon, 1980); Claire Weinstein, "Elaboration Skills as a Learning Strategy," in *Learning Strategies*, ed. Harold F. O'Neil (New York: Academic Press, 1978).

43. Mikulecky, *Job Literacy*, p. 24.

IMPROVING SKILLS BEFORE HIGH SCHOOL

One approach would be to place even greater pressures on the elementary grades and junior high schools to prepare students for more advanced learning through basic skills improvement. The minimum competency approach and efforts already being made to prevent problems rather than to remediate them in later grades may have considerable impact over the next years. The task of vocational educators a decade from now thus may be only fostering continued growth of vocabulary and fluency in using basic skills, a task that may be accommodated easily when students are prepared better to begin with. The extent to which these efforts will be effective is unknown, however, and it seems likely that even if the problem of lack of basic skills is reduced, it will not be entirely eliminated in the early grades.

SOMEONE ELSE'S JOB

A second approach would be to argue that vocational education has an important but limited responsibility in basic skills development. The responsibility might be limited to continuing the reasonable development of vocabulary and fluency in applied skill use for students whose basic skills are adequate or better. Such students should not fall behind; opportunities would be provided to enhance literacy for employability, but primary responsibility for students with serious basic skills problems would be seen as that of remedial programs for such youth or of the appropriate departments in high schools, community colleges, and technical/vocational schools. The content of such remedial programs might well be developed cooperatively with vocational educators, and reflect what is known about literacy for employability, but completion of such courses might be *prerequisites* to enrollment in vocational programs. Such an approach might be most compatible with present practice, and with a time when declining enrollments are not of concern. It may be less than forthcoming, however, where the need for skilled workers is high and where vocational programs may want to attract a larger number of learners.

At least one authoritative spokesperson for vocational education at the national level argues strongly for this view:

While there are students who take vocational courses (often referred to as vocational students), these students also and simultaneously take general and academic courses. . . . There is a growing tendency to indicate that the total school system and especially the general and academic parts of the system have little or no responsibility for a student once he or she enrolls in a vocational course. While vocational education should and does have some responsibility for basic skills and development (both literacy and employability), it is quite clear to me that general education and academic education have a much larger responsibility for teaching at least the basic literacy skills.[44]

GREATER INVOLVEMENT WITH BASIC SKILLS IMPROVEMENT

A third approach would be to assume a more direct role in basic skills improvement. Such a choice would mean fairly considerable departures from current practice. The first departure would be the investment in development of adequate curricular materials. The second would be training vocational educators in how to combine basic skills and technical training, perhaps building on the work done by Sticht and his colleagues for the military. The third would be greater attention to assessing students' basic skills on enrollment, during training, and as part of the criterion of program effectiveness for which vocational and occupational educators would accept accountability. A fourth difference would be expansion of the time students currently spend in vocational programs, since integrating technical skills with basic skills development might be more instructionally efficient but is unlikely to yield twice the learning in the same time. A fifth would be the need for greater individualization: except for programs serving groups homogeneous with regard to the need for improvement in basic skills, vocational education might be more in the posture of opening enrollments and widening the range of abilities within usual classes. Using new computer-based instructional technologies

44. Glen Boerrighter, personal communication, 1981. Boerrighter also emphasizes that the purposes of vocational education extend beyond the basic ones of job-entry training, technical training, and upgrading job skills, all of which may imply some responsibility for literacy development. He notes that vocational education "in fact often has moved into or taken on purposes related to economic development, entrepreneurship development, concern for reindustrialization, and developing person power for the military as well as specific businesses and industry." His comment suggests that the effectiveness of vocational education should be judged against criteria considerably more complex than improving basic skills needed for employability.

might be considered, but the costs in retooling and in student instructional management would not be negligible. In addition, the difficulties of engaging some youth in any kind of basic skills instruction can not be underestimated. Taggart has argued that for those whose school experience has been a series of failures, it may be necessary to provide instruction in alternate settings, reducing to a minimum what might seem like "here we go again" direct instruction.[45]

One argument favoring such involvement has not been raised to this point, but seems appropriate to consider. Both experience and at least some research suggest that when students do not believe education is instrumental to achieving a place they want in society, even those from advantaged backgrounds will not engage sufficiently in school to learn. Ogbu has made this case in particular in the context of education and employment: in communities where students do not see education as leading anywhere for them, almost nothing schools can do in the way of better curricula or extended schooling hours seems to work.[46] The potential of occupational training and vocational education to lead to somewhere worthwhile, it could be argued, is great if the skilled human services and technical trades expand. Integrating basic skills instruction *with* vocational education thus finds support from fundamental inquiry as well as arguments reaching back to the early days of vocational programs. At least on a pilot basis, the time may be now to bring together these lines of reasoning into programs for youth, showing what schools—and vocational education programs—*can* do to improve the basic skills needed for employability.

45. Taggart, *Youth Employment.*

46. John Ogbu, "Context and Ethnography of Urban Reading Problems" (Paper presented at a National Institute of Education Roundtable on Urban Reading, November, 1980).

CHAPTER VIII

The Equity and Effectiveness of Secondary Vocational Education

SUE E. BERRYMAN

Introduction

In this chapter the equity and work establishment effectiveness of secondary vocational education for youth in general and for selected youth subgroups are assessed. We address three sets of questions that we would expect to be relevant to the policy debate on the reauthorization of the federal Vocational Education Act.

1. Relative to their preplacement abilities and preferences, are students misassigned to the alternative high school curricula? Does this misallocation have consequences for their postsecondary outcomes?

2. Does the vocational curriculum organize high school resources so as to assure that students with particular abilities and postsecondary destinations are treated as clients of the school? Does it do so in ways that unduly segregate its enrollees socially and educationally from the rest of the student body?

3. What work establishment payoffs might we expect from vocational education, given employer hiring and internal market behaviors? Are vocational education resources now organized to deliver these payoffs?

We assess the equity and effectiveness consequences of vocational education because these considerations represent important values in American society. Vocational education has often been

---

This chapter is based on a paper presented at the 1979 Aspen Workshop on Vocational Education Policies, held at the Aspen Institute in Aspen, Colorado. The Office of the Assistant Secretary for Planning and Evaluation, U.S. Department of Health, Education, and Welfare funded the study through the Aspen Systems Corporation. The study was published as a Rand Corporation Note, N-1475-ASC.

judged solely on its work establishment effectiveness,[1] as evidenced by policy concerns with "in-field" employment, projections of occupational vacancies, and employment and wage effects. However, secondary vocational education is also part of the tracking system in high schools. As such, it is a vehicle for the differential treatment of students. Differential treatment always carries the potential for inequity. Thus, an adequate policy assessment of vocational education requires looking at what differential treatment buys in work establishment effectiveness at what costs in equity.

Even if we ignore federal vocational education objectives that do not directly involve students (for example, community economic development), we recognize that federal objectives clearly go beyond work establishment. The basic purpose of the nation's education and training system, including vocational education, is to humanize and prepare our children for their multiple adult roles of citizen, consumer of goods and services, spouse, and parent, as well as for a labor force role.

A primary objective of vocational education, however, has always been the employability of its graduates. The labor force role is also central for males and increasingly central for females. Of youth who were eighteen years old in 1977, males had a life expectancy of 53.1 more years and a working-life expectancy of 37.7 years; females, a life expectancy of 60.5 more years and a working-life expectancy of 27 years.[2] Thus, at age eighteen males

1. We use Freedman's definition of *work establishment*: (a) attachment to an occupation or organization, (b) employment stability, that is a minimum shelter against economic risk, and (c) earnings sufficient to enable the worker to support himself/herself and dependents according to accepted standards of health and decency. See Marcia Freedman, *The Process of Work Establishment* (New York: Columbia University Press, 1969).

2. These numbers represent preliminary estimates from an increment-decrement model of the tables of working life. Shirley J. Smith, demographic statistician with the Office of Current Employment Analysis, Bureau of Labor Statistics, Department of Labor, kindly supplied us with these estimates. The labor force estimates for eighteen-year-old males and females are based on the 1977 labor force status and transitions in and out of the labor force by older adult cohorts in 1977. Since number of years in the labor force is declining for males and increasing for females, regardless of marital and parental status, the labor force expectancies for eighteen-year-olds in 1977 represent an upper bound for males and a lower bound for females.

can expect to spend 71 percent and females 45 percent of their remaining lives in the labor force.

If we hold any of our secondary education accountable for student employability, secondary vocational education is most suitably judged on that contribution. Vocational graduates enter the labor force directly from high school at higher rates (60 percent employed in October of the year of graduation) than graduates of the general curriculum (48 percent employed) or of the academic curriculum (15 percent employed). Of the 30 percent who enter postsecondary education, half of these enroll in postsecondary vocational/technical programs that are usually of short duration. Thus, for 75 percent of secondary vocational graduates, high school is their last or almost their last experience in the educational system.

We define *youth* as individuals fourteen to twenty-four years of age. Our different questions involve different parts of this range. *Vocational education* refers to all formal, work-oriented education that is conducted in public secondary schools and is targeted at occupations requiring no more skills than can be obtained at the secondary level or in limited postsecondary programs. Thus, the term encompasses training called "vocational," "technical," "distributive," or "business and commercial."

We restrict our assessment to secondary vocational education because secondary and postsecondary vocational education should be assessed separately. Clients differ in age and ability, and the services and delivery institutions differ. Since about 67 percent of the federal appropriation for vocational education goes to the secondary level, we concentrate on that level.

Obviously, measures of students' high school curricula enter into our discussions of all three sets of questions. We do not know how sensitive the results of the analyses reported here are to different measures. The *National Longitudinal Study of the High School Class of 1972 (NLS 1972)* measures student perceptions of their curricula, school records of the students' curricula, and detailed information on the courses taken. Meyer reports discrepancies among all three coding schemes.[3] Obviously, the different mea-

3. Robert H. Meyer, "Vocational Education: How Should It Be Measured?" Project Report (Washington, D.C.: Urban Institute, August, 1981).

sures are useful for different analytic purposes. However, not only do data bases often not allow analysts to choose the most appropriate measure, but analysts who have worked with the major data bases have often been unaware of the discrepancies in coding schemes. Thus, results reported in this chapter could change if different curricular measures were used, for example, measures of actual time in particular vocational courses.

We rely entirely on the published literature and available data, and we synthesize these materials around the issues initially described at the beginning of this section.

Fairness of Student Curricular Assignments

Members of society judge the fairness of any allocation relative to cultural agreements about who should get what. We can use at least three different norms to judge the fairness of high school curricular assignments. For example, we can use a compensatory norm. In this case we might consider assignments fair if we see students registered in courses that could be expected to reduce preassignment differences among students. We can have an equality objective. In this case we would consider assignments fair if we could not distinguish students on the basis of the courses they take. Finally, we could have a tracking objective, that is, training that is differentiated according to students' abilities and postsecondary preferences. In this case we would consider assignments fair if they matched variations in abilities and preferences.

In this chapter the fairness of curricular assignments is judged according to a tracking objective. This decision does not imply that tracking is the only or necessarily the most appropriate basis for allocating students among high school educational opportunities. However, tracking represents a major assignment norm in American high schools.

We recognize that tracking creates unease because of a concern that the vocational track restricts its enrollees to the less attractive postsecondary opportunities available in the society. We argue, however, that the policy question is not whether students should be prepared for the less attractive jobs in the nation. To pretend that a substantial proportion of any youth cohort will not end up in these jobs is to mislead youth and misallocate our education and training resources.[4] Rather, the questions are these: Do curricular placements in high schools and the experiences associated with the different curricula misallocate a cohort's talents and preferences among postsecondary educational and occupational opportunities? Do they significantly restrict a student's ability to implement changes in his or her preferences that might occur during or after high school?

CONDITIONS FOR INEQUITY

Under a tracking system, inequity is possible under either of two situations. In the first situation, students are allocated among curricula on bases other than ability and preferences (for example, on the basis of status characteristics such as race and sex); the different curricula (vocational, general, and academic) have effects on talents, preferences, and behaviors independent of differences that existed prior to curricular placement; and the different curricula are associated with different postsecondary educational and occupational outcomes.

In the second situation, students are properly assigned to curricula on the basis of abilities and preferences. The different curricula, however, create differences among students that did not exist prior to curricular enrollment and unnecessarily restrict their postsecondary opportunities.[5]

It is easier to determine inequity in the first situation than in the second. The problem with the second case lies in the concept "unnecessarily." For each youth cohort, high school immediately precedes its first major branching into homemaking, college, or full-time work. One of the presumptive points of high school tracking is to facilitate this branching. Under these conditions it would not be surprising to observe increased differences between

4. Of the total jobs in the nation, two-thirds represent blue-collar, low-level white collar, or service jobs. U.S. Department of Commerce, *Statistical Abstracts of the United States, 1978* (Washington, D.C.: U.S. Government Printing Office, 1978).

5. This situation illustrates differences between compensatory and tracking objectives for the high school curricula. In the tracking case, inequity occurs when curricula increase initial differences unnecessarily, not when they maintain them. It occurs in the compensatory case when the curricula increase or maintain (that is, fail to reduce) initial differences.

students in the different tracks. If such differences occur, the difficulty arises in deciding when they are inevitable, not inequitable. If we differentiate training in response to unequal abilities of students, their postsecondary preferences, and their postsecondary opportunities, when are increased differences developmental in nature and unavoidable? When are they excessive, given these realities?

We suspect that social unease about tracking derives in part from the difficulty of distinguishing the inevitable from the inequitable. We cannot assess this issue well from the available data. Observers' social values will also strongly affect any equity decision here.

However, we can assess the first situation empirically. We also anticipate that most observers, regardless of values, will see tracking as inequitable if students are allocated among curricula on bases other than ability and preferences, if curricula have effects on talents and aspirations independent of initial differences, and if these effects translate into different postsecondary outcomes.

In the rest of this section we examine the evidence on: (a) the bases for initial curricular assignments; (b) the effects of curriculum, independent of preenrollment differences; and (c) the relationship between the high school curriculum and postsecondary outcomes. The evidence on these questions comes primarily from the analyses by Alexander, Cook, and McDill of data from the Academic Growth Study.[6] This longitudinal study was conducted by the Educational Testing Service from 1965 to 1967. It measured students in the fall of the ninth grade (that is, prior to track assignment), in the fall of the eleventh grade, and in the winter of the twelfth grade. These analyses indicate potential misallocation of students among postsecondary opportunities.

INITIAL CURRICULAR ASSIGNMENT

The Alexander, Cook, and McDill analyses indicate that ability, ninth-grade achievement, and ninth-grade curriculum plans account for less than half of the variance in track placement and that un-

6. Karl L. Alexander, Martha Cook, and Edward L. McDill, "Curriculum Tracking and Educational Stratification: Some Further Evidence," *American Sociological Review* 41 (February 1978): 47-66.

measured variables account for over half. These analyses also indicate that sex, but not family socioeconomic status and race, directly determines curricular placement. Family socioeconomic
status and race affect placement indirectly via their direct effects
on ability, ninth-grade achievement, and ninth-grade curricular
plans.

To assess the basis for initial curricular placement, Alexander,
Cook, and McDill used several ninth-grade measures from the
Academic Growth Study: father's and mother's education; father's
occupation; the student's sex, race, verbal and quantitative ability;
ninth-grade achievement; high school curriculum plans (dichoto-
mized as academic and other); peers' college plans; and father's and
mother's encouragement of college plans.

Within this system of variables they found that the major direct
determinants of high school curriculum placement were ability,
achievement, and ninth-grade curriculum plans. The effects of
socioeconomic status (as measured by variables such as father's occupation and father's and mother's education) and race were indirect via these direct determinants. Sex was the only demographic
variable for which the effect was independent of these determinants.

In other words, if we accept ability and curricular preference
as appropriate placement bases, these students are generally appropriately placed in terms of the placement variance for which
these variables account. However, the direct determinants of placement only accounted for less than 40 percent of the variance in
placement, leaving 60 percent unexplained. If we assume that the
Academic Growth Study measured these determinants well, these
results indicate that students of equal ability, achievement, and curricular preference can end up in different curricula.

UNIQUE CURRICULUM EFFECTS ON ACHIEVEMENTS
AND PREFERENCES

Alexander, Cook, and McDill found that track placement affects
achievements and postsecondary preferences, independent of precurriculum differences. Using Academic Growth Study measures
at the ninth (precurriculum enrollment), eleventh, and twelfth
grades, Alexander, Cook, and McDill estimated curriculum effects
on eleventh- and twelfth-grade outcomes, independent of precur-

riculum differences. For the eleventh grade they found that, relative to the nonacademic track (vocational and general curricula), the academic track largely—but not entirely—transmits prior influences. This track uniquely enhances eleventh-grade achievement (by one-fourth of a within-school standard deviation), even when ability and ninth-grade achievement are controlled. It also uniquely increases associations with peers who plan to go to college and (at least the student's perception of) parental encouragement of going to college.

For the twelfth grade they found that curriculum uniquely affects mathematical, but not verbal, achievement. (The academic track is worth 27 percent of a pooled within-school standard deviation on the P/SAT quantitative battery.) The academic track also increases by about 30 percent the chances that seniors will expect to go to college.

SECONDARY CURRICULUM AND POSTSECONDARY OUTCOMES

Analyses of the major longitudinal data bases, such as Project TALENT, the *National Longitudinal Survey (NLS)*, the *National Longitudinal Study of the High School Class of 1972 (NLS 1972)*, show strong correlations between high school curriculum and postsecondary outcomes. For example, table 1 shows the distribution of primary activities of the *NLS 1972* cohort in the October after high school graduation. Relative to general and academic curriculum students, graduates from the vocational high school programs are less frequently enrolled in school and more frequently working as apprentices, in the military, or in a job.

However, these analyses fail to reveal whether postsecondary outcomes are independent of individual differences prior to track placement. The Academic Growth Study unfortunately has no measures of postsecondary outcomes. It does have measures of outcomes proximate to postsecondary outcomes: plans to attend college, application to a college, and acceptance by a college.

Using these data, Alexander, Cook, and McDill found an effect of curriculum placement on all three outcomes, independent of precurriculum differences. Net of initial differences, curriculum placement accounts for 40 percent of the variance in college plans,

TABLE 1

Postsecondary "Primary Activity" in October 1972, by High School Curriculum

Status after High School (October 1972)	Total	Percent of Students in Various Curriculums		
		Vocational	General	Academic
Enrolled: school or college	(57.3)	(28.6)	(40.1)	(80.9)
Four-year	29.9	5.4	11.9	52.1
Two-year	14.6	9.1	15.1	16.8
Other	12.8	14.1	13.0	12.0
Not enrolled: military, apprentice, working	(34.7)	(59.4)	(47.6)	(15.4)
Military	3.1	3.6	5.2	1.7
Apprentice or on-the-job trainee	9.6	16.1	13.1	4.4
Working full-time	17.9	32.6	24.1	7.2
Working part-time	4.1	7.1	5.2	2.1
Not enrolled: not working at a job	(8.0)	(12.0)	(12.3)	(3.6)
Homemaker	2.4	3.0	3.9	1.0
Other	5.6	8.4	8.4	2.6
Total	100.0	100.0	100.0	99.9

SOURCE: F. Reid Creech et al., *Comparative Analysis of Postsecondary Occupational and Educational Outcomes for the High School Class of 1972* (Princeton, N.J.: Educational Testing Service, 1977), p. 3.3.

34 percent in application to college, and 16 percent in college acceptance.

These data indicate an independent effect of track placement on outcomes that should be related to actual college attendance. However, they also indicate a declining effect of curriculum on outcomes that increasingly predict actual college attendance. Thus, the unique contribution of curriculum on actual college attendance, that is, contribution net of initial differences, is probably much smaller than table 1 suggests.

CONCLUSION

In sum, student ability and curricular preferences account for only 40 percent of the variance in initial placement. Curricula have small but unique effects on abilities and preferences, that is, effects independent of initial differences in enrollees. Finally, these unique effects probably translate into differences in postsecondary outcomes although into much smaller differences than earlier studies without preenrollment controls indicated.

Thus, students may be misallocated among curricula. However, until we identify unmeasured determinants of placement, we cannot necessarily conclude that substantial misallocation occurs. For example, we do not know if controlling on characteristics of the high school reduces the unexplained variance in placement. Schools differ in their distributions of talent. If they place students relative to the distribution of talent in the individual school, students of equal ability and achievement at different schools can end up in different curricula. In this case misallocation may occur, but at the national, not the within-school level. It is not clear that national misallocation represents the same sort of inequity as within-school misallocation.

Alexander, Cook, and McDill also based their estimates of the match between curricular preference and actual curricular assignment on ninth-grade preferences. We do not know to what extent changes in students' curricular preferences between ninth grade and the year of actual curricular placement might account for (or increase) the unexplained variance. None of the national surveys determines in which grade students actually enter a differentiated track. The greater the time elapsed between a ninth-grade measure of preferences and actual track placement, the greater the chances that students will change their curricular preferences. Obviously, changes can increase or decrease the match between track preference and actual placement.

In assessing the unexplained variance in placement, it is important to remember the Alexander, Cook, and McDill findings on status characteristics. Critics of the nonacademic curricula have worried that status characteristics, not talent and preferences, account for placement. However, the Academic Growth Study measures major status characteristics (parental socioeconomic status, sex, race). If we can assume these to be well measured, the Alexander, Cook, and McDill analyses indicate that the direct effects of these characteristics on placement are negligible, except for the direct effect of sex. In fact, if precurriculum ability is controlled, blacks are somewhat more likely than whites to enroll in the academic program. Thus, precurriculum talent and preferences may account for only 40 percent of the variance in placement. However, a status basis for placement has also been assessed and, except for sex, found to be trivial.

Other unknowns affect our estimates of the extent and meaning of misallocation. For example, if curricular misallocation occurs, we do not know how much high school policies or staff are responsible for the misallocation.

We also do not know the extent of intercurricular migration that represents "midcourse corrections," that is, adjusts initial misplacements. We also do not know whether the different curricula present different barriers to midcourse corrections. We have data on the amount and nature of migration among majors at the college level.[7] However, the major national surveys yield a confusing picture on the volume and direction of change at the secondary level.[8] For example, these surveys do not always differentiate initial curricular branching from migration among the specialized curricula.

Thus, we cannot assess how much apparent track misplacement is remedied. We also cannot assess whether the different curricula have different midcourse correction rates and, if so, why. Do teachers or counselors differentially encourage migration out of or into the different curricula? Are the courses in some curricula, for example, the academic curriculum, so different in content and so hierarchical in sequence that they allow out- but not in-migration? Although we lack data to assess these questions, they are crucial to the misallocation issue. They are also related to a question that we raise in the next section about whether the vocational track unduly segregates its enrollees educationally.

Vocational Curriculum as High School Niche

We expect the nation's schools to educate youth who come from the full socioeconomic range of families, who represent the full range of normal intelligence, who will select from the full range of postsecondary alternatives, and who will fill the full range of

7. James A. Davis, *Undergraduate Career Decisions* (Chicago: Aldine Publishing Co., 1965); Alexander W. Astin and Robert J. Panos, *The Educational and Vocational Development of College Students* (Washington, D.C.: American Council on Education, 1969).

8. John T. Grasso and John R. Shea, *Review and Discussion for Planning the NIE Vocational Education Study* (Washington, D.C.: National Institute for Education, 1977).

occupations. In other words, we expect our high schools to treat all youth as their clients, regardless of their talents or postsecondary destinations.

At the secondary level the youth cohort approaches its first major branching in activities. Thus, the differentiated curricula can potentially assure that students with different postsecondary destinations remain clients of the school by organizing school resources in ways consistent with those divergent futures.

The questions, then, are:

1. Does the high school student body consist of individuals with different needs that are best addressed by differentiated school services?

2. Does vocational education seem to provide services that fit the needs of an identifiable subgroup of students?

3. Do vocational programs minimize the educational and social segregation of their clients that differentiated curricula inevitably produce?

In this section we argue: (a) that an examination of any high school student body reveals subgroups with *qualitatively* different motivations and capacities; (b) that these differences represent the effects of different curricula far less than refinements of differences that these subgroups brought to the curricula; (c) that vocational programs apparently provide an educational and social niche in the high school for particular subgroups; (d) that vocational education can represent a *mechanism* by which these students can transform their preferences and relative capacities into a viable adulthood; (e) that vocational students appear segregated educationally and socially from other students; and (f) that on the basis of available data, we cannot draw conclusions about the extent and necessity of this segregation.

We use the *NLS 1972* base year and first-year follow-up data to assess points (a), (c), (d), and (e). With regard to point (b), data cited in the preceding section indicate that although curricula have effects independent of preenrollment differences, they primarily transmit prior differences.

Echternacht reports the means and standard deviations by curriculum for the *NLS 1972* variable system.[9] These data show that vocational students differ strongly and primarily from academic students. However, they also differ from general education students on some telling variables.

Vocational students evidence substantially lower school performance and measured ability than academic students. Although vocational and general curriculum students have similar reasoning, verbal, and quantitative scores, vocational students have higher grades and a higher class ranking. They derive from families of much lower socioeconomic status than those of academic students and from ones of somewhat lower status than general students. They are disproportionately black while the academic group is disproportionately white.

They show more self-esteem than academic students, but have less sense of control over events that affect them.

They value occupational security and family happiness more than both the academic and general groups. They value occupational contacts and steady progress in work more than the academic group.

They rated the overall quality of the school about the same as academic students and higher than the general students. They were less alienated from school and felt less channeled into their curriculum than general students. They rated the schools' counseling and job placement services higher than either the academic or general students. They participated in extracurricular activities the least of all groups, especially relative to the academic students.[10]

State employment officers influenced their postsecondary plans more than academic students, counselors less than academic students, and teachers more than general students. They talked over their postsecondary plans with parents less than academic students.

As table 2 shows, their postsecondary plans differed substan-

9. Gary J. Echternacht, *A Vocational Re-Evaluation of the Base Year Survey of the High School Class of 1972: Part II, Characteristics Distinguishing Vocational Students from General and Academic Students* (Princeton, N.J.: Educational Testing Service, 1975).

10. The tabular results for the base year *NLS 1972* show that they participated more than either the general or academic students in only one of nine different kinds of activities: vocational clubs such as Future Homemakers and Farmers of America.

tially from those of the academic group and somewhat from those of the general group. Relative to the academic group, many more planned to work full time, become homemakers, and attend postsecondary vocational and trade schools. Many fewer expected to attend four-year colleges; somewhat fewer expected to attend junior colleges.

TABLE 2

PLANS FOR FIRST POSTSECONDARY YEAR BY HIGH SCHOOL CURRICULUM

PLANNED ACTIVITY	PERCENT OF STUDENTS IN VARIOUS CURRICULUMS[a]		
	Vocational	General	Academic
Working full time	46.6	33.3	8.6
Entering an apprenticeship or on-the-job training program	3.6	4.7	1.2
Going into regular military service (or service academy)	4.2	4.8	2.3
Being a full-time homemaker	4.7	3.9	0.9
Taking vocational or technical courses at a trade or business school full time or part time	14.9	11.0	4.7
Taking academic courses at a junior or community college full time or part time	5.3	10.9	13.6
Taking technical or vocational subjects at a junior or community college full time or part time	6.0	5.8	4.9
Attending a four-year college or university full time or part time	6.5	16.7	60.4
Working part time, but not attending school or college	2.7	3.1	1.0
Other (travel, take a break, no plans)	5.4	5.7	2.3

SOURCE: William B. Fetters, *National Longitudinal Study of the High School Class of 1972: Student Questionnaire and Test Results by Sex, High School Program, Ethnic Category, and Father's Education* (Washington, D.C.: National Center for Education Statistics, 1975), p. 43.

[a] Students are categorized by curriculum on the basis of high school records, not self-report.

In terms of the first postsecondary year, table 1 shows that, of the three groups, vocational students are *most* apt to be working and *least* apt to be in school. Of those in school, about a third were enrolled in vocational-technical schools, a third in junior colleges, and a fifth in four-year colleges.

Graduates who were not attending postsecondary schools were asked why they had not continued their schooling. Compared to graduates of the academic and general tracks, vocational students much more frequently gave reasons indicating that they wanted to work *and* did not want to go to school. They were more likely to say that they wanted to make money and were offered a job that they wanted. They were less likely to say that they could not afford college, that they needed money for further education, or that they wanted practical experience before continuing their education.

As table 3 shows, vocational students had the highest labor force participation rates and the lowest unemployment rates of all three curricular groups in October 1972 and October 1973. Of all those employed in each curricular group, more vocational graduates in both years supplied ≧ thirty-two hours of labor per week. Unfortunately, Creech et al. do not report hourly wages. However, of those employed, vocational students had the highest median weekly earnings, although only slightly higher than those of general students.[11]

TABLE 3

ESTIMATED LABOR FORCE PARTICIPATION RATES AND UNEMPLOYMENT RATES OCTOBER 1972 AND OCTOBER 1973

SUBGROUP	LABOR FORCE PARTICIPATION RATE OCT. 1972 (in percent)	UNEMPLOYMENT RATE OCT. 1972 (in percent)	LABOR FORCE PARTICIPATION RATE OCT. 1973 (in percent)	UNEMPLOYMENT RATE OCT. 1973 (in percent)
Males				
General	78	11	80	8
Academic	54	9	62	9
Vocational	84	10	86	6
Females				
General	65	17	70	13
Academic	50	19	62	13
Vocational	76	16	80	10

SOURCE: Creech et al., *Comparative Analysis of Postsecondary Occupational and Educational Outcomes for the High School Class of 1972*, p. 2.60.

Relative to general curriculum students, vocational males were more concentrated in the craft and operator and less in the service occupations; vocational females, more in the clerical and less in the sales and service occupations.

On job satisfaction measures that could range from −2 to +2,

11. Wage rates in the immediate postsecondary years have a small variance, a characteristic that makes them a less interesting outcome variable for our purposes.

all curricular groups showed substantial intragroup variance and no statistically significant differences. However, despite the failure of formal significance, table 4 reveals a consistent pattern for male and female vocational students. With one exception, they report consistently higher job satisfaction than either academic or general students, for jobs as a whole, and for specific job dimensions.

When we look at this array of variables, we see a group that, relative to one or both of the other curricular groups, comes from the socioeconomically lower-status families in the community; does not do well at what schools tend to define as their highest status mission—cognitive development; is not part of the high school's extracurricular structure except for that part directly related to the vocational curriculum; rates the quality of the school positively; is not alienated from the high school; does not regard itself as having been channeled into its curriculum; wants money, steady work, and a happy family out of life; prefers to work after high school; selects practical (technical/vocational) postsecondary education; has higher postsecondary employment rates and higher numbers of hours worked per week; and is more satisfied with jobs as a whole and with their specific dimensions.

We suggest that the vocational curriculum "accounts" for this surprising combination of "outcomes." It gives these students a niche in the high school and a future direction with which they can identify.

If we conceive of high school dropouts as individuals unable to "connect" with the high school, we can theoretically test the idea of the vocational curriculum as niche by looking at dropout rates by curriculum. Unfortunately, as shown in the next section, we are unclear about the relationship between curriculum and dropping out, net of preenrollment differences associated with high school noncompletion (for example, low ability).

Vocational programs may provide a social and educational home for a particular subgroup of high school students. However, data from the preceding section and this section indicate that the vocational track may also tend to segregate its students educationally and socially within the high school. Data presented in the last section indicate that vocational programs have a small, but statistically significant, independent, and negative effect on their clients' aca-

TABLE 4

INDICES OF JOB SATISFACTION FOR OCTOBER 1973 JOBHOLDERS

SUBGROUP (CURRICULUM × SEX)	PAY AND FRINGE BENEFITS	IMPORTANCE AND CHALLENGE	WORKING CONDITIONS	OPPORTUNITIES FOR PROMOTION AND ADVANCEMENT (EMPLOYER)	OPPORTUNITIES FOR PROMOTION AND ADVANCEMENT (OCCUPATION)	SECURITY AND PERMANENCE	OPPORTUNITIES TO DEVELOP SKILLS	JOB AS A WHOLE
Males								
General	.51	.44	.62	.25	.31	.47	.42	.64
Academic	.52	.38	.76	.24	.19	.47	.30	.70
Vocational	.59	.58	.68	.32	.42	.63	.56	.74
Females								
General	.42	.46	.85	.15	.16	.66	.39	.76
Academic	.41	.27	.88	.03	.05	.54	.20	.67
Vocational	.53	.70	.94	.29	.41	.86	.61	.87

SOURCE: Creech et al., *Comparative Analyses of Postsecondary Occupational and Educational Outcomes for the High School Class of 1972*, p. 2.56.

demic achievements. If we had data on intercurricular migration flows, we could assess the extent of educational segregation better. In the meantime, we can surmise that an effect of differentiated curricula is a specialized faculty with a specialized student clientele. The vocational faculty may not see basic skill training as their responsibility; the academic faculty may not see vocational students as their clients.

As observed in this section, vocational students also have a pattern of extracurricular participation that implies social segregation within the high school (high participation in vocational clubs and low participation in all other types of activities). However, we know that precurriculum characteristics are related to extracurricular participation, for example, youth from higher socioeconomic status families participate at higher rates. Thus, in the absence of precurriculum controls, we do not know if the vocational curriculum is responsible for this segregation.

Work Establishment Effects

The work establishment process reflects labor supply and demand factors and defines what effects any formal or informal education or training can have. We do not understand the effects of the human resource policies of employers on this process as well as the effects of applicant or employee characteristics, especially for noncollege youth. In this chapter we therefore concentrate on the implications of employers' hiring behaviors for what effects we can expect from vocational education as currently organized or in restructured form.

To assess hiring payoffs of vocational education we need to know whether: (a) vocational training improves the fit of noncollege youth with employer hiring preferences; and (b) whether the quality of the fit is better for some groups of youth or for some kinds of employment (for example, some kinds of occupations or types of firms).

Theoretically, factors that affect employer hiring represent information variables that employers use to project an applicant's value as an employee, for example, his training costs, "troublemaker" costs, job performance, employment stability, promotability. To infer an applicant's value, employers may assess a variety of applicant characteristics: educational credentials; academic skills (verbal and mathematical skills); job skills (general human capital or firm-specific skills); work habits (effort, reliability, willingness to take direction, cooperation with coworkers); interpersonal skills; "troublemaker" qualities; and previous work experience.

To assess the feasible and actual contribution of secondary vocational education, we ask several questions of each hiring criterion: Is the characteristic just an indicator variable, that is, just a proxy for some other characteristic valued by employers? Is the characteristic trainable in a circumscribed training program, such as employer-sponsored training or secondary vocational education? Do firms expect to select job applicants with the skill or train them themselves?

Answers to these questions determine if vocational education has a training role for that characteristic. If a hiring criterion, X, primarily signals characteristic Y, the policy question is, What is the most efficient way to convey the information about Y that employers need? To create more X may increase youth employability, but very inefficiently. Vocational education might have an information role, but not a training role, for X.

If a characteristic is not trainable in a circumscribed program, vocational education might have an information role, but not a training role, for that characteristic. If firms expect to hire the skill, vocational education has a training role. Secondary vocational education may only train basics of the skill, postsecondary training being required to produce a "job ready" candidate. If firms expect to train the characteristic themselves, vocational education might have a preskill training role of some kind, but not a credible training role for the skill itself.

In the next subsections we discuss each of the seven factors listed earlier, assessing each in terms of the questions just identified.

HIGH SCHOOL COMPLETION

We know that high school completion increases youth employment rates.[12] Presumably, however, the high school degree has no value, independent of what it conveys about other characteristics,

---

12. *Employment and Training Report of the President* (Washington, D.C.: U.S. Departments of Labor and Commerce, 1978), p. 246.

such as additional human capital acquired in additional schooling or better work habits (for example, persistence, acceptance of institutional constraints).

We see two questions here. First, is the high school diploma a valid signal about the applicant's value to an employer? Data on the All Volunteer Force (AVF) indicate that if mental ability is controlled, educational attainment has only a small effect on performance in entry-level jobs.[13] Thus, at least for entry-level jobs, high school completion predicts job performance primarily through any effects it might have on academic ability. AVF data also show that high school completion predicts disciplinary problems and turnover, dropouts evidencing more of both. For the enlisted cohort of fiscal year 1977, of the I-IIIA mental group, 19 percent of the high school graduates and 37 percent of the high school dropouts had left the military by December, 1978 (that is, before the end of their three-year enlistment contract).[14]

Second, does secondary vocational education increase the completion rate of dropout-prone students? Both Project TALENT and *NLS* data show that dropouts come disproportionately from the general, not the vocational, curriculum. In the TALENT sample, 75 percent of the male and two-thirds of the female dropouts came from the general curriculum. The vocational curriculum produced 15 percent of the male and 25 percent of the female dropouts.[15] The *NLS* data show similar results: the general curriculum accounted for 82 percent of the white and 76 percent of the black dropouts; the vocational curriculum, 13 percent of the white and 18 percent of the black dropouts.[16]

In the absence of controls on student characteristics prior to track placement, we cannot conclude from these data that the vocational track reduces dropout rates. Relative to the vocational

13. David Armor, personal communication.

14. Richard V. L. Cooper, *A National Service Draft?* (Santa Monica: Rand Corporation, 1977).

15. Janet Combs and William W. Cooley, "Dropouts: In High School and After School," *American Educational Research Journal* 5 (May 1968): 343-63.

16. John T. Grasso, *The Contributions of Vocational Education, Training, and Work Experience to the Early Career Achievement of Young Men* (Columbus: Center for Human Resource Research, Ohio State University, 1975).

track, the general track may simply enroll disproportionate numbers of students disposed to drop out, with neither track affecting dropout rates. Analyses of the *NLS* data that introduce some preplacement controls yield contradictory results on the effects of vocational programs on school completion. These analyses also fail to control for other potentially important preenrollment characteristics.[17]

In the absence of appropriate analyses, we can look at pretrack characteristics that distinguish students who drop out of high school from those who do not. Do these characteristics imply that potential dropouts may fit the vocational track better than the general one?

In fact, data from the longitudinal *Youth in Transition* (*YIT*) study suggest that dropout rates may be relatively impervious to any curriculum.[18] At tenth grade, future dropouts differ from nondropouts in ways that probably simultaneously affect curricular assignment, response to their curriculum, and their attachment to high school.

The *YIT* data show that dropouts are more apt to come from stressed families and to perceive their relations with their parents as stressful. Dropouts' families are more apt to be poor. Even if family socioeconomic status is controlled, dropouts' families tend to be larger and are less apt to be intact. One in five students from broken homes drops out, but only one in nine from intact homes. Dropouts are more likely to report less good relationships with their parents, perceived parental punitiveness being the primary dimension of parental relations that is associated with dropping out. (Parental punitiveness may contribute to dropouts' poor school adjustment or be a response to it.)

Dropouts perform less well in school and show more negative school attitudes and behaviors. Both the *YIT* and *NLS* studies find that dropping out is strongly associated with lower mental ability. Dropouts have lower vocabulary skills and reading comprehension.

17. Grasso and Shea, *Review and Discussion for Planning the NIE Education Study*.

18. Jerald G. Bachman, Swazzer Green, and Ilona D. Wirtanen, *Youth in Transition: Vol. III, Dropping Out—Problem or Symptom?* (Ann Arbor: Institute for Social Research, University of Michigan, 1971).

They are more apt to have been held back a year in school. Forty percent of those held back a grade, versus 10 percent of those not held back, dropped out of school. Dropouts have a history of lower average school grades: 50 percent of those with a D average in the ninth grade but only 2 percent of those with an A average dropped out before graduation. Dropouts have more negative self-concepts of their school abilities, more negative school attitudes, and engage in more rebellious behaviors in school.

Relative to high school graduates, dropouts have other characteristics that signal less functional adjustments. They have less sense of personal efficacy, lower self-esteem, lower occupational aspirations, more frequent somatic symptoms, more self-reported aggressive impulses, and more delinquent behaviors in school. Of all characteristics that differentiate dropouts from graduates, the latter behavior (school delinquency) most differentiates the two groups.[19]

In sum, dropouts have several characteristics that predate and contribute to dropping out. Together, these characteristics account for 40 percent of the variance in educational attainment in the sample. At the same time, potential dropouts may fit the vocational track better than the general one.[20] The general track appears to lack purpose and structure, if the Project TALENT questionnaire defines it[21] as general track students experience it.[22] The personal characteristics of future dropouts suggest that they may particularly need purpose and structure. Relative to the vocational curriculum, the general track also sets tasks that are more academic than practical. As the YIT study shows, future dropouts do not do well on such tasks.

19. Ibid.

20. The vocational track may have a characteristic that could increase dropout rates. If the vocational track gives easier access to part-time work, enrollees who do badly in school (that is, those with an incentive to leave) have more chances to substitute work for school (that is, more chances to drop out).

21. The questionnaire defined the general curriculum as one that "does not necessarily prepare you either for college or for work, but in which you take subjects required for graduation and many subjects you like."

22. The Echternacht data cited earlier showed that vocational students were less alienated from school and more oriented to the working world than the general students.

The military provides a test of the effect that the vocational curriculum might have on dropouts. It provides training in practical jobs and has substantial structure. Although a substantial proportion of enlisted high school dropouts respond to military enlistment as to high school, the majority successfully complete their first term of service.

ACADEMIC SKILLS

Controlling on educational attainment, we know that verbal and mathematical skills differentiate the noncollege employed from unemployed in the first postsecondary year.[23] These skills are of value in themselves, not proxies for other characteristics. In a study of New York city industries, employers stressed the importance of communication skills in their entry-level hiring decisions.[24] By communication skills they meant a level of communication ability once demanded only of managers: a command of English vocabulary, spelling, sentence structure, arithmetic calculations, the functions of codes and symbols, and the ability to think.[25] This and other studies indicate that employers think that these skills are trainable.[26] However, they want to hire the skills, not train them themselves.

The Alexander, Cook, and McDill data presented earlier show that the nonacademic curricula have small, but statistically significant, negative effects on basic skills, net of preenrollment ability differences. They also show that nonacademic enrollees have lower academic skills at curricular entry than academic enrollees.[27] Other

23. F. Reid Creech et al., *Comparative Analysis of Postsecondary Occupational and Educational Outcomes for the High School Class of 1972* (Princeton, N.J.: Educational Testing Service, 1977).

24. The New York city economy is not representative of the national economy. However, the jobs assessed in the study certainly occur across the nation: clerical, computer-related, banking occupations; jobs in food service, home health care, and horticulture-floriculture industries; occupations in building maintenance, major appliance repair, and advanced business machine repair; and occupations in the garment, printing, and machinery industries.

25. Edith F. Lynton et al., *Employers' Views on Hiring and Training* (New York: Labor Market Information Network, 1978).

26. Seymour Lusterman, *Education in Industry* (New York: The Conference Board, 1977).

27. Alexander, Cook, and McDill, "Curriculum Tracking and Educational Stratification: Some Further Evidence."

analyses indicate that vocational enrollees have the lowest academic skills of entrants into all three curricula.[28]

Thus, lower-skill youth enroll in the vocational curriculum and that curriculum increases the academic skill gap between vocational and academic students. Vocational education not only does not contribute to their enrollees' employability on this dimension, but actually impairs it.

JOB SKILLS

A major rationale for secondary vocational education is its job skill training. The data indicate that job skills affect entry-level hiring decisions less than characteristics such as work habits and attitudes, communication skills, and interpersonal skills. They affect hiring for general human capital jobs (for example, secretary), more than specific human capital jobs. Employers consider job skills trainable. However, they think that secondary vocational programs do not train low-skill, repetitive jobs well. Although they do not expect secondary vocational programs to produce "job ready" applicants for high-skill jobs, they do not think that these programs mesh their training well with the training sequence required to produce such skills.

Thurow argues that for entry-level, noncollege jobs the elasticities of substitution between labor of different skills are high. In other words, employers are not responsive to specific skills, such as those presumably produced by the vocational curriculum. Thus, the job market for youth is essentially a market for training opportunities, not fully developed job skills. In other words, in general employers hire the ability to *acquire* job skills, not the skills themselves.

Thurow goes on to say that skills for some jobs (for example, secretary) are typically acquired in formal training and sold to a prospective employer. Thus, he argues that some, but not most, jobs

28. Rupert N. Evans and Joel D. Galloway, "Verbal Ability and Socioeconomic Status of 9th and 12th Grade College Preparatory, General, and Vocational Students," *Journal of Human Resources* 8 (Winter 1973): 24-36; Jerald G. Bachman, *Young Men in High School and Beyond: A Summary of Findings from the Youth in Transition Project* (Washington, D.C.: Bureau of Research, Office of Education, Department of Health, Education, and Welfare, 1972).

require skills that vocational education typically provides.[29]

To us, the data support Thurow's view of the youth labor market. They also indicate that the female occupations are more apt to require preemployment training.

Several data fragments support the training opportunities image of the market. The data already cited on employers' responsiveness to academic skills can be interpreted as responsiveness to applicants' trainability. Analyses of the same data found, not only that academic skills distinguished the employed from the unemployed, controlling on educational attainment, but also that secondary and postsecondary vocational education did not affect employment status.[30] Since we know that some jobs require the kind of preemployment training that secondary or postsecondary vocational education provides, this result may simply reflect a poor measure of training. It may also reflect a very low ratio of jobs that require preemployment training to ones without such requirements.

These analyses also do not report a test for an interaction between ability and vocational training. Vocational education may have different effects, depending on individual ability level. Grasso and Shea report a test for interaction effects between curriculum and wages (not hiring). They find that academic aptitude makes a much greater contribution to the wages of vocational than to the wages of general or academic curriculum students.[31] In other words, relative to the other curricula, vocational education increases pay for the academically able students, but not that for less able students. This result suggests that academic ability may represent a relatively "nonnegotiable" hiring criterion for employers. If the applicant passes this "gate," then vocational skills at least increase wages (and probably employment rates).

The Lynton study of New York city employees supports this interpretation. Across a range of industries the study found that

29. Lester C. Thurow, "Vocational Education as a Strategy for Eliminating Poverty," in *Planning Papers for the Vocational Study*, ed. Henry David (Washington, D.C.: National Institute of Education, Department of Health, Education, and Welfare, 1979).

30. Creech et al., *Comparative Analysis of Postsecondary Occupational and Educational Outcomes for the High School Class of 1972*.

31. Grasso and Shea, *Review and Discussion for Planning the NIE Vocational Education Study*.

in hiring entry-level workers, employers cared first about the applicant's work attitudes, communication skills, interpersonal skills, and interest in the firm's industry. Only after ascertaining these qualities did employers, whose jobs required technical skill, assess the applicant's technical training. If applicants met the initial criteria, a lack of technical training only barred them from jobs that required high levels of technical training. For many entry-level technical jobs employers were willing to supply the technical training for applicants who possessed the other desired qualifications.[32]

Access to occupations also indicates whether the noncollege youth labor market is a market for previously developed skills or training opportunities. Do vocational graduates with training in one occupational family tend to end up with jobs that do not use their training? Although data of these kinds have been used to assess the relevance and quality of vocational education, these same data show whether youth can get jobs without occupationally specific skills. Do general and academic high school graduates without job skills have approximately the same entry-level occupational distributions as vocational graduates? Do youth migrate across occupations with dissimilar skills?

These are all questions about the elasticities of labor substitution among occupations. Although data exist that could be analyzed to estimate these elasticities for entry-level jobs and youth labor, we do not know of any completed analyses. Grasso and Shea analyzed *NLS* data for employed youth who had exactly twelve years of schooling. As they observe, the occupational distributions of the male graduates of the three curricula resemble each other to some extent, especially for white males. For example, variations in curricula do not substantially affect participation in the craft occupations (vocational, 36 percent; general, 31 percent; and academic, 29 percent), although the commercial curriculum reduces it (22 percent). The academic curriculum reduces participation in the operative occupations (15 percent), but the vocational, commercial, and general curricula do not differentially affect participation (31 percent, 32 percent, and 28 percent, respectively). Thus, for noncollege males, especially white males, the elasticities of substitution among youth seem relatively high.

32. Lynton et al., *Employers' Views on Hiring and Training.*

Black and white female high school graduates show more differential occupational participation by curriculum. Especially for white females, the commercial (or business and office) curriculum substantially increases clerical employment (74 percent), although the majority of general and academic graduates are also employed in the clerical occupations (52 percent and 55 percent, respectively).[33] We interpret these data below in our discussion of general human capital skills.

Finally, Freedman reports data that imply relatively low barriers to interoccupational migration, that is, relatively high elasticities of substitution between labor with different skills. Freedman classified job changes for a sample of eighteen- to thirty-one-year-olds, noncollege male workers who had not come directly from high school to the firms under study. Since the ages of the sample did not allow many internal market moves (for example, promotions), she restricted the analyses to changes involving employer shifts. She defined the principal shift of interest to us, an occupational shift, as a change across not narrowly defined occupations but across broad job families: blue collar, inspection and research, vehicle operation, sales, clerical, personal service, and other services, and farm. She found that 77 percent of the job shifts involved occupational family shifts, that is, shifts across occupations with very different characteristics.[34]

In general, then, the data suggest that trainability affects hiring far more than training does. At the same time, previously acquired skills seem to affect hiring and wages, at least in some traditionally female occupations. Grasso and Shea report a possible employment advantage for those particular training programs most apt to be associated with "male" and "female" jobs where employers expect to hire developed skills. Their *NLS* analyses suggest that white male vocational (but not distributive education) and female business and commercial (but not vocational) graduates may experience less unemployment than their general curriculum counterparts.

Grasso and Shea also report that for females business and commercial training confers an hourly and annual wage advantage rela-

33. Grasso and Shea, *Review and Discussion for Planning the NIE Vocational Education Study.*

34. Freedman, *The Process of Work Establishment.*

tive to their general and academic curricula counterparts, but that neither vocational nor commercial training confers such a wage advantage on males.[35]

Using actual course enrollments as a measure of vocational education, and for the NLS 1972 sample, Meyer found that commercial, but not technical or home economics education, had a positive wage and employment effect for females. The effect estimates for males are quite unstable, but trade and industrial arts seem to generate initial income gains.[36]

We can interpret these data when we note that: (a) as reported earlier, 74 percent of female business and commercial graduates were employed in the traditionally female clerical occupations; and (b) employers historically have hired developed skills in these occupations. Employers have regarded females as high turnover employees, that is, ones from whom they could not recoup training costs. In turn, females have needed general human capital skills that allowed them to move in and out of the labor market as family composition changed or their husbands' job locations changed.

Against this history we would expect to see in the data what we do see: employment and wage payoffs to traditionally female skills that can be acquired in secondary vocational education.

We cannot yet conclude that vocational education can affect employment and wages in only limited circumstances. We first need to determine if the general lack of relation between skills created in vocational programs and employment signals a lack of demand for previously acquired skills or a lack of adequately acquired skills. The Lynton study reports that employers perceive most vocational education as the wrong kind.[37] For low-level technical jobs that require repetitive operations, such as production typing, sewing machine operation, or lower-level food process-

35. Grasso and Shea, *Review and Discussion for Planning the NIE Vocational Education Study.*

36. Robert H. Meyer, "The Labor Market Effects of Vocational Education," Project Report (Washington, D.C.: Urban Institute, August, 1981).

37. We can probably generalize what qualities New York city employers want for different jobs to requirements for these same jobs in other parts of the country. However, their experiences with New York city vocational programs probably heavily determine their views of secondary vocational programs. If these programs are not typical, their views of the adequacy of these programs are not generalizable.

ing, vocational programs do not provide enough repetitive, intensive drill to give the trainee the speed required to justify entry-level wage rates. For high-level technical occupations, such as advanced business machine repair or printing, secondary vocational programs cannot produce "job ready" candidates. However, they can coordinate their training much better than they now do with postsecondary training, provided either by postsecondary schools or employers.[38]

WORK ATTITUDES AND HABITS

New York city employers identified work attitudes and habits as the most important of several criteria for hiring entry-level workers.[39] However, we do not know how employers assess candidates' attitudes and habits—from the job interview, proxies such as high school completion, or by some reference system, such as calling the applicant's previous employers.

We do not know whether and in what ways vocational programs deliberately try to affect work habits, let alone the success of any such efforts. We also do not know if we might reasonably expect vocational programs to affect work habits. If poor work habits reflect a student's lack of information about the economic costs of such habits, vocational programs may be able to alter them. If they reflect fundamental behavior patterns, however, they may be beyond the reach of secondary teachers.

Finally, we do not know what, if any, information (or referencing) role vocational programs play for employers—with regard to work habits or other student characteristics. However, vocational programs might usefully play such a role. High schools operate as reference systems for those students who go on to college. There is no reason that this function cannot be extended to employers, especially for qualities such as work habits that are difficult for employers to ascertain in other ways.

School success requires many of the same qualities as work success. Thus, even if vocational staffs have no opportunity to observe the student in a work setting (for example, in a work-study program), they have substantial chances to observe relevant be-

38. Lynton et al., *Employers' Views on Hiring and Training.*

39. Ibid.

haviors in school. Students reveal their reliability by their school attendance records, class arrival times, and record of meeting homework and project deadlines. They reveal task motivation by the effort they expend on classroom and homework assignments. They reveal their probable responses to work superiors and coworkers in their relationships to teachers, school rules, and peers.

INTERPERSONAL SKILLS

For entry-level hiring, interpersonal skills generally matter more than job skills. Depending on the industry and occupation, employers require one or both of two kinds of interpersonal skill: ability to work as a team member and skill in dealing with customers. As the economy becomes more service-oriented, customer relations skills become increasingly important.

Employers generally try to select, not train, interpersonal skills. They use prior experience in customer relations and extracurricular activities as two indicators of interpersonal skills. Apparently they do not rely on school training as an indicator. They argue that schools train students as though they will work in isolation. They do not stress customer relations in their training for jobs that particularly require these skills.

Employers do not regard interpersonal skills as untrainable. At least service-intensive industries such as airlines argue that pre-employment training could substitute for and probably be superior to prior work experience in customer relations. They see prior experience as having limited generalizability to a new firm or job and believe that training could provide an array of interpersonal skills and the basis for choosing appropriate ones for particular situations.[40]

TROUBLEMAKER QUALITIES

Survey data and common sense indicate that employers assess whether a job applicant might victimize coworkers, superiors, or the firm.[41] We would expect employers to worry about theft,

40. Ibid.

41. Daniel E. Diamond and Hrach Bedrosian, *Industry Hiring Requirements and the Employment of Disadvantaged Groups* (New York: New York University, 1970).

violent acts, sabotage—and perhaps the individual's potential for bringing affirmative action suits in cases of dismissal. Again, we do not know how much this dimension affects hiring, or how employers assess it, aside from applicant questions about police records.

We have no data on relationships between the vocational curriculum and troublemaker variables. If relationships exist, we do not know to what extent they reflect precurriculum differences in character and to what extent effects of the curriculum net of initial differences. However, at least at the extreme we are talking about delinquent behaviors. Experience with a variety of interventions indicates that these are intractable behaviors in the teenage years. Thus, we have little reason to expect that vocational or any educational intervention can affect this dimension.

Again, we do not know if vocational staffs play an information role for employers on this dimension. However, they have the knowledge of students necessary to play such a role. Students leave as much of a troublemaker trail in school as they do an achievement trail.

HIGH SCHOOL WORK EXPERIENCE

We do not know what role vocational programs now play in high school work experiences. We also do not really understand the effects of high school work experience on work establishment, independent of other individual characteristics that affect employment. Accordingly, we cannot decide what high schools, including vocational programs, should do that they are or are not already doing in this area.

Potential employers may use previous work experience as a reference system, that is, as previous employers that they can call. If employers believe that a young person's school record generalizes to his workplace performance, vocational staffs can substitute for previous employers as references.

Employers may use part-time high school jobs as probationary employment, that is, as a way to identify individuals that they want to add to the full-time labor force. If employers need part-time workers anyway, they can use part-time work opportunities to cut their search costs for full-time workers. Or high school work experience may signal a cheaper employee, that is, one for whom previous employers have absorbed the "break in" costs associated with new entrants to the labor market. Part-time high school work apparently has an independent positive effect on work attitudes, thus enhancing the value of a young applicant.[42]

If high school work experience provides probationary opportunities or reduces "break in" costs, vocational programs can enhance hiring in two ways. They can increase enrollees' participation in work-study programs and provide more aggressive part-time job placement services. Data from the NLS 1972 indicate that vocational students could use more of both of these services. Twenty-one percent of the vocational students reported no hours of work over the school year; 9 percent reported less than six hours of work per week. Only 17 percent reported ever having participated in a Cooperative Vocational Education program, and only 22 percent in a work-study program. Although vocational students reported more satisfaction with high school job placement services than students in the other curricula, over half of the vocational enrollees rated these services as poor (28 percent) or only fair (25 percent).[43]

Employers respond to good basic skills. We can therefore ask what effects high school work experience has on these skills. Some data tentatively suggest that part-time work during school negatively affects school attendance and academic performance. The latter effect seems stronger for poorer students and for students who work long hours. At the same time work has positive effects on "practical" literacy (business practices, money matters, and consumer arithmetic), especially for poorer students.[44]

At least for some jobs employers may be more interested in

42. Ellen Greenberger and Lawrence D. Steinberg, "Part-Time Employment of In-School Youth: A Preliminary Assessment of Costs and Benefits" (Unpublished paper, Program in Social Ecology, University of California at Irvine, 1979).

43. William B. Fetters, National Longitudinal Study of the High School Class of 1972: Student Questionnaire and Test Results by Sex, High School Program, Ethnic Category, and Father's Education (Washington, D.C.: National Center for Education Statistics, 1975).

44. Greenberger and Steinberg, "Part-Time Employment of In-School Youth."

practical literacy than in more academic verbal and mathematical skills. In this case the negative effect of work on academic performance may matter less. The practical literacy effect does imply that schools can use the job "curriculum" to improve basic skills, especially for poor students. This idea has been frequently advanced.[45] These data suggest that it may be feasible.

Summary

The discussions of this and the last section indicate that secondary vocational programs can *potentially* affect their enrollees' work establishment in three and possibly four ways:

1. *By integrating a particular subset of students into the high school.* Vocational programs organize high school resources to serve students with a different distribution of talents and postsecondary destinations than those who traditionally enter the academic curriculum. As such, they can assure that the educational needs of this group are addressed. If some potential dropouts feel more "at home" in the vocational program than in the other curricula, vocational programs can increase high school completion.

2. *By developing academic and general human capital job skills.* The data indicate that verbal and mathematical skills affect employment, independent of educational attainment. They also indicate that the vocational programs negatively affect their enrollees' acquisition of these skills. However, the vocational curriculum does not inherently have to affect basic skills adversely. We suspect that academic skills of vocational students will increase if the "academic" and vocational faculties *jointly* focus on ways to generate these skills in the vocational context.

The data indicate that the job market for noncollege youth, especially for male youth, is more a market for training opportunities, not developed job skills. We now invest unknown (but probably not insignificant) vocational resources in providing specific skills that employers generally do not try to purchase. This implies that vocational programs need to: (a) identify what skill

45. David R. Olson and Jerome S. Bruner, "Learning through Experience and Learning through Media," in *Media and Symbols: The Forms of Expression, Communication, and Education,* ed. David R. Olson, Seventy-third Yearbook of the National Society for the Study of Education, Part I (Chicago: University of Chicago Press, 1974), pp. 125-50.

training local employers want to purchase that secondary vocational programs can provide; (b) determine what quality of training meets local employer standards; and (c) for occupations that require a secondary and postsecondary training sequence, coordinate the secondary with the postsecondary training required.

This does not mean that we should discontinue all vocational training that employers do not buy. Some courses can be seen as consumption, not investment, courses. Others may be particularly suitable vehicles for transmitting academic skills and work habits.

3. *By creating good work habits and interpersonal skills.* As we indicated earlier, we do not know if vocational (or any secondary) programs can affect work attitudes and habits. Effects depend on the origin of poor work habits. However, vocational programs can and should make explicit for students the economic costs of poor work habits. If vocational staffs assume the information role for employers that we suggest below, students can see the relevance of work habits to the workplace more easily.

Although vocational programs apparently do not now train the interpersonal skills desired by employers, employers do regard them as trainable.

4. *By operating as an information system for employers and a reference system for students.* For employers, the hiring process is an evaluation process. They will use various information to project an applicant's training costs, "troublemaker" costs, job productivity, turnover, and promotability. As we observed earlier, schools already function as reference systems for students who go to college and information systems for the colleges to which they apply. There is no reason that this function cannot be extended to employers and students who go directly from school to work.

Evaluation systems have their abuses. They can degenerate into pro forma or inflated and consequently meaningless assessments. Teachers can use them to enforce idiosyncratic standards of behavior. They can operate like police records, that is, make it difficult for students with negative histories to escape the past.

However, like it or not, employers will judge applicants, and they may use less valid information than schools possess. When employers lack better information, they probably use information statistically, that is, they judge an individual by characteristics statistically associated with groups to which he belongs (for example, youth, females, black males, graduates of schools associated with violence). Even if the group in question possesses a particular characteristic, teachers know how it varies among members of the group. For example, an applicant may come from a troubled inner-city school. However, his teachers know if he has taken his schooling seriously and has stayed out of trouble, at least in the school context.

A reference function for vocational education can also help teachers communicate the importance of work habits and non-deviant conduct. Poor work habits or delinquent conduct will catch up with students, either in the hiring interview or on the job. If students understand that employers use schools to evaluate these dimensions, the consequences of their behavioral choices should become apparent to them earlier. Students applying to college know that grades, references, and SAT scores affect their chances. It is not certain that vocational students have as clear an image of what skills and behaviors they need to increase their employment chances. If employers can use the schools for information, the connection between what employers want and what potential workers should possess becomes clearer.

It can be argued that employers will not regard vocational staffs as credible sources of information about applicant characteristics of concern to employers. In this case, employers will fail to use any potential reference services that schools might provide. However, any lack of credibility should not arise out of any inherent disjuncture between the qualities that youth need for school success and those that employers want.

CHAPTER IX

Evaluation of Postsecondary Vocational Programs

WELLFORD W. WILMS AND SUSAN REDELMANN BERG

Vocational training (by which we mean skill training of less than baccalaureate degree level that is aimed at subprofessional employment) is conducted in a vast array of American institutions. Public and private vocational schools, employers, prisons, labor unions, and the armed forces train millions of men and women each year to become productive parts of society. Since the early twentieth century, vocational training has been considered an antidote to unemployment and underemployment. A key assumption that has supported vocational training is that there are plenty of "good" jobs to go around. The job of training according to that assumption is simply to equip job seekers with vocational skills so they can successfully enter and move up on a career ladder. But, over the past decade, a dramatic increase in highly credentialled job seekers and a relatively slow growth of "good" jobs has shaken that assumption,[1] forcing educators and policy makers to reexamine links between education and work. In this chapter we synthesize research findings about training effectiveness in three major training sectors—public postsecondary vocational training, proprietary (profit making) vocational school training, and employer training. Though the military, apprenticeship, and prison training represent enormous training resources, they are relatively insulated, politically and socially, from public policies geared to improving the fit between education and work, and have been omitted.

While institutions in each of these sectors have interests in providing effective training, their incentives, purposes, and methods

1. James O'Toole, *The Reserve Army of the Underemployed: A Policy Agenda for the Next Decade* (Los Angeles: Center for Futures Research, University of Southern California, 1974).

vary widely. Therefore it is not surprising to find an absence of studies upon which comparisons between sectors can be made. We describe briefly each of the three major sectors, detailing how each works, for whom, and within limits of available data, how well, and at what cost. We then assess the strengths and weaknesses of past research and suggest ways of improving future research efforts.

Public Vocational Education in Postsecondary Schools

ADMINISTRATION, SCHOOLS, STUDENTS, AND COSTS

The vocational education system set up under the Smith-Hughes Act in 1917 has changed remarkably little over the past sixty years. Vocational education is administered from a separate division within the U.S. Department of Education. Federal funds are funneled through a pipeline to nine regional offices and then to separate state boards for vocational education, where they are combined with state and local funds. (Often the state board for vocational education and state board of education are synonymous.)

State boards delegate authority for administration and supervision of vocational education to administrative divisions within state departments of education, which are organized along specialized lines that now include agriculture, distributive education (marketing), health, home economics, technical fields, and trade and industry. Since 1968 states must appoint advisory councils to broaden the interests in planning and evaluation.

States are mandated to center their programs around a five-year plan developed from broad-based participation. In theory this planning process should help local districts and the state to gear programs to real labor market needs, to set priorities within federal guidelines, and to measure progress toward these goals. However, the state planning process has been heavily criticized as being superficial, carried out in isolation, and out of touch with local labor market demands.[2]

2. Michael Kirst, *Research Issues for Vocational Education: Compliance and Enforcement of Federal Laws*, Planning Papers for the Vocational Education Study (Washington, D.C.: National Institute of Education, U. S. Department of Health, Education, and Welfare, 1979); Controller General of the United States, "What is the Role of Federal Assistance for Vocational Education," Report to the Congress (Washington, D.C.: U.S. Department of Health, Education, and Welfare, 1974); Arthur M. Lee, *Learning a Living across the Nation*, vol. 5 (Flagstaff, Ariz.: Project Baseline, Northern Arizona University, 1976).

Vocational education costs are hard to extract because of wide variations in definitions and in procedures for counting students. In schools that have only vocational training, like regional occupational centers, students can be counted only once. In more comprehensive schools like community colleges that offer both vocational and academic programs, students may be counted more than once. Hence cost figures must be interpreted with caution. A few studies have tried to assess vocational education costs, but most of them have been done at the secondary level. We found no reliable studies that compared costs of postsecondary vocational and academic programs. The few studies that tried to measure postsecondary vocational program costs compared them with secondary vocational programs. They conclude that current (operating) costs of postsecondary vocational programs are almost five times greater than those of secondary vocational programs.[3]

While secondary vocational program enrollments grew only 1.5 percent between 1975 and 1977, postsecondary enrollments grew 25 percent to a total enrollment of 2.4 million during the same time.[4] Some of the drop in secondary and the increase in postsecondary enrollments was due to the movement of the baby bulge through the educational system. But a major part of the growth in postsecondary vocational education was no doubt due to the combined effects of employers' preferences for older workers and the simultaneously rising national educational attainment. Postsecondary enrollments were concentrated most heavily in office occupations, followed by trade and industry, technical (which includes such diverse occupations as interior decorating, aviation, electronics, and oceanography), and health. No doubt fueled by proliferating licensing of nurses, X-ray technicians, and other health workers, enrollments in health led other postsecondary vocational education enrollments, growing 88 percent between 1971 and 1974.

Two-year vocationally oriented degrees increased rapidly in proportion to four-year college degrees during the 1970s. During

3. Theodore Abramson et al., *Handbook of Vocational Education Statistics*, Research Foundation of the City University of New York (Beverly Hills, Calif.: Sage Publications, 1979).

4. National Center for Education Statistics, *Digest of Education Statistics* (Washington, D.C.: U.S. Department of Health, Education, and Welfare, 1979).

1969-1970, 6.4 bachelors degrees were awarded for each two-year vocational degree. Six years later, only 3.8 bachelors degrees were awarded for each two-year vocational degree.[5]

Social scientists generally agree that vocational students are the least advantaged in the postsecondary system. For example, Hansen and Weisbrod found in California that whites from higher socioeconomic backgrounds are most likely to attend prestigious four-year colleges, while those from less advantaged backgrounds are more likely to attend two-year colleges.[6] Within two-year colleges, economically disadvantaged students are most likely to enroll in vocational programs.[7]

OUTCOMES

Economic benefits (successful job placement and increased earnings) are not the only important measures of the effectiveness of vocational programs. Vocational students may enjoy greater job satisfaction and self-confidence, for example. But vocational education is usually publicly justified on the basis of its presumed economic benefits. Furthermore, economic benefits seem deceptively simple to measure compared with more murky psychological outcomes. Consequently, it is not surprising to find that most studies aimed at assessing the effectiveness of programs focus on economic outcomes.

A chief means for evaluating program effectiveness is following students into the labor market and analyzing their occupational success. As the Carnegie Council on Policy Studies in Higher Education observed, there are only a few such studies.[8] Pincus points out that only two of twenty-four issues of the *Community and*

5. Fred Pincus, "The False Promises of Community Colleges: Class Conflict and Vocational Education," *Harvard Educational Review* 50 (August 1980): 382-61; Bureau of Labor Statistics, *Occupational Projection and Training Data*, Bulletin 2020 (Washington, D.C.: U.S. Government Printing Office, 1979).

6. W. Lee Hansen and Burton Weisbrod, "The Distribution of Costs and Direct Benefits of Public Higher Education: The Case of California," *Journal of Human Resources* 4 (Spring 1969): 176-91.

7. Jerome Karabel, "Community Colleges and Social Stratification," *Harvard Educational Review* 42 (November 1972): 521-62.

8. Carnegie Council of Policy Studies in Higher Education, *The Federal Role in Postsecondary Education: Unfinished Business, 1975-1980* (San Francisco: Jossey-Bass, 1975).

Junior College Journal published between 1976 and 1978 reported on systematic follow-up studies of vocational students.[9] A recent federal policy paper reviewed forty-eight major studies of vocational education and found that only four tried to assess the quality or effectiveness of programs.[10] Those studied confined their evaluations to economic benefits. In short, not only are effectiveness studies scarce, but most are narrowly focused on economic benefits alone.

This section reviews research on the economic benefits (student persistence, job placement, earnings, and unemployment) of vocational education and also noneconomic benefits from a study of cooperative vocational education programs. With a few exceptions, research on student persistence in public community colleges, the site of most postsecondary vocational training, has focused on combined persistence rates for vocational and academic students (those preparing to transfer to a four-year college). From the few studies that treated vocational and academic students separately, however, the combined persistence rates appear to be similar to persistence rates for vocational students. For example, a study done for the state of California in 1955 found that 66 percent of all students entering community colleges were lost in the first year. By the end of the second year, the authors estimated 75 to 86 percent would have fallen by the wayside.[11] Medsker reported that 66 percent of all students entering community colleges did not graduate two years later,[12] and Clark found that 83 percent of all students entering San Jose College did not complete two years of work.[13] Citing American Association of Junior Colleges data, Medsker and Tillery reported that between 1958 and 1967, 50 percent of the

9. Pincus, "The False Promises of Community Colleges."

10. Lawrence Brown et al., *Research and Data Resources in Vocational Education: An Assessment*, Technical Analysis Paper No. 8 (Washington, D.C.: Office of the Assistant Secretary for Planning and Evaluation, U.S. Department of Health, Education, and Welfare, February 14, 1980).

11. *A Restudy of the Needs of California in Higher Education* (Sacramento: California State Department of Education, 1955).

12. Leland L. Medsker, *The Junior College: Progress and Prospect* (New York: McGraw-Hill, 1960).

13. Burton Clark, *The Open Door Colleges: A Case Study* (New York: McGraw-Hill, 1960).

students who entered community colleges nationally did not complete two years of work.[14] Astin reported similar findings from a national survey, showing that 61.6 percent of community college students leave school before completing their studies.[15] In one of the few studies that disaggregated vocational and academic students, Hakanson reported that 60 percent of the vocational students in California community colleges dropped out before graduation.[16]

Wilms's longitudinal study of postsecondary students in six vocational programs reported that two and one-third years after enrolling 46 percent of the students had graduated, 40 percent had dropped out, and 14 percent remained in school.[17]

Studies that link student persistence and later job placement and earnings are even fewer. Noeth and Hanson successfully followed up 60 percent of a large national sample of students who had enrolled in vocational, technical, and transfer postsecondary programs five years earlier.[18] Though the authors did not report on completion rates or students' later earnings, they reported a relatively high placement rate for both graduates and dropouts in a wide range of vocational programs. The meaning of Noeth and Hanson's findings is unclear, however, as they reported "successful" placements in ways that may overlook important differences in job training requirements, job status, and pay. For example, the authors reported that 72 percent of accounting graduates got their first jobs in the "business detail occupational group," the meaning of which was not explained.[19]

14. Leland L. Medsker and Dale Tillery, *Breaking the Access Barriers: A Profile of Two-year Colleges* (Toronto: McGraw-Hill, 1971).

15. Alexander Astin, *College Dropouts: A National Profile* (Washington, D.C.: American Council on Education, 1972).

16. John W. Hakanson, "Selected Characteristics, Socioeconomic Status, and Levels of Attainment of Students in Public Junior College Occupation-Centered Education" (Doct. diss., University of California, Berkeley, 1967).

17. Wellford W. Wilms and Stephen Hansell, "The Unfulfilled Promise of Postsecondary Vocational Education: Graduates and Dropouts in the Labor Market," University of California, Los Angeles, 1980.

18. Richard J. Noeth and Gary Hanson, "Occupational Programs Do the Job," *Community and Junior College Journal* 47 (November 1976): 28-30.

19. Ibid., p. 29.

One of the few studies that attempted comparisons between public school dropouts' and graduates' earnings was recently reported by Pincus.[20] By comparing state-reported earnings of community college vocational graduates and nongraduates in Virginia, Illinois, Maryland, and South Carolina, he found that nongraduates in Virginia and Illinois earned more on both their first and most recent jobs than graduates. In Maryland, Pincus found that, for students who began new jobs, graduates initially earned more than dropouts, though over time the gap substantially narrowed. Maryland graduates who kept the same jobs they had in school, fared worse than dropouts both in initial and later earnings. Though findings from Pincus's separate analyses converge on the overall conclusion that graduates generally earn no more than dropouts, care must be taken, as Pincus himself observes, in interpreting these findings. Because the analysis relied on data collected from secondary sources, students' background characteristics and other extrinsic factors could not be controlled, and the data could be presented only as simple cross tabulations.

Wilms's recent study, which attempted to improve on earlier studies by following students longitudinally and controlling for key differences in their backgrounds, also compared dropouts' and graduates' job placement and earnings.[21] The study followed 87 percent of a sample of students from six vocational programs through fifty public community colleges and technical and proprietary schools for two and one-third years. In addition to completion rates cited earlier, the study reported that placement rates for men and women in upper-level jobs (accounting, programming, and electronic technician training) were equally low for graduates and dropouts alike. Wilms found, however, that in lower-level female occupations (secretary, dental assistant, cosmetologist) placement rates for graduates were substantially higher than for dropouts. Finally, after controlling for important student differences that were found to have affected students' earnings, such as their job tenure, sex, age, ethnicity, education, socioeconomic status, and ego development (a motivational measure), Wilms

20. Pincus, "The False Promises of Community Colleges."

21. Wilms and Hansell, "The Unfulfilled Promise of Postsecondary Vocational Education."

found that students' earnings were unrelated to whether or not they graduated. While this study was an improvement over many earlier studies because such key student background variables were statistically controlled, it is likely that other unmeasured variables affected students' earnings. Also, generalizations drawn from a six-occupation sample of programs in urban schools are necessarily limited. Further, while Wilms' sample included public community colleges and the more single-purpose technical skill centers, the small sample does not allow them to be disaggregated.

Finally, two studies followed postsecondary vocational students into the labor market and analyzed earnings of students who were in jobs related to their training. After controlling for selected background characteristics, Somers found that postsecondary vocational graduates earned no more than high school vocational graduates in all fields studied except allied health.[22] He also reported higher incomes among nongraduates but his sample was too small to produce reliable results. A second study by Wilms, based on the same design as that used in his 1980 study, followed 2,270 vocational school graduates into the labor market and assessed their postgraduation earnings.[23] He found low placement rates for men and women who studied for upper-level jobs and high placement rates for women who studied for lower-level jobs, which suggests that the fit between vocational education and work may be better at the lower end of the occupational structure where less training is needed.

Unemployment rates can also be seen as indicators of program effectiveness. Pincus analyzed unemployment rates of former vocational students from twelve separate studies on state data banks and concluded that postsecondary vocational graduates were less likely to be unemployed than high school graduates, but probably no more likely to be unemployed than college graduates.[24] Pincus,

---

22. George G. Somers et al., *The Effectiveness of Vocational and Technical Programs* (Madison, Wis.: Center for Studies in Vocational and Technical Education, 1971).

23. Wellford W. Wilms, *Public and Proprietary Vocational Training: A Study of Effectiveness* (Lexington, Mass.: Lexington Books, D.C. Heath and Co., 1975).

24. Pincus, "The False Promises of Community Colleges."

however, noted that these data did not control for students' ages and educational backgrounds.

One of the very few studies that has attempted to evaluate noneconomic benefits of postsecondary vocational programs was Walsh and Breglio's follow-up of 309 former postsecondary students in cooperative vocational education programs.[25] (Cooperative vocational education refers to an organized educational program that integrates academics and on-the-job training.) The students were first identified by Frankel in his initial appraisal of high school cooperative programs.[26] Walsh and Breglio compared these former students in a cooperative program with 243 students from the same schools who were not in such a program with respect to employment status and satisfaction with job and school. They reported that former students in a cooperative education program earned more on their jobs after school than their classmates who were not in cooperative programs and that they also were more satisfied with their jobs. Finally, Walsh and Breglio reported that minority postsecondary students in cooperative education programs were more satisfied with their jobs and with school than white postsecondary students not in cooperative programs. These findings need to be interpreted cautiously, as Walsh and Breglio did not control for important background characteristics as they analyzed earnings and satisfaction. For example, in the analysis of former students' earnings, only sex was controlled. The superior earnings of students in cooperative education may have been due to other unmeasured characteristics like age, ethnicity, prior work experience, and so forth. Students' satisfaction ratings were also not controlled by background variables that could have influenced them. While students in cooperative education appear to be more satisfied with their schools and jobs than those not in cooperative programs, they were a self-selected group, making it difficult to attribute their superior satisfaction to schooling. But some con-

25. John Walsh and Vincent J. Breglio, *An Assessment of School Supervised Work Education Programs, Part II: Urban Cooperation Education Programs and Follow-Up Study, Executive Summary* (San Francisco: Olympus Research Center, 1976).

26. Steve M. Frankel et al., *Executive Summary: An Assessment of School Supervised Work Programs* (Santa Monica, Calif.: Systems Development Corporation, 1973).

sideration is due that explanation because similar findings of superior satisfaction of students in cooperative education appear in studies of secondary programs that did attempt to control for differences in students' backgrounds that could have affected their satisfaction ratings.[27]

Proprietary Schools

Proprietary vocational schools, organized as profit-making institutions, have always been regarded skeptically and kept at arms length by traditional educators. Since the debates that preceded the 1917 Smith-Hughes Act, proprietary schools have faced stiff opposition on three main grounds.

First, organized labor argued that private schools, lying outside of public control, would be used to circumvent the unions and foment antiunion sentiments among their students. Labor feared that private vocational schools would be used by employers to train scabs to break strikes.

Second, the public sector was considered more efficient in providing vocational training. Educators assumed its enormous resources could better coordinate more effective vocational training than the piecemeal approach found among competing private schools.

Third, labor and social reformers felt that because most private schools operated for profit, the bottom line of the schools' income statement would overshadow students' educational needs—an attitude that persists today. Contemporary experience with proprietary schools has to some extent confirmed that fear. Many veterans returning from World War II with GI Bill entitlements in hand were taken advantage of by unscrupulous schools and these incidents eventually provoked government intervention. On the other hand, recent research suggests abuses are not as widespread as horror stories in the press suggest and that the private sector offers important benefits in vocational training. As academic and business

27. Harry F. Silberman, "Job Satisfaction among Students in Work Education Programs," *Journal of Vocational Behavior* 5 (1974): 261-68; Irwin L. Herrnstadt, Morris A. Horowitz, and Andrew Sum, *The Transition from School to Work: The Contribution of Cooperative Education Programs at the Secondary School Level* (Washington, D.C.: U.S. Department of Labor, 1978).

interests have merged over the past decade, the opposition of public policy makers and educators to proprietary schools has softened.

Despite a century or more of ostracism by public educators, proprietary schools have not only survived but have flourished. Estimates of this large and diverse sector indicate that the more than 10,000 proprietary schools enroll from 1.3 million[28] to 1.5 million students, and in 1978 produced gross annual revenues of 3.2 billion, on which substantial corporate and personal income taxes were paid.[29]

As public schools have encountered shrinking budgets, they have looked to the private sector for effective recruiting techniques to bolster sagging enrollments and management practices to squeeze more mileage out of fewer dollars. Proprietary schools have been increasingly recognized in state master plans for education and in legislation on financial aid for students.

SCHOOLS AND REGULATION

Proprietary schools (we have omitted the much smaller number of private, nonprofit schools) have at least two essential characteristics in common. They are driven by the profit motive to offer short-term vocational training, and they must have some sort of government sanction to operate.

Unlike public schools that have few incentives to adjust programs to changing student and labor market conditions, proprietary schools have built-in incentives to seek out markets not served by nearby competing public schools. For the most part, they are free from weighty investments in equipment and tenured teachers that characterize public vocational education, and can shift resources quickly to meet new demands. The profit motive dictates, in theory, that they be able to recruit, train, and successfully place their graduates in jobs to make a return on their investment.

Proprietary schools are a risky business. Hyde studied the economics of proprietary schools and found that while the average rate of return exceeded the 10 percent return of manufacturing firms

28. National Center for Education Statistics, *Digest of Education Statistics.*

29. SRI (Stanford Research Institute) International, "The Outlook for the Proprietary School Industry," (Discussion draft prepared for the National Education Corporation, Menlo Park, Calif., July 1979).

by only 4 percent, they were highly volatile.[30] Some extremely profitable schools reported return rates that exceeded 100 percent, while during the same period a quarter of the schools suffered losses. During the late 1960s, large firms like Bell and Howell acquired small, formerly independent proprietary schools, but a few years later, the trend reversed itself as parent firms found these schools less profitable when managed at a distance. To corroborate this observation, Hyde found that successful schools were not parts of larger corporations, but were most often owned and managed by one person, and had small enrollments and low capitalization.

A growing web of disconnected government regulations designed to protect the public interest apparently tends instead to distort the delicate market mechanisms of proprietary schools. Federal student aid has shifted from schools to students and proprietaries have become eligible receivers, but the federal dollars also have meant more federal control. As a first line of defense against student abuse, proprietary schools that receive student aid must be accredited by an accrediting association approved by the U.S. Department of Education. There are four agencies—the National Association of Trade and Technical Schools, the Association of Independent Colleges and Schools (business schools), the Cosmetology Accrediting Commission (cosmetology and barber schools) and the National Home Study Council (correspondence schools). These four accrediting associations, however, cover only a small proportion of profit-making schools, many of which choose to forego student aid and avoid the time-consuming and conformity-producing accreditation process. In rare cases, the U.S. Department of Education grants direct approval to schools. Accredited schools that receive federal student aid must observe added federal guidelines embedded in individual aid programs, which may diminish schools' incentives to seek out unserved markets for short-term training. For example, schools accredited by the National Association of Trade and Technical Schools could not until recently accept high school dropouts, thereby depriving this already disadvantaged group of an important option for vocational training.

30. William D. Hyde, Jr., *Metropolitan Proprietary Schools: A Study of Functions and Economic Responsiveness* (Lexington, Mass.: Lexington Books, D.C. Heath and Co., 1975).

Further, schools that accept Basic Opportunity Grants must make their programs last six months, independent of employers' needs. And, guidelines for federally guaranteed student loans equate longer programs with stability and arbitrarily insist that training last at least 300 clock-hours. These brief examples illustrate how well-intentioned regulations may on the one hand help protect the public interest, while on the other hand they may interfere with market signals that create efficiencies. Further, approval of the Veterans Administration, independent of accreditation, is needed by schools that want to attract GI Bill students. This regulatory function, subsidized by the Veterans Administration, is vested most often in state departments of education.

Though generally ineffective, state licensing, which is most often assigned to state departments of education, serves as a second line of defense against unscrupulous schools.

As a third line of defense, the Federal Trade Commission promulgated a trade regulation rule in 1980 that called for all proprietary schools to substantiate advertised claims about graduates' earnings, to disclose dropout rates, and to provide a cooling-off period for prospective students. The rule also established a *pro rata* refund policy. Schools charged that the rule unfairly discriminates against proprietaries, thereby placing them at a competitive disadvantage with nearby publicly subsidized vocational schools. The rule was returned by the courts to the Federal Trade Commission for redrafting.

PROGRAMS, COSTS, AND STUDENTS

The array of proprietary vocational training that ranges from bartending to zookeeping is staggering. The Federal Trade Commission record documents at least 13,000 different courses offered through proprietary schools. About three-quarters of them fall into the following categories: 30 percent in correspondence courses (widely disparate in and of themselves), 25 percent in business and office school courses, 10 percent in cosmetology and barber school courses, and 9 percent in trade school courses. Most courses end with a certificate, although there is a trend for accredited schools to seek state approval to grant associate degrees, which often results in programs being lengthened unnecessarily.

Direct costs likewise run the gamut from over $3,000 for computer programming, to less than $500 for cosmetology.

As Wilms found, however, on-site proprietary school programs are, on the average, half as long as comparable programs in the public sector.[31] Motivated to use their resources efficiently, proprietary school programs demand more class hours each day, making them more intense than public programs. Lacking much general education found in public programs, proprietaries pack concentrated skill training into relatively few hours. Wilms reported evidence that suggested proprietary schools were keenly sensitive to the costs of instruction and minimized them by paying their teachers, on the average, 65 percent of their counterparts in the public sector. They also deployed their teaching staffs with costs clearly in mind by using their low-cost teachers more intensively than their higher-cost teachers. In all cases, proprietary school instructors carried a substantially heavier teaching load than vocational instructors in public schools. Further, Wilms found that proprietary schools hire, retain, and promote their teachers on their demonstrated ability to teach. Instructors in proprietary vocational schools do not get tenure, and students and school management evaluate them frequently.

Student characteristics, like costs, vary largely with vocational programs. On balance, proprietary vocational students appear to be remarkably similar to their counterparts in public schools. They generally come from the lower ends of the range of socioeconomic status and academic ability.[32]

OUTCOMES

Allegations of extraordinarily high dropout rates for both correspondence and residential proprietary schools have been reported in the popular press and before congressional committees for years. The Federal Trade Commission cites gross dropout rates, collected by the Department of Health, Education, and Welfare, that showed 60 percent of students in proprietary schools had withdrawn prior to completing one-quarter of the course. Given the nature of correspondence programs that require rigorous self-discipline and the

31. Wilms, *Public and Proprietary Vocational Training.*

32. Ibid.

vulnerability of low-income students to the schools' hard-sell techniques, high dropout rates seem entirely plausible. But when gross enrollment and dropout figures collected by the Veterans Administration and the Department of Health, Education, and Welfare are broken down by type of school and program it appears proprietary students persist as well, if not better, than students in public vocational schools.

On the other hand, Schaefer and Kaufman reported that in Massachusetts 61 to 100 percent of the residential proprietary students completed their courses. This study, however, is of a limited sample of schools in one state.[33] In his study of accredited trade and technical schools, Belitsky found that the median completion rate for day students was 86 percent and 80 percent for night students.[34] Further, Belitsky reported that 75 percent of the students who had dropped out of high school and were enrolled in proprietary schools completed their training. His study was confined to trade schools accredited by the National Association of Trade and Technical Schools. In a study of "successful" business schools, Erickson et al. reported similar findings, that is, that about 85 to 90 percent of all proprietary school students at the schools visited completed their programs.[35] Wilms's comparative study of public and proprietary students (excluding correspondence students) from six vocational programs in accredited and nonaccredited urban schools shows that after controlling statistically for students' backgrounds, vocational program, and labor market variations, proprietary school students were 1.5 times more likely to complete their programs than public school students.[36] Although Wilms's study improved on past studies of proprietary schools by sampling a more heterogeneous group of schools and controlling for students' backgrounds, his study may have been affected by a

33. Carl J. Schaefer and Jacob J. Kaufman, *Occupational Education for Massachusetts* (Boston: Massachusetts Advisory Council on Education, 1968).

34. Abraham H. Belitsky, *Proprietary Vocational Schools and Their Students* (Cambridge, Mass.: Schenkman, 1969).

35. Richard W. Erickson et al., *Proprietary Business Schools and Community Colleges: Resource Allocation, Student Needs, and Federal Policies* (Washington, D.C.: Inner City Fund, 1972).

36. Wilms and Hansell, "The Unfulfilled Promise of Postsecondary Vocational Education."

sampling error that could have been obviated only by random assignments of students to public or proprietary schools. For example, although Wilms attempted to measure and control for motivational and other important differences between public and proprietary students, one group paid for its training and the other group received it nearly free. It is therefore difficult to attribute student outcomes solely to their schooling.

Wilms's 1980 study also confirms the findings of his 1975 study that proprietary students (excluding those in correspondence schools) have about the same experiences in the labor market as public students, although they are in school, on the average, only half as long as their public school counterparts. In both studies, Wilms found that proprietary schools can cut their programs to at least half the length of public programs with no loss in placement or earnings for their graduates. Of course, in the absence of controls on students' characteristics prior to selection of school program, we also cannot conclude from these data that the type of program itself influenced placement or earnings. Length of program does not appear to be related to subsequent labor market experience.

Employer Training

Private employers have long been a major source of occupational training. By 1920, industrial giants like Western Electric, Goodyear Tire and Rubber, Ford, Packard, Winchester Repeating Arms, and Carnegie Steel were operating massive programs that included "vestibule schools" to meet their own demand for skilled workers who would boost production and improve safety.

The employer training model seems to combine the best of all worlds. Learning, much of which happens informally, takes place in a real workplace, directed to specific objectives. This hands-on model is wholly consistent with the best educational theory, and offers constant feedback on performance to the trainees.

Private employers, like proprietary schools, are under strong pressure to do the job as efficiently as possible. Trainees' salaries can represent up to 90 percent of training costs, so employers try to keep course time to an absolute minimum. Private employers routinely supplement expensive classroom teaching with programmed self-study, using techniques considered "innovations" in the public school sector.

Decentralized and privately controlled, training by employers operates under virtually no outside regulation. Training, which evolved out of the corporate backwaters of industrial safety offices, seems finally to have outgrown its second-class citizenship and to have come into its own in the eyes of top managements. Training has grown rapidly over the past twenty years. The American Society for Training and Development (ASTD), the main professional training group, reports that its 1943 membership was only fifteen, but by 1967 it had grown to 5,000 members and now stands at over 20,000.[37] ASTD officers estimate at least 50,000 training professionals are employed in private training outside of the schools.

Employer training, like proprietary schools, is also big business. In 1974, firms that employed over 500 people, accounting for over half the private employment (about 32 million jobs), spent an estimated $2 billion in direct costs on training. Jobs in these medium and large firms are growing rapidly. They expanded about 30 percent between 1965 and 1973.

PURPOSES

Most employers make heavy investments in training so they can control the supply of trained employees to offset natural turnover and growth, improve productivity, and comply with growing federal regulations such as are found in the Occupational Safety and Health Act and the Equal Employment Opportunity Act. In a Conference Board study of a national sample of firms that employ more than 500, Lusterman found that from 30 to 40 percent of the surveyed firms used training to increase the job opportunities for women and minorities.[38] Lusterman affirms that equal employment legislation and affirmative action regulations have had a marked effect on expanding corporate training. It appears, too, that private employers' investments in training are resistant to changing economic conditions. As Lusterman observed, during the 1974-1975

37. Telephone interview with Public Affairs Director, ASTD, Madison, Wisc., February, 1981.

38. Seymour Lusterman, *Education in Industry* (New York: Conference Board, 1977).

recession only a quarter of the firms in his study cut back on train-ing expenses.

Such massive corporate investment in training suggests careful personnel planning. However, in a thoughtful review of private sector training, Freedman points out that what little corporate planning does happen centers around professional and managerial personnel, rather than around sales, production, and clerical work-ers who are generally available and quickly trainable.[39] She also claims that few firms with less than 500 employees have any per-sonnel planning.

PROGRAMS, PARTICIPATION, AND COURSES

The investment of firms in training varies considerably, both by size and type. Lusterman found that the average training expense per employee was $60, but the median was only $16.[40] The differ-ence can be traced to the upward pull on the average by a few giant firms that invest heavily in training.

Similarly, in financial institutions, in which the work force con-sists mostly of clerical and service workers who must pay close attention to routine detail, the median expenditure for training was $56, far more than in wholesale and manufacturing firms, where the median expenditure was only $11.

Formal training, however, touches surprisingly few lives of the 32 million potential private sector employees. Lusterman reported that overall, only 13 percent of employees participated in in-house programs. Participation rates varied only a little by firm size, but markedly by type. A full 20 percent of employees of financial firms participated in in-house training, compared with only 7 per-cent of the employees of manufacturing firms.

Interestingly, while 60 percent of the firms in Lusterman's study reported that they had management development or supervisory courses and 54 percent said they had technical-functional courses (which most closely resemble vocational training), almost three-quarters of all in-house training funds went toward technical-func-

---

39. Marcia Freedman and Anna Dutka, "Training Information for Policy Guidance" (New York: Conservation of Human Resources, Columbia Uni-versity, 1979).

40. Lusterman, *Education in Industry.*

tional training—a full $1.3 billion in 1975. Nineteen percent of the firms reported having basic remedial or "other" courses (English as a second language and economic education, for example), but they accounted for only 2 percent of total training expenses. However, proportions understate the investment in the remedial and "other" courses. In absolute dollars, they totaled $30 million in 1975. Of the $1.3 billion firms invested in technical-functional courses in 1975, 90 percent was spent on existing employees.

Freedman points out that firms rely heavily on informal, low-cost training for new employees in entry-level jobs. She attributes this disparity to the need for short-term training that characterizes many entry-level jobs. For example, the tasks of assembly line workers, stock clerks, and waitresses are limited and specific. Besides a certain level of physical strength and basic literacy, skill requirements can be learned in weeks. Freedman shows that these jobs, which require only limited training for entry, account for more than one-third of total employment in United States—an important consideration for vocational educators.

EMPLOYERS AND THE SCHOOLS

Lusterman's study pinpointed a major concern of private employers, namely, that the schools should do a better job of preparing students for work. His study revealed an interesting paradox. On the one hand, three-quarters of the employers heartily endorsed the trend toward further vocationalizing school curricula. On the other, at least half the firms faulted schools for doing a poor job of preparing students to read, communicate, and write. Lusterman states:

If any generalization can be made, it is that, at all levels of schooling, too many employees lack the language capabilities that executives think they should have. Entry-level blue-collar workers may be functionally illiterate; clerical workers may spell or punctuate poorly, speak or write ungrammatically; supervisors, managers, scientists, and other professionals may be unable to organize and present ideas well, orally or in writing.[41]

When asked their beliefs about how well the schools prepare young people for later work roles, over half the firms gave high

41. Ibid., p. 62.

marks to four-year engineering programs and two-year vocational programs. Private vocational schools ranked much lower (29 percent of the employers gave them high ratings) followed by high school vocational programs. Four-year college liberal arts programs and high school academic programs ranked lowest. Lusterman points out that business is not faulting collegiate liberal arts and academic high school programs for lacking a vocational component. Rather, he thinks these programs garner little support because in employers' eyes, they do a bad job of what they claim to do best—develop students' competence in using their minds and the language. The key issue in employers' minds is: how to get schools to teach the basics in addition to fundamental reasoning processes. As an officer in a large manufacturing firm said:

It's impossible to know what our manpower needs will be in five or ten years, and therefore the basic need is for flexible people who have been trained in reading, writing, basic computational skills, and thinking. We can teach them the rest.[42]

Even though firms report that they do very little training that in their estimation the schools should do, 35 percent of the large firms (those with over 10,000 employees), and particularly financial and insurance companies, said they provided basic or remedial training.[43] These firms described their training as an outgrowth of hiring large numbers of minorities for jobs that require well-developed language, communication, and computational abilities.

Firms are modest about the results of these remedial efforts. Most claim the results are mixed, and some employers acknowledge that they "cream" the market. Lusterman illustrates this point with an example of a firm that screened 300 youngsters for twenty-four clerical jobs, and then hired the most promising candidates.

Freedman's analysis of the future job market and its training needs, coupled with Lusterman's study and a recent study of employer hiring practices in New York City that found employers were primarily interested in entry-level workers' ability to read and write,[44] converge on a key point. In the future, entry to jobs

42. Ibid.

43. Ibid.

44. Edith Lynton et al., *Employers' Views on Hiring and Training* (New York: Labor Market Information Network, 1978).

will likely depend less on narrow skill training, and more on access to the system and basic literacy and computational skills.

Conclusions and Suggestions for Further Research

A number of conclusions emerge from this review:

1. There is little evidence that public postsecondary vocational programs result in superior economic student benefits. There is some evidence that students in cooperative vocational education programs may earn more than their classmates from conventional programs.

2. There is growing evidence that, like students from high school cooperative programs, students from public postsecondary cooperative programs may enjoy greater noneconomic benefits, including satisfaction with job and school.

3. Students in proprietary vocational schools, whose programs average half as long but include more class hours per day than public programs, appear to complete their programs successfully as frequently or more frequently, and earn the same or more, than students in public postsecondary vocational schools.

4. Private employers place a heavy emphasis on informal, on-the-job training for entry-level jobs. They appear, however, to be mixed in their views about how schools should prepare young people for work. One employer viewpoint is that the schools should emphasize vocational training for entry-level employment. Another viewpoint is that the schools should deemphasize vocational training and instead emphasize teaching students how to read, write, compute, and get along on the job.

These findings are uneven, however, and each study is limited because of the difficulty of conducting experimental research in natural settings. Only by comparing results of vocational programs across programs in which respondents are randomly assigned to control and treatment groups could we confidently attribute observed differences in outcomes to program effects rather than to alternative explanations such as a self-selection bias. No doubt the results of all of the studies we have reported have been to some extent affected by self-selection and other unmeasured variables. But, even if we were able to detect completely and perfectly the results of programs, we would probably be hard pressed to understand the reasons that lie behind them. Complex social phenomena usually elude purely quantitative social science analysis, and there is the need for a more comprehensive research approach.

Research results we have reported provide an outline for a future research agenda. First, research efforts should be focused on a systematic assessment of noneconomic student rewards from vocational programs that combine work and study. Already completed research suggests such benefits exist but they need to be better assessed and understood. For example, cooperative education programs may be more able to help students see connections between academics and classwork, thereby fostering a greater sense of intellectual curiosity than classwork alone. Cooperative programs may result in greater student self-awareness and confidence. Cooperative programs may help students develop a better sense of their relationship to others and a sense of interdependence on the job. Finally, research should seek to understand whether or not cooperative programs are more successful in helping students navigate post-school employment than conventional programs.

Second, research should be directed toward better understanding private sector entry-level training efficiencies suggested by past studies. Incentive structures unique to private schools and employers that may result in improved student persistence and placement in some programs need to be better understood.

Qualitative research efforts can help provide a deeper understanding of these processes, and should be given high priority. We are not advocating one research methodology over another. Rather, efforts should be made to combine both qualitative analyses of small-scale observations with quantitative treatments of survey data to provide both the scope and depth of understanding necessary for complex social problems.

CHAPTER X

A Message of Marginality: Black Youth, Alienation, and Unemployment

JULIA WRIGLEY

The educational system has been considered the guarantor of the egalitarian promise of American society. Enormous differences in wealth and power have been justified on the basis of equal access to educational opportunities. In the last decade, however, even as young blacks have been rapidly closing the gap in schooling between them and white youth,[1] their employment prospects have worsened both absolutely and relative to whites.[2] All measures of the unemployment situation of black teenagers and young adults show unemployment rates for them that are extreme even by the standards of the Great Depression.[3] In 1978, 38.6 percent of black teenagers were unemployed, as were 21.7 percent of black adults

I would like to thank Cara Anderson, Eric Chester, Merrilee Finley, Candido Gomez, and Harry Silberman for their helpful comments on an earlier version of this chapter.

1. W. Vance Grant and Leo J. Eiden, *Digest of Education Statistics 1980* (Washington, D.C.: National Center for Education Statistics, 1980), p. 16.

2. Paul Osterman, "The Employment Problems of Black Youth: A Review of the Evidence and Some Policy Suggestions," in Vice President's Task Force on Youth Employment, *A Review of Youth Employment Problems, Programs, and Policies* (Washington, D.C.: Employment and Training Administration, U.S. Department of Labor, 1980), vol. 2, pp. 1-25, to be cited hereafter as *Review of Youth Employment*; National Commission for Employment Policy, *Expanding Employment Opportunities for Disadvantaged Youth*, Fifth Annual Report to the President and the Congress (Washington, D.C.: National Commission for Employment Policy, 1979); Kim Clark and Lawrence H. Summers, "The Dynamics of Youth Unemployment" (Paper presented at a conference of the National Bureau of Economic Research, March 1980).

3. Robert Lerman, "An Analysis of Youth Employment Problems," in *Review of Youth Employment*, vol. 1, p. 22.

aged twenty to twenty-four.[4] These unemployment rates were somewhat over two and a half times those for white youth. Even more disturbingly, the proportion of black men who are in the labor force has declined substantially, far more than can be explained by the rising enrollment of blacks in school. This indicates that increasing numbers of young black men are detached from the major institutions of the society, finding work either in the illegal economy or eking out marginal existences through official or unofficial aid.

This chapter focuses on the connections between high rates of unemployment and alienation among black youth. It will suggest that, rather than seeing joblessness as a product of alienation, black youth express high aspirations that are only gradually eroded as the realities of unemployment rates in the range of 30 to 40 percent hit home for them. The contrast between expectations and reality is particularly great for black youth; they have occupational aspirations that are not much lower than those of white youth, yet they gain poorer jobs and they experience much more unemployment.[5] Further, their job problems persist on a large scale through their early adulthood. The discouraging job prospects for many inner-city youth weaken the ability of the schools to motivate black youth to learn.[6] This problem is exacerbated because those black youth who are employed disproportionately hold jobs in the secondary labor market that require little skill. The leverage of the schools is reduced when the skills that they teach are occupationally irrelevant for many ghetto youth. Participation in the secondary labor market in itself has a negative effect on the expectations and work attitudes of black youth, thus helping to foster attitudes of cynicism and alienation that government programs have seldom addressed effectively.

4. U.S. Department of Labor and U.S. Department of Health, Education, and Welfare, *Employment and Training Report of the President* (Washington, D.C.: U.S. Government Printing Office, 1979), p. 270.

5. Paul J. Andrisani, "The Establishment of Stable and Successful Employment Careers: The Role of Work Attitudes and Labor Market Knowledge," in U.S. Department of Labor, *Conference Report on Youth Unemployment: Its Measurement and Meaning* (Washington, D.C.: U.S. Government Printing Office, 1978), p. 98.

6. John Ogbu, *Minority Education and Caste: The American System in Cross-Cultural Perspective* (New York: Academic Press, 1978).

The first section of this chapter will review the employment status of young blacks and whites. The second section will consider the schooling experiences of ghetto youth in relation to their job prospects, and the last section will consider the promise and the performance of government programs directed toward unemployed black youth.

Unemployment Rates for White and Black Youth

There is surprisingly little certainty about the scope of unemployment for black youth. This is because of the way that government data have been both categorized and collected. First, in Bureau of Labor Statistics data until the late 1970s blacks were usually lumped in a "nonwhite" category that included American Indians, Eskimos, and Orientals, a highly diverse group with quite different schooling and employment experiences.[7] Blacks make up roughly 89 percent of this group; for the purposes of this chapter, the "nonwhite" category will be referred to as black. Second, different data sources have reported quite different employment figures. Monthly Current Population Surveys (CPS) differ from the National Longitudinal Survey (NLS) in their estimate of the disparity between the unemployment rates of black and white youth. The NLS, a survey in which 20,000 people divided into four age-sex categories are interviewed by the Census Bureau under contract with the Labor Department, is conducted differently from the CPS; in particular, the youth themselves, rather than their parents or guardians, are interviewed about their work experiences. This survey shows significantly higher labor participation rates among young men and women and a smaller racial disparity in employment than does the CPS.[8] The different findings make it difficult to develop explanations of the reasons for the differences in rates. Other sources are skeptical of each of the official sources, arguing that minority unemployment rates are far higher than reported. Pines, Ivry, and Lee organized a project in Baltimore that

7. Steven P. Zell, *The Growth of Youth Unemployment: Characteristics and Causes* (Kansas City: Federal Reserve Bank of Kansas City, 1979), p. 23.

8. Michael E. Borus, Frank L. Mott, and Gilbert Nestel, "Counting Youth: A Comparison of Youth Labor Force Statistics in the Current Population Survey and the National Longitudinal Surveys," in U.S. Department of Labor, *Conference Report on Youth Unemployment*, pp. 15-34.

guaranteed in-school youth a job at the federal minimum wage if they met certain low-income criteria. The response they received was far greater than would have been predicted from the official statistics on the percentage of the population that fell within the guidelines.[9]

Acknowledging these limitations, the data do give a broad sense of unemployment trends. Employment statistics show that the unemployment rates of white teenagers, both male and female, did not change dramatically in the twenty-five years from 1954 to 1979.[10] As more young whites entered the labor market than previously, although the unemployment rate remained roughly the same, the employment situation of white teenagers actually improved.[11] White young adults, aged twenty to twenty-four, also experienced relatively stable unemployment rates, with those for males decreasing and those for females rising. Black male teenagers, on the other hand, experienced a sharp rise in unemployment beginning in the early 1970s. Their unemployment rate had dipped during the expansionary years of the mid-1960s (when a significant proportion were also enrolled in the military), but it rose during the economic slowdowns that characterized the 1970s. By 1978, it had reached 38.6 percent, which represented a drastic deterioration of their position.[12] Black female teenagers also registered a sharp upturn in unemployment over the period, going from 28.4 percent in 1958 to 41.0 percent in 1978.[13] The unemployment rates of both male and female whites dropped substantially for those in their early twenties; this was true also for blacks, but the unemployment rates of black young adults remained far higher than those of white young adults.

Unemployment rates for all youth, male and female, white and

9. Marion W. Pines, Robert Ivry, and Joel Lee, "The Universe of Need for Youth Employment: The Reality behind the Statistics," in *Review of Youth Employment*, vol. 1.

10. David H. Swinton, "Towards Defining the Universe of Need for Youth Employment Policy," in *Review of Youth Employment*, vol. 1.

11. Frank Levy and Robert Lerman, "An Analysis of the Black Youth Employment Problem," in *Review of Youth Employment*, vol. 2, p. 2.

12. Ibid., p. 3.

13. U.S. Department of Labor and U.S. Department of Health, Education, and Welfare, *Employment and Training Report of the President*, p. 270.

black, have been high over the last twenty years. Unemployment rates of teenagers have not fallen below 11 percent since 1954.[14] White teenage males have typically had unemployment rates of two to three times those of white adult males; black teenage males have had unemployment rates that have usually been three to four and a half times the black adult rate.[15] In the last five years, there has been a slight improvement in youth unemployment rates, but this has been due entirely to improvement in the employment status of white youth.[16] The adult and youth unemployment rates both fluctuate with the business cycle, but the youth rate fluctuates both more widely and more frequently than does the adult rate.[17] Youth unemployment takes longer to recover from business downturns and usually only begins to respond to upturns some years after the onset of the improved economic conditions.[18] Unemployment among black youth is particularly sensitive to the overall economic situation; black employment-population ratios are estimated to be about 50 percent more sensitive to cyclic variations than are white youth employment-population ratios.[19]

In addition to variations in the unemployment rate reported by different surveys, there is a more basic problem with relying on statistics based on the unemployment rate. Most importantly, those who have given up looking for work are not counted as being unemployed. These "discouraged workers," who are reported as not being in the labor force, may make up a significant part of certain categories of the population. In particular, those groups, such as

14. "An Analysis of Youth Employment Problems," p. 2.

15. Swinton, "Toward Defining the Universe of Need for Youth Employment Policy," p. 1.

16. Michael L. Wachter, "The Dimensions and Complexities of the Youth Unemployment Problem," in American Assembly, *Youth Employment and Public Policy* (Englewood Cliffs, N.J.: Prentice-Hall, 1980), p. 37.

17. Congressional Budget Office, "The Unemployment of Nonwhite Americans: The Effects of Alternative Policies," Background Paper no. 11 (Washington, D.C.: Congress of the United States, July 19, 1976), p. xi; Zell, *The Growth of Youth Employment*, p. 23.

18. Wachter, "The Dimensions and Complexities of the Youth Unemployment Problem," pp. 40-41.

19. Richard B. Freeman, "Why Is There a Youth Labor Market Problem?" in American Assembly, *Youth Employment and Public Policy*, p. 22; Paul Osterman, "The Employment Problems of Black Youth," p. 8.

minorities, with the highest unemployment rates, also include the highest number of discouraged workers.[20] The size of this group is hard to estimate. Its existence is, however, demonstrated by the fact that when economic conditions improve, the labor market swells as more people enter who had previously been discouraged. This entry of additional workers into the labor market can result in a minimization of the overall reduction in unemployment during upturns. It has been estimated, for example, that the unemployment rate for black men aged sixteen to twenty-one would have fallen from 31 percent to about 15 percent in 1977-79 if more young blacks had not been drawn into the labor force. As it was, the unemployment rate for this category of black youths fell only from 30.6 percent to 26.3 percent because of new entrants into the labor market.[21]

Because of this and other difficulties, the employment-population (EP) ratio provides information that gives a broader sense of the labor market conditions facing different categories of workers. The EP ratio is computed by expressing the number employed in a certain age or sex category as a percentage of the total number of people in that category. The EP ratio shows that the share of black youth who are employed has fallen since the mid-1950s, while the EP ratios of white youth have remained roughly the same or risen.[22] The decline in the EP ratio for black males sixteen to nineteen is particularly striking. Between 1955-59 and 1978 their EP ratio fell from 47.5 to 29.8. During the same period the EP ratios for male and female whites increased. White male teenagers increased their labor force activity only slightly. Teenage white women entered the work force in greatly increasing numbers, however, with their EP ratio going from 36.9 in 1955-59 to 48.7 in 1978. Even while the EP ratio for white female teenagers was increasing, that for black women aged sixteen to nineteen declined

20. Congressional Budget Office, "The Unemployment of Nonwhite Americans," p. 3.

21. Lerman, "An Analysis of Youth Employment Problems," pp. 7-8.

22. See Clark and Summers, "The Dynamics of Youth Unemployment," on the particular advantages of using the employment/population ratio in discussing the employment situation of teenagers. See also, Freeman, "Why Is There a Youth Labor Market Problem?" p. 29.

slightly. Among young adult women, both whites and blacks worked in increasing proportions from 1955 to 1978. The white women registered dramatic gains in EP ratio, from 43.0 to 60.5, while the blacks marked only a small increase from 40.1 to 45.4. The great increases in employment for young white women show that the economy is capable of generating a significant number of jobs.

The reduction in the EP ratio for black male youth can be partially explained by their increased enrollment in school. In-school black youth have lower labor force participation ratios than do white students.[23] This does not explain the bulk of the decline for any segments of black youth, however, except for those aged sixteen to seventeen. For those who are older, the decline in the EP ratio has far outstripped what can be attributed to the effect of increased schooling.[24] An estimated 30 percent of young adult black men in 1978 were neither working nor enrolled in school.[25]

This broad overview makes it evident that while unemployment is a significant problem for all youth, male and female, white and black, it is black youth for whom unemployment problems are most serious. The effect of coming from an economically disadvantaged background is seen in the fact that white youth from poor families also face very high unemployment rates.[26] Economically disadvantaged white youth from sixteen to twenty-four had an unemployment rate of 25.5 percent in 1978. In the same year, however, the unemployment rate for black youth from economically disadvantaged families was 40.8 percent, pointing up again the particular severity of their problems. By whatever measure, whether unemployment rates or EP ratios, black youth, particularly black male youth, have faced a major decline in their employment fortunes over the last decade.

23. George Iden, "The Labor Force Experience of Black Youth: A Review," *Monthly Labor Review* 103 (August 1980): 14.

24. Wachter, "The Dimensions and Complexities of the Youth Unemployment Problem," p. 59. See also, Freeman, "Why Is There a Youth Labor Market Problem?" p. 28.

25. Levy and Lerman, "An Analysis of the Black Youth Employment Problem," p. 9.

26. Lerman, "An Analysis of Youth Employment Problems," p. 3.

A final point raised by unemployment statistics requires discussion before we turn to a consideration of the complex ties between schooling and work. Teenage unemployment is often dismissed as not being serious because age is assumed to deal with the major problem. Government programs or schools have sometimes been characterized as "aging vats" that enable teenagers to get through difficult employment years, only to emerge as employable young adults. There are categories of youth, however, for whom the characteristic teenage pattern of spells of unemployment followed by job-holding does not apply. It is necessary to consider the cases of in school and out-of-school youth separately, as their labor market experiences are quite different.

In-school teenagers who are looking for part-time work often display a very casual commitment to the labor market. This is revealed by their high rate of withdrawal from the labor force if they fail to find a job quickly. Nearly half of unemployed male youth who are going to school drop out of the labor force within a month. This compares to only 18 percent of out-of-school unemployed youth who drop out of the labor force within a month if they fail to find work. Data on the relative success of new labor force entrants in finding jobs compared to the unemployed also strongly suggest that many teenagers enter the labor force only when a job is presented, rather than engaging in determined searches.[27]

The situation of out-of-school youth is different and here there is more likely to be a hard core of unemployed youth. The average number of weeks of unemployment for out-of-school youth is 50 percent greater than for in-school youth.[28] While in general youth unemployment is of shorter duration than adult unemployment, a minority of unemployed youth face long stretches without a job.[29] These youth account for a highly disproportionate share of the weeks of unemployment. Their experience belies the notion of a period of productive labor market experimentation during which teenagers efficiently explore the labor market without committing

27. Clark and Summers, "The Dynamics of Youth Unemployment," pp. 9, 12.

28. Ibid., p. 26.

29. Lerman, "An Analysis of Youth Employment Problems," pp. 11-12.

themselves to any particular job. Instead, a minority of youth bear most of the burden of unemployment. Those young workers with fifteen or more weeks of unemployment in a given year accounted for between 70 percent and 80 percent of the total weeks of unemployment. While many teenagers suffer from brief periods of unemployment while changing jobs, these short periods out of work account for only quite a small part of the total weeks of nonemployment.

There is increasing inequality in the distribution of unemployment among the black population. A significant minority has great difficulty in obtaining any job. Among black men from sixteen to twenty-four in 1977, one-third of total unemployment was accounted for by men who held no job at all during the year. The problem persists beyond the teenage years. The drop in the EP ratio for black men sheds some light on this. For black men aged twenty to twenty-four, in the decade from 1967 to 1977, the percentage who worked at least one week per year declined from 86 to 74.[30] Black male teenagers suffered an even greater drop, from 60 percent to 47 percent, over the same period. There was also a sharp reduction in the percent of black young women who worked at all during the year, but there was not the same pattern of increasing inequality within the black female population because the number of weeks employed per worker also dropped for young black women.

The increasing concentration of long-term unemployment among a segment of the black population has occurred during the same period in which the wages of black youth have approached parity with those of white youth.[31] The relative wage equalization between blacks and whites may be due in part to the fact that the wages of young white workers have dropped relative to those of adult workers. The baby boom and the resulting surplus of young people has led to a swollen labor market in which teenagers and young adults have had little bargaining power. One consequence

30. Ibid., p. 30.

31. Wachter, "The Dimensions and Complexities of the Youth Unemployment Problem," p. 45; Richard B. Freeman and David Wise, *Youth Unemployment*, Summary Report of a conference on Youth Joblessness and Employment, Airlie House, Virginia, May 1979 (New York: National Bureau of Economic Research, 1979), pp. 3-4.

of the increasing wage equalization across races is to reinforce patterns of inequality within the black community. Those black youths who find jobs do not do much worse than their white counterparts, but those without jobs do not share in this benefit.

School and Work for Black Youth

One of the key supply-side variables affecting employment is education. Here, in a quantitative sense, blacks have been quickly catching up with whites. The school enrollment figures of all age and sex categories of black youth now outdistance those of whites. This is a remarkable turnaround; as recently as 1965, black youth had uniformly lower enrollment rates than white youth.[32] This has led to a marked narrowing of the school attainment gap between blacks and whites. Between 1957 and 1977, the median educational attainment of nonwhites rose from 8.4 to 12.2 years. White school attainment also rose, but not as rapidly. During the same period, there was an increase from 12.1 to 12.6 years for whites. The 1957 gap of 3.7 years in median educational attainment thus decreased over twenty years to .4 years.[33]

The increasing enrollment of black youth in school in itself belies the notion of a radical level of alienation among the majority of this population. Black youth generally share the American cultural consensus on the value of education.[34] Numerous researchers have reported on the high educational aspirations found among black youth and the conviction that schooling represents the best way to get ahead.[35] The emphasis on education may have particular roots in the black experience. There is a relative lack of black access to some alternative routes of upward mobility that have been extensively used by immigrants, such as the ownership of small

32. Wachter, "The Dimensions and Complexities of the Youth Unemployment Problem," p. 58.

33. Swinton, "Towards Defining the Universe of Need for Youth Employment Policy," p. 9.

34. Paul Bullock, *Youth in the Labor Market: Employment Patterns and Career Aspirations in Watts and East Los Angeles* (Los Angeles: Institute of Industrial Relations, University of California, 1972), p. 126.

35. Dorothy K. Newman et al., *Protest, Politics, and Prosperity: Black Americans and White Institutions, 1940-1975* (New York: Pantheon, 1978), p. 79.

businesses or, to some degree, the building of political machines. While black politicians began during the late 1960s and the 1970s to gain control over a number of industrial cities, they began gaining this control at a time when many of the cities, such as Detroit, were in severe decline. This makes political control a less valuable prize than it was in an earlier period when immigrant control over booming cities guaranteed access to patronage and other forms of economic rewards. The emphasis of the civil rights movement on the need for equal and integrated schooling also served to legitimate education as a means of social and individual advance.

Other factors besides a positive valuation of education have probably contributed to closing the schooling gap between blacks and whites. In particular, the development of community colleges as cheap, open-access forms of postsecondary education helped to make college more attainable to blacks. In 1978, for example, roughly 42 percent of those blacks enrolled in postsecondary education attended two-year institutions, as compared to roughly 34 percent of whites.[36]

Lastly, on the negative side, the increased enrollment of blacks in school can be attributed in part to lack of jobs. Where leaving school means to be unemployed, the incentive to stay in school is greater than if an attractive job were available. Just as school enrollment rose during the Great Depression, so the depressed conditions that have hit urban ghettos can help to account for the rise in attendance figures.[37] School and work serve as partial substitutes for each other.

The school attainment figures of blacks and whites are now sufficiently similar that differences in attainment can account for only a relatively small proportion of the unemployment gap between black and white youth. One author estimates that if in 1977 black youth had had the same educational attainment distribution as whites, the gap between their unemployment rates would have fallen by only about 8 percent.[38]

36. Grant and Eiden, *Digest of Education Statistics 1980*. Computed from table 93, p. 101.

37. Lerman, "An Analysis of Youth Employment Problems," p. 20.

38. Swinton, "Towards Defining the Universe of Need for Youth Employment Policy," p. 20.

Black youth taken as a whole have demonstrated sufficient confidence in schooling to increase their enrollment rates, yet, at least until recently, the benefits of high school graduation were not clear. In 1964, the unemployment rates of high school dropouts and high school graduates were almost identical (18.1 percent and 18.8 percent, respectively).[39] This contrasted with the situation for whites, where the benefits of graduating from high school were immediate. While in 1964, 13.6 percent of white high school dropouts were unemployed, only 8.9 percent of high school graduates were. Several studies covering the late 1960s and early 1970s similarly came to the conclusion that blacks did not appear to gain greatly from high school graduation.[40]

By the mid and late 1970s, however, blacks were beginning to register gains from completing high school. In 1977, 22 percent of nonwhite high school graduates aged sixteen to twenty-four were unemployed, compared to 31.5 percent of high school dropouts.[41] In other words, black high school graduates still had a very high risk of unemployment—much higher than in the 1960s—but their relative position vis-á-vis dropouts had improved. It is interesting to break the figures on unemployment rates for graduates and dropouts down by age, for they reveal that among males it is only in the older category that graduates score particular employment benefits. In 1978, nonwhite high school graduates who were sixteen to nineteen were only slightly more likely to have jobs than were dropouts. The unemployment rate for graduates was 28.1 percent and that for dropouts was 33.7 percent. *Recent* black graduates tend to have very high unemployment rates. The Current Population Survey estimates the figures for March 1978 to be roughly 40 percent for blacks compared to 10 percent for recent white graduates.[42] For the twenty- to twenty-four-year-old age range, however, the benefits of graduation were much clearer. The unemployment rate was 17.3 percent for graduates, while for dropouts it remained close to what it had been just after leaving

39. Freeman, "Why Is There a Youth Labor Market Problem?" p. 10.

40. Lerman, "An Analysis of Youth Employment Problems," p. 37.

41. Freeman, "Why Is There a Youth Labor Market Problem?" p. 10.

42. Iden, "The Labor Force Experience of Black Youth," p. 14.

school, 28.7 percent.[43] Black women gained more from graduating, even in the sixteen to nineteen age range. This may be because graduation gave women more access to clerical jobs. The unemployment rate of black women is higher than that of black men, with female high school dropouts aged sixteen to nineteen having an unemployment rate of 43.2 percent in 1978. Graduates had an unemployment rate of 31.4 percent, not much below that for black male dropouts. In the twenty to twenty-four age range, the figures for black women graduates and dropouts are closer to those for black men: a 26.5 percent unemployment rate for dropouts compared to a 17.5 percent rate for graduates. There is a long-run earnings gain from completing high school, regardless of the type of program taken.[44]

In short, for black males the employment benefits of high school graduation appear to be delayed, while this is not so much the case with females. In both cases, the unemployment rate of both young graduates and dropouts is so high that students, assuming that they were in some sense weighing costs and benefits of staying in versus leaving school, would have to be willing to consider their employment prospects in strongly relative terms. For black males, they also have to be willing to take a long-range view of the benefits of high school graduation. The fact that more black youth are staying in school indicates that they are willing to take a long-range perspective for the most part. They are ultimately rewarded, in that young adult black men who have graduated not only have significantly lower unemployment rates than those who have not, but they also have higher earnings. High school graduation does pay off, but only in the context of unemployment rates that are far above those that occurred for black youth in the expansionary years of the mid-1960s.

The issue of why unemployment rates are so high for all categories of black youth is too complex to be addressed here. Further, it is an issue on which economists are deeply divided.

43. Lerman, "An Analysis of Youth Employment Problems," table 13, facing p. 25.

44. Stephen M. Hills, Lois B. Shaw, and Kezia Sproat, "Teenagers: What Are Their Choices about Work?" in *Review of Youth Employment*, vol. 1, p. 3.

The hypotheses that have been offered seldom seem adequate to account for the rapid rise in unemployment rates.[45] There are a number of partial explanations that deserve brief mention, however, before returning to the question of how schooling and work experiences of black youth react upon each other. First, there is discrimination against black workers, which, although hard to measure quantitatively, contributes to the disproportionate unemployment rates.[46] Second, there is no question but that the overall stagnation of the economy during the 1970s took a particular toll on black youth employment. As mentioned previously, black youth employment has historically been highly sensitive to the overall level of aggregate demand.[47] Third, the surplus population of youth arising from the baby boom gave employers more options in choosing whom they would hire. This allowed room for more discriminatory judgments. Fourth, young ghetto residents may suffer from a particular job paucity because industries and firms have moved to the suburbs in increasing numbers. This explanation is bolstered because ghetto youth often cite transportation problems as making it hard for them to find work.[48] Fifth, there may be competition within the secondary labor market. As an example, black adults may compete with black youth for low-wage jobs that would not interest most white adults. A representative of McDonalds, for example, reported that the fast-food chain receives job applications from adults in central cities, but not in suburbs.[49] The increasing racial disparity in youth unemployment rates may also be due to changes in the structure of the youth labor market, with a decline in jobs considered appropriate for young workers. In a shrinking job market for youth, whites may have been able

45. Norman Bowers, "Young and Marginal: An Overview of Youth Employment," *Monthly Labor Review* 102 (October 1979): 4-18; Levy and Lerman, "An Analysis of the Black Youth Employment Problem." See also, Congressional Budget Office, "The Unemployment of Nonwhite Americans," pp. xi-xv.

46. Congressional Budget Office, "The Unemployment of Nonwhite Americans," pp. 21-23.

47. Osterman, "The Employment Problems of Black Youth."

48. Hills, Shaw, and Sproat, "Teenagers: What Are Their Choices about Work?" p. 7.

49. Lerman, "An Analysis of Youth Employment Problems," p. 26.

to capture a disproportionate share of the remaining jobs.[50] Other economists have cited the minimum wage as causing a downturn in the number of youth jobs available, but this argument has led to considerable dispute among economists.[51] Lastly, researchers sometimes attribute much of black youth unemployment to supply-side problems of worker attitudes, skills, and motivation—problems to which we shall return.

While there are quite diverse views on the causes of youth unemployment in general, and of black youth unemployment in particular, there is broad agreement that the employment situation of young blacks as a whole has worsened even while their educational situation has improved. This apparent paradox, while in part certainly stemming from discrimination, may also reflect in some measure differences in the quality of schooling received. Black youth, even while staying in school longer, may have fewer incentives than white youth have to invest their energies heavily in studying because their expectations of what schooling will bring them are lower. The job barrier may corrode the schooling process itself. Given the possible routes upward out of poverty, schooling may appear to be one of the most likely; it also receives the broadest cultural sanction. Yet even middle-class students, who receive intensive parental support for school achievement, often suppress boredom and alienation in school only because they perceive school success as being directly related to later career success. Ninety-one per cent of the students in one sample of several thousand enrolled in two elite high schools in Boston reported that they agreed with the statement: "What we do in high school is essentially preparation for what will come later; the payoff will be in college or on the job."[52] While expressing little enthu-

50. Osterman, 1980, "The Employment Problems of Black Youth," pp. 11-12.

51. Terence Kelly, "Youth Differentials to the Minimum Wage: A Summary of the Arguments," in *Review of Youth Employment*, vol. 1.

52. Buford Rhea, "The Myth of Institutional Paternalism in High School," *Urban Review* 2 (February 1968): 13-15, 34. See also Arthur Stinchcombe, *Rebellion in a High School* (Chicago: Quadrangle Books, 1964). For discussion of the pressure many middle-class parents place upon their children to do well in school, see Ray C. Rist, *The Invisible Children* (Cambridge, Mass.: Harvard University Press, 1978).

siasm for school work as such, the students were highly motivated to compile good high school records that would serve them well later. In this enterprise, even extracurricular activities were viewed instrumentally and in future-oriented terms as a means of demonstrating their "roundedness" to college authorities. Middle-class students with good academic skills may rebel by trying to outsmart the teacher; even their alienation can be expressed in academic terms.[53]

Students from poorer backgrounds seldom have the option of expressing resentment by challenging the teacher on academic terrain. Instead, they may gain status within an alienated subgroup by sullenly or defiantly resisting school directives. A careful ethnographic study of fifty-six white and black high school gang members found that they rejected students who appeared to be interested in conforming to school rules and to winning the approval of teachers.[54] While they responded positively to teachers who appeared to be genuinely interested in helping them learn and who were perceived as grading fairly, they did not share the tolerance of many of the other students for school activities that struck them as boring or meaningless. Similarly, a study of tracking in a junior high school reported that the low-track students (mainly black) did not understand how the curriculum related to them; they had little incentive to try in school, because to do so would only invite failure in an enterprise whose whole meaning seemed unclear. Metz writes, "for those who remained in the lower tracks, not only the content of the curriculum in fields like English, social studies, and the arts, but also the full range of skills to be learned seemed alien and of little use. They could not see the world of their elders, let alone their own current concerns, reflected in what the school was telling them they needed to become adults."[55]

The ambivalent attitude of many low-track students toward

53. Mary Haywood Metz, *Classrooms and Corridors: The Crisis of Authority in Desegregated Secondary Schools* (Berkeley: University of California Press, 1978), p. 107.

54. Carl Werthman, "Delinquents in Schools: A Test for the Legitimacy of Authority," *Berkeley Journal of Sociology* 8 (1963): 39-60.

55. Metz, *Classrooms and Corridors*, p. 84.

school—on the one hand, resenting it, and on the other hand, hoping to do well even without understanding the connection between what they are taught and what they will later need to know —is reflected in the frequently reported finding that such students express particular hostility toward teachers who do not really try to teach them.[56] The students recognize that the school is transmitting the educational requirements of the larger society; if it is officially acknowledged, through the teachers' behavior, that these requirements are not relevant to the students, it symbolizes their exclusion from the society. This leads students to dislike teachers who do not trouble to maintain educational illusions even more than they dislike teachers who are rigid and punitive. The frequency with which even students who are doing very poorly in school say that they aspire to middle-class professional occupations indicates that it is difficult to give up the idea of success through schooling; the student may well have given it up in a practical, day-to-day sense, by not working hard and not linking the material studied to later career plans, but it is far more devastating to have teachers who make it clear that they have already given up the idea of occupational success on behalf of the students.

The failure of many ghetto schools is reflected in high rates of functional illiteracy among their students. The National Assessment of Educational Progress conducted a study of reading ability among seventeen-year-olds. It judged 91.8 percent of the whites to be functionally literate, while concluding that only 58.4 percent of the blacks were.[57] Mathematics skills of black students were also much lower than those of whites.[58] In ghetto schools, there tends to be a high degree of emphasis on the formal procedures of learning, while there is less actual time-on-task or attention to the subtleties of subjects than in middle-class schools. In ways that are not likely to escape students, teachers often value order over originality, neatness over ambitious effort, and most seriously,

56. Ibid., pp. 87-88; Werthman, "Delinquents in Schools"; James Herndon, *The Way It Spozed to Be* (New York: Bantam, 1969).

57. Justine Farr Rodriguez, "Youth Employment: A Needs Assessment," in *Review of Youth Employment*, vol. 1, p. 24.

58. Grant and Eiden, *Digest of Education Statistics 1980*, p. 27.

the semblance of learning rather than learning itself. On the basis of a participant-observer study of a ghetto school in New York, Levy writes:

The teachers' preoccupation with routines and control leads inevitably to evaluating children's work almost exclusively on its form. Children are rarely rewarded for content. The emphasis is always on neatness in handwriting and arithmetic calculation, clearness in speech, and formulaic answers in social studies and science.[59]

The problems that lead teachers to discouragement and an emphasis on routine are serious and not always within their control; the reality remains that it is possible for a good many students to go through ten or more years of schooling and not learn basic skills. Students cannot help but be aware that they are not performing at a high level. For many, school thus becomes a confining and punishing experience. Dislike of school and a high degree of alienation from it are correlated with later law breaking. Glaser reports that "a poor school record has become more closely related to delinquency than belonging to a lower socioeconomic class or a minority group."[60]

Few students who are doing poorly in school have the energy or will to subject themselves continually to a painful experience. The students with the most trouble in reading or writing usually drop out as soon as it is legally possible for them to do so. In a study of functional illiteracy, Fisher found that many students who were unable to read and comprehend simple materials left school at age sixteen.[61] These students constitute the core of the functional illiteracy problem, although clearly some high school graduates also lack command over basic skills, a fact that has given rise to a demand for proficiency tests before graduation in many states.

The high degree of segregation of schools helps to concentrate

59. Gerald Levy, *Ghetto School: Class Warfare in an Elementary School* (Indianapolis: Bobbs-Merrill, 1970), p. 88.

60. Daniel Glaser, "Economic and Sociocultural Variables Affecting Rates of Youth Unemployment, Delinquency, and Crime," in U.S. Department of Labor, *Conference Report on Youth Unemployment*, p. 134.

61. Donald L. Fisher, *Functional Literacy and the Schools* (Washington, D.C.: National Institute of Education, 1978), p. 16.

youth from poverty stricken homes in a narrow range of schools where they are not exposed to others from different economic backgrounds. Pettigrew has pointed out that the social costs of this go beyond reinforcement of racial barriers.[62] In an environment where unemployment and dependency on welfare are the norm, or at least are frequent occurrences, it is difficult for students to generate confidence that their expectations can be met. Ghetto youth do not as often have faith in schooling reinforced by observation of parental occupational success as do middle-class children. Studies have shown that where parents are unemployed, children have a much higher rate of unemployment than do others whose family heads have obtained work.[63] Concentration of poor youth in a narrow range of schools also deprives students of contact with middle-class youth who are more plugged in to the job world through their families and friends. Black students often lack access to the kinds of informal social networks that later in life help to provide access to and information about jobs. It also creates a schooling environment in which many youth have a less than adequate view of the labor market because their experience of it has been so partial.[64]

The frequent result of the unhappy schooling experiences of ghetto youth is the existence of two layers of beliefs and values in regard to education. On the one hand, students abstractly value education and they express high aspirations; on the other hand, the possible rewards from long-range academic effort do not seem secure enough to warrant full-scale commitment. One study of ghetto youth in Los Angeles found that few imagined the attainment of a large income through steady progress toward a career goal.[65] Instead, large incomes were viewed as accruing through either the illegal economy or through personal talent, luck, or

---

62. Thomas Pettigrew, *Report to the Superior Court of the State of California for the County of Los Angeles* (Los Angeles, Calif.: Los Angeles County Superior Court, 1978).

63. Lerman, "An Analysis of Youth Employment Problems," p. 29.

64. National Commission for Employment Policy, *Expanding Employment Opportunities for Disadvantaged Youth*, pp. 103-7; Andrisani, 1978, "The Establishment of Stable and Successful Employment Careers," pp. 91-96.

65. Bullock, *Youth in the Labor Market*, p. 129.

"connections." As academic work requires steady application in the absence of much immediate return (particularly given the often dull curriculum of high schools), it is hard for many ghetto youth to muster this application in the face of the unemployment and low earnings that are pervasive in their milieu. Educational ambivalence is essential to the functioning of many ghetto schools; if the students lose faith entirely, they become impossible to control, yet the teachers do not want to foster hopeless illusions about their students' possible success.[66] Thus, students are praised for work that might actually be below par, even while a climate of failure and misdirected application hangs over the entire school. It is not necessarily the student's *own* experience of unemployment that can undercut educational ambitions; it is, rather, the social context of poverty and unemployment and uncertain educational reward.

The dilemmas and tensions that exist for all youth with high aspirations and low prospects are particularly acute for black teenage women. They face educational and occupational decisions that are difficult by the standards of any other age-sex group. They have the highest unemployment rates of any element of the youth population.[67] They also earn the lowest wages and are the most likely to be out of the labor force. This combination of negative conditions can account in part for the high pregnancy rate among black teenage women. Educational level and age of women at first birth are negatively related;[68] black women without desirable job options do not have the incentive to postpone birth that many more favorably situated white women have. Having a baby can serve as a symbol of adult status, where otherwise the transition from girlhood to adulthood is hard to mark.[69] Middle-class girls can mark the transition by moving from the family home to the college dormitory, or by obtaining a job that enables the young woman

66. Levy, *Ghetto School*, p. 89.

67. Freeman, "Why Is There a Youth Labor Market Problem?" pp. 10-11.

68. Ronald R. Rindfuss, Larry Bumpass, and Craig St. John, "Education and Fertility: Implications for the Roles Women Occupy," *American Sociological Review* 45 (June 1980): 431-47.

69. Carol B. Stack, *All Our Kin: Strategies for Survival in a Black Community* (New York: Harper, 1974), p. 7.

to be self-supporting. There are fewer available symbols of adult status for that large number of black teenage women who have trouble finding work. While teenage unemployment may have transitory consequences for many white youth, it helps to create conditions that lead many teenage black women to early mother-hood and thus often lays the basis for long-term poverty and un-employment.

Does Alienation among Black Youth Help to Cause Their Unemployment?

Some economists have focused on supply-side problems of ghetto youth in finding jobs. They have argued that employers may reject some black youth because they are poorly prepared educationally or lack proper work attitudes. The youth may show up for work late or may disdain what they perceive to be menial employment. Expectations may be unrealistically high, giving rise to alienation and inefficiency on the part of young employees when confronted with the types of routine jobs generally available.

There is some reason to doubt that these supply-side factors account for a significant part of joblessness among black youth. First, the great majority of youth, including black youth, take the first job that they are offered, indicating that their job demands are not unrealistic. One study found that 90 percent of young black and white job seekers took the first job they were offered and that if jobs were not available at their desired wage, they ad-justed their wage expectations downward.[70] Second, while evi-dence on this point is scanty, several authors who have researched the wage expectations of youth have not found wage demands of blacks to be unrealistically high. The fact that a significant group of young black workers are employed at less than the minimum wage indicates that there is not a general refusal to take low-wage jobs.[71] Third, several researchers have reported on the basis of survey data that the attitudes of young workers toward work are

70. National Commission for Employment Policy, *Expanding Employment Opportunities for Disadvantaged Youth*, p. 62.

71. Robert B. Hill, "Discrimination and Minority Youth Unemployment," in *Review of Youth Employment*, vol. 2, p. 1; Hills, Shaw, and Sproat, "Teen-agers," p. 5; Kelly, "Youth Differentials to the Minimum Wage," p. 2.

very similar to those of older workers.[72] The majority of both old and young workers report themselves to be satisfied with their jobs and both groups of workers reported similar patterns of satisfaction and dissatisfaction with particular aspects of their jobs. There is no discernible pattern of particular youth alienation from work on the basis of these data.

In the area of educational preparation for their jobs, it again is not clear that educational deficiencies of young black workers account for their position at the end of the labor queue. Most jobs available to youth require little in the way of academic qualifications or particular skills. There are indications that most job growth in central cities has occurred among semiskilled and low-skilled occupations such as those in the sales, clerical, operative, and service areas.[73] Further, specific studies of youth employment have demonstrated that the great majority of young people work in retail and service jobs that require very little training.[74] A careful and detailed examination of what a sample of young employees actually did on their jobs revealed that they were almost never required to read, write, or use arithmetic skills on the job. Most spent their time cleaning or carrying objects; interaction with others was limited. While there is no question but that it is a sizeable handicap in contemporary society to have deficient academic skills, particularly in the areas of reading and writing, young employees are seldom called upon to exercise these skills. It has been suggested that for many young job seekers, filling out a job application may actually require more literacy skills than doing the job.[75] This is particularly the case as hiring policies become more institutionalized; the ironic consequence may be that even as the level of job skills re-

72. Andrisani, "The Establishment of Stable and Successful Employment Careers," p. 109; Patricia Miller and William Simon, "Do Youth Really Want to Work?" in U.S. Department of Labor, *Supplementary Papers from the Conference on Youth Unemployment: Its Measurement and Meaning* (Washington, D.C.: U.S. Department of Labor, 1978).

73. Bowers, "Young and Marginal," p. 16.

74. Laurence D. Steinberg, "Whither the Workplace? The Promise and Problems of Work Experience for Adolescents," in *Reconsidering Compulsory Schooling for Adolescents: Studies in Social Science, Education, and Law* (New York: Academic Press, forthcoming).

75. Rodriguez, "Youth Employment," p. 26.

quired remains the same, the function of education as a screening device intensifies.

Two final factors make it unlikely that antiwork orientations of young black job seekers are responsible for a major part of their high unemployment. When there is an economic upswing and more jobs become available, young blacks who were previously out of the labor force enter again and compete actively for the new jobs.[76] This provides strong behavioral evidence of a willingness to work if work is available. And lastly, the emphasis on deficient attitudes and educational preparation of ghetto youth cannot explain the worsening position of young black men and women compared to whites. School enrollment rates for blacks have been rising, as discussed earlier; this has not, however, resulted in improved job prospects. Even if one adopts a very cynical view of ghetto education, it is hard to argue that increased schooling could be commensurate with *poorer* educational preparation than in previous decades.[77] Further, in 1978 white high school dropouts had a lower unemployment rate than black youth with some college experience.[78] Here again it is hard to argue that the white youth were better equipped for jobs.

I have suggested that great disparities between the unemployment rates of white and black youth cannot be adequately explained in terms of poor work attitudes of black youth. Demand and not supply factors seem to be most significant in explaining the racial gap in youth employment. It is, however, possible to argue that the poor job prospects of young black men and women help ultimately to create increased alienation and cynicism. The social and personal costs of unemployment are very high, and it would not be surprising if unemployment, or long-term confinement to the secondary labor market, would lead to growing alienation. This is particularly the case because there are so many ancillary benefits

76. Osterman, "The Employment Problems of Black Youth."

77. There is considerable evidence to indicate that the quality of black schooling compared to that of whites has improved over time. See James P. Smith and Finis R. Welch, "Black-White Male Wage Ratios: 1960-1970," *American Economic Review* 67 (June 1977): 323-38.

78. Hill, "Discrimination and Minority Youth Unemployment," p. 9.

attached to job holding that the unemployed suffer particular deprivation in a wide range of areas.

The costs of unemployment are both economic and psychological. In the United States, those who have never held a job cannot collect unemployment insurance, which is a fact with particular relevance to the youth labor market. This contrasts with the situation in Europe, where most countries provide unemployment coverage to new labor force entrants.[79] In addition to this problem of lack of coverage for new entrants into the labor force, blacks generally collect less in unemployment benefits than do whites. This is because they are disproportionately employed in industries not covered by unemployment compensation and they often have more intermittent work histories than whites. It also occurs because benefits are geared to earnings.[80] Those without work, or those employed in small-scale or marginal establishments, also do not have access to health insurance programs; again, in Europe, these benefits are not linked to the job in the same way that they are in the United States. Pension plans are also strongly job-linked in the United States. Additionally, many skills are taught on the job. This means that access to a good job helps to increase one's valuation in the labor market over time; restriction to dead-end jobs in the secondary sector, or lack of access to jobs at all, means that those so situated are unable to gain the benefits of a vast system of informal training.[81] One observer of ghetto youth culture has argued that ghetto youth cannot accept jobs in the secondary sector with the same insouciance as can middle-class youth. While the inner-city residents are likely to accept the job, in keeping with the finding that most young workers take the first job they are offered, to them it can serve as a dead-end option rather than as a broadening experience.[82]

Dismay or resignation over the prospect of a low-skill, low-

79. Beatrice G. Reubens, "Review of Foreign Experience," in American Assembly, *Youth Employment and Public Policy*, p. 113.

80. Congressional Budget Office, "The Unemployment of Nonwhite Americans," p. xiv.

81. Bowers, "Young and Marginal," p. 16.

82. Elijah Anderson, "Some Observations of Black Youth Employment," in American Assembly, *Youth Employment and Public Policy*, pp. 64-87.

wage job in the secondary sector is understandable given that
many black workers do remain stuck in these jobs long after their
white counterparts have left them. For white youth, labor market
problems characteristically decline with age. In their teenage years,
when most are enrolled in school and looking for part-time work,
they face high unemployment and relegation to low-wage jobs.
As they enter adulthood, though, most make the transition fairly
easily to more stable, more carefully chosen, more economically
rewarding work.[83] It is this transition that occurs more irregularly
and uncertainly for blacks. Before the 1969-70 recession, unemployment rate trends for black young adults were similar to those
for whites in the same category.[84] Beginning in the 1970s, however,
there was a secular decline in the employment prospects for black
young adults that paralleled the decline in the employment prospects for black teenagers. The decline in the employment-population
ratio for black young adults was particularly marked. Further,
young black adults who are employed do not so often find the
kind of "bridging" jobs that help enable many white youth to
leave the unskilled sector for better jobs. The National Commission
for Employment Policy reports that the growth in earnings between the eighteen-to-nineteen age group and the twenty-five-to-
twenty-six age group is twice as large for whites as for blacks.[85]
Studies based on data from the National Longitudinal Survey found
that while approximately a fifth of one cohort of young white
men who started job-seeking in the mid-1960s remained in the
secondary labor market several years later, two-fifths of the black
youth did.[86]

Confinement to the secondary sector is associated with increas-

83. National Commission for Employment Policy, *Expanding Employment
Opportunities for Disadvantaged Youth*, p. 41.

84. Morris J. Newman, "The Labor Market Experience of Black Youth,
1954-78," *Monthly Labor Review* 102 (October 1979): 20.

85. National Commission for Employment Policy, *Expanding Employment
Opportunities for Disadvantaged Youth*, p. 47.

86. Paul J. Andrisani, "The Secondary Labor Market's Effects on the
Work-Related Attitudes of Youths," in Industrial Relations Research Association, *Proceedings of the Thirty-Second Annual Meeting*, Atlanta, December
1979 (Madison, Wis.: Industrial Relations Research Association, 1980), pp.
245-46.

ingly negative attitudes toward work.[87] Even after the personal characteristics of youth (such as years of schooling, years of service with the employer, completion of formal occupational training, marital status, aspirations, and other characteristics) were controlled, those youth who remained in the secondary labor market developed more critical attitudes toward work than did their more successful counterparts. Andrisani reports that:

While moving through the youth labor market in the late 1960s, those youth who held higher status jobs and received promotions, regardless of the income and job security the job provided, tended to be less inclined than ostensibly comparable youths to have negative attitudes toward their jobs. Thus, labor market segmentation, causing comparable youths to vary widely in occupational status and promotions, was found to be consistently linked to levels and changes in youths' attitudes toward their jobs.[88]

Those youth with poor labor market experiences tend to lower their aspirations. The stated aspirations of many blacks remain relatively high, however, even after some experience in the job market. The gap between black aspirations and outcomes is much higher than that between white aspirations and outcomes.[89] This is the type of situation that could be expected to lead to increased alienation if poor labor market conditions continued. One study found that among older men attitudes toward work were strongly influenced by the nature of the jobs they held. Those who experienced upward mobility, increased earnings, and no unemployment increased their commitment to values characterized as being part of the Protestant work ethic. Those who had more negative job experiences also developed a more negative set of work attitudes. The authors concluded that the sentiments of young workers were even more likely to be shaped by their work experiences.[90]

Most studies of the attitudes of the poor toward work have

87. Ibid.

88. Ibid., p. 246.

89. Andrisani, "The Establishment of Stable and Successful Employment Careers," p. 98.

90. Reported in Andrisani, "The Secondary Labor Market's Effects on the Work-Related Attitudes of Youth," pp. 246-47.

been so methodologically flawed as to be almost valueless.[91] Survey data have often been inadequate because variables have been poorly specified, there have been no adequate control groups, or the questionnaires have been administered to nonrepresentative samples. The personnel in charge of government programs such as the Job Corps did not always share the desire of social scientists to gather data and did not cooperate with evaluation programs.

Given the paucity of other sources of data, ethnographic accounts have perhaps the most to offer us. These tend to indicate that there are respects in which clashing life-styles and values create employment tensions for some young blacks.[92] In particular, black youth have been subjected to conflicting pressures. The civil rights movement created a new sense of collective pride and racial awareness. Black youth became unwilling to accept demeaning or subordinate behavior that they associated with generations of oppression. Employers often consciously or unconsciously affronted young black employees, some of whom were not willing to conform to conventional styles of behavior. Compared to other employees who were near the end of the labor queue, such as undocumented aliens, urban blacks conveyed a more militant and political image that could disturb employers. This more militant image was compounded by the common identification of young black men with urban crime. As Anderson writes,

The young black person, especially the male, both through portrayals in the mass media and, to an important degree, through personal experiences of urban whites has come to symbolize danger and to evoke fear in the minds of many urban and suburban whites. The stereotype is now strong and is often applied indiscriminately to unknown blacks in the urban milieu.[93]

This stereotype means that there are suspicions on both sides of the employer-employee relationship; the young black employees are on the watch for discrimination and slights, and the employers

91. Leonard Goodwin, "The Social Psychology of Poor Youth as Related to Employment," in *Review of Youth Employment*, vol. 1.

92. Anderson, "Some Observations of Black Youth Employment"; Elliot Liebow, *Tally's Corner: A Study of Negro Streetcorner Men* (Boston: Little, Brown, 1967).

93. Anderson, "Some Observations of Black Youth Employment," p. 71.

are on the watch for signs of untrustworthiness or unreliability. The frequent tensions between black employees and their employers help to undermine further the employment position of black youth.[94] It is not that the attitudes of black youth are anti-work, but that work is not to be accepted on any and all conditions, if those conditions are interpreted as demeaning. The availability of income through the illegal economy can help to undergird determination not to tolerate employment conditions that are interpreted as offensive.[95] The undermining of the employment position of black youth through suspicion and tensions between employer and employee in turn serves to create conditions of unemployment or restriction to low-skill jobs that can breed cynicism and alienation on a new and deeper level.

Government Employment Programs

The social problems identified with very high levels of unemployment for ghetto youth have impressed themselves sufficiently firmly on the national consciousness that the government has established a considerable range of youth employment programs.[96] Many Congressmen have made remarks indicating that they have thought of these programs as "riot insurance."[97] Most, but not all, of the programs are targeted disproportionately toward disadvantaged youth. The six major youth employment programs are: (a) Young Adult Conservation Corps, for sixteen- to twenty-four-year-olds to do conservation work on public lands; (b) Youth Community Conservation and Improvement Projects, for sixteen- to nineteen-year-old economically disadvantaged youth to do community and neighborhood projects; (c) Youth Incentive Entitlement Pilot Project, an experimental program operating in a small number of cities that guarantees employment to youth from low-income families, aged sixteen to nineteen, who are in school or willing to return to school; (d) Youth Employment and Training Programs for sixteen-

94. National Commission for Employment Policy, *Expanding Employment Opportunities for Disadvantaged Youth*, p. 101.

95. Bullock, *Youth in the Labor Market*, pp. 162-97.

96. *Employment and Training Report of the President*, p. 270.

97. Newman et al., *Protest, Politics, and Prosperity*, p. 48.

to twenty-one-year-olds, providing services primarily for in-school youth; (e) Summer Youth Employment Program, designed for economically disadvantaged youth between fourteen and twenty-one; and (f) the Job Corps, a residential program for disadvantaged youth between fourteen to twenty-one.[98]

There is a tension in these programs between the goal of making youth more employable through developing skills and good work attitudes and that of simply providing youth with jobs.[99] In fact, the programs have operated much more in the latter capacity than in the former. They have served as a means of reducing unemployment on a fairly large scale; Killingsworth and Killingsworth estimate that in the absence of these programs, the teenage unemployment rate for 1976 would have been 3.9 percentage points higher than the actual figure.[100] There is no persuasive evidence, however, that they have led to changed attitudes or greater skill development. This is not surprising, as the programs generally employ youth at quite low-level jobs. As discussed previously, there is little to indicate that employment in such jobs leads to more positive work attitudes; some have argued that over time, it is perhaps equally likely to lead to a lowering of ambitions and expectations and a more negative view toward work.[101]

In spite of a widespread conviction that the employment problems of minority youth stem at one point or another from failures in work socialization, it is noteworthy that there are almost no evaluations of the successes or failures of government youth employment programs in socializing youth into good work values.[102]

98. Ernst W. Stromsdorfer, "The Effectiveness of Youth Programs: An Analysis of the Historical Antecedents of Current Youth Initiatives," in American Assembly, *Youth Employment and Public Policy*, pp. 94-95.

99. National Commission for Employment Policy, *Expanding Employment Opportunities for Disadvantaged Youth*, pp. 35-36.

100. Charles C. Killingsworth and Mark R. Killingsworth, "Direct Effects of Employment and Training Programs on Employment and Unemployment: New Estimates and Implications for Employment Policy," in U.S. Department of Labor, *Conference Report on Youth Unemployment*, pp. 249-86.

101. Andrisani, "The Secondary Labor Market's Effects on the Work-Related Attitudes of Youth," pp. 245-46.

102. Goodwin, "The Social Psychology of Poor Youth as Related to Employment."

This can only lead one to the view that in reality the socializing functions of these programs are subordinate to the income-transfer functions. The programs have been shaped, or misshaped, by political pressures to do something about youth unemployment and the perceived problems of crime and social disruption that it has brought in its wake.[103] The most direct, easiest, and cheapest way to do something is simply to provide jobs for a segment of the most volatile youth during the period of their greatest hardship and social explosiveness—the teenage years and early twenties. With few exceptions, such as the Job Corps, there is little evidence that these programs aid youth beyond the period of their enrollment.[104] In contrast to the Works Projects Administration of the 1930s, there are no recognizable projects of broad social scope or purpose identified with the programs. While in the 1930s the WPA projects included the building of New York's Central Park Zoo, San Francisco's Aquatic Park, Chicago's waterfront, the Philadelphia Art Museum, the restoration of Independence Hall in Philadelphia and Faneuil Hall in Boston, the subsidizing of artists and musicians, and the building of thousands of miles of woodland trails, in the 1960s and 1970s little of such scope and collective endeavor was accomplished through the youth employment programs.[105] Young people simply worked at unskilled or semiskilled jobs for periods and received, in some cases, special but unevaluated services to help them adjust. Even the Job Corps, the most ambitious of the job programs, and the only one that is considered to have a significant positive effect on enrollees after their period of enrollment, has had little lasting impact on the employment of black Corps members.[106]

Conclusions

There is a paradoxical quality to employment and education statistics over the last decade. Even as educational levels of black

103. Stromsdorfer, "The Effectiveness of Youth Programs," p. 92. See also, Christopher Weeks, *Job Corps: Dollars and Dropouts* (Boston: Little, Brown, 1967), for a description of the political shaping of the Job Corps.

104. Steinberg, "Whither the Workplace?"

105. Newman et al., *Protest, Politics, and Prosperity*, pp. 47-48.

106. Stromsdorfer, "The Effectiveness of Youth Programs," p. 104.

youth have risen, their employment prospects have worsened. Staying in school pays off for black graduates in terms of higher earnings and greater likelihood of finding a job. These benefits accrue only in the context of a rapid rise in unemployment rates for black youth taken as a whole. The 1970s witnessed also the penetration into the young adult labor market for blacks of the same kinds of employment problems that have characterized the teenage labor market.

Alienation does not appear to cause or even substantially contribute to the special labor force difficulties of most young black men and women. Black teenagers have high job aspirations and show increasing willingness to stay in school. They take low-paying jobs when these are what are available. A significant minority hold jobs that pay less than the minimum wage. There is reason to believe that the alienation/unemployment connection runs in the reverse direction: high unemployment and restriction to a narrow range of jobs help to convey the message that academic skills are only marginally relevant to youth success. Students may want the credential, but may not find their classroom experience tolerable if they do not perform well. Many ghetto youth operate in an educational environment where teachers and administrators implicitly accept the idea that there is little occupational future for their students. The increasing inequality in the distribution of unemployment in the black youth population, and the increasing number of young black men who are neither in school nor in the labor force, indicate that there is a minority of youth who are marginal to the established institutions of the society. They do not share in the links created by school and work, but represent an alienated subcore of the population.

The identification of black youth with crime and militancy, a common phenomenon among employers as well as among other segments of the society, helps further to restrict employment options for black youth. A cycle of lack of opportunity is created that can only help to provide daily evidence of superfluity. Government programs have thus far failed to address this cycle in a way that offers a decisive break. The programs have helped youth to obtain some job experience and, most importantly, some income. They have been more patchwork than far-reaching, however, and have not come to grips with the problem of youth who have received a message of marginality. As "riot insurance" the programs may work; as training mechanisms, they do not. Without a major commitment to providing jobs with economic futures, black youth will continue to remain at the end of the labor queue, on the edges of the productive institutions of the economy.

CHAPTER XI

Lessons from Experience with Employment and Training Programs for Youth

ROBERT TAGGART

Experience under the Youth Employment and Demonstration Projects Act of 1977 (YEDPA) and experience with youth employment and training programs provide a number of lessons concerning the effectiveness of alternative activities and strategies in meeting youth employment needs. These lessons provide the basis for restructuring and reorienting the youth employment and training system, as well as the background for budget and policy choices.

The Program Elements: What We Have Learned

There are four major building blocks of youth employment and training programs: preemployment assistance, work experience in the public sector, remedial training and education, and private sector access activities. A range of approaches are subsumed by these categories. Most programs and projects contain elements of all four. Yet in each category, there are some generalizations that seem warranted by experience.

PUBLIC AND NONPROFIT SECTOR WORK EXPERIENCE

Part-time school year and summer jobs for students, plus year-round "aging vat" or "bridge" jobs for high school dropouts or graduates not ready for career entry, constitute the primary activity in federal employment and training programs for persons twenty-one and under. These public and nonprofit sector jobs are generally temporary and of limited intensity. The school-year jobs usually last less than the school term and are typically ten hours weekly. Summer jobs average twenty-six hours per week for nine weeks. The length of stay in out-of-school work experience is normally less than six months, with thirty-five hours of work weekly.

There is no evidence of substantial short-term postprogram gains in employment and earnings as a result of work experiences of such limited duration. Available measurement tools cannot isolate the modest expected impacts of such activities. Also, the immediate results may not be indicative of full program efforts. Nonparticipants tend to be looking for work and have some probability of finding it by the time participants leave the program and begin experiencing frictional joblessness. Hence, comparisons of pre/post changes for participants and nonparticipants may yield little evidence of impacts. Basically, however, these short-term jobs do not lead to employment tracks any more than other short-term jobs held during the teen years. They simply contribute to a cumulative experience. But these long-term effects are difficult, if not impossible, to measure, just as it is difficult to determine the future employment and earnings consequences of any teenage work experience.

In contrast, the *direct* effects of work experience are measurable and significant. Well-run youth projects can be highly productive, paying back social costs in useful products. Recent work valuation estimates have documented a surprisingly high output level ranging from $2.98 per hour of work for the Summer Youth Employment Program (SYEP) to $3.57 for Young Adult Conservation Corps (YACC). Jobs can reduce the likelihood and consequence of negative events such as crime. Findings from work programs featuring intensive support services for youth in the criminal justice system suggest a noticeable in-program decline in arrests. Findings from another federally supported experiment guaranteeing jobs to low-income youths who stay in high school or return indicate that jobs can be used to lure youth back to school and to forestall early leaving. It is estimated that the effective dropout rate has been reduced by up to 10 percent in such program sites, and that one-third of eligible dropouts have been lured back to school. Because youth employment programs pay minimum wages for limited hours of work, significant reductions in measured unemployment can be achieved per dollar of public expenditure.

Youth work experience programs are not always well run. YEDPA put increased emphasis on supervision and disciplined work experience, and there is evidence that there were improvements in these as well as in existing efforts. The summer program was ignored for many years and loose standards prevailed for worksite activity. In the summers of 1979 and 1980 there were enormous improvements, which provided encouragement about the possibility of running large-scale work experience programs with disciplined and productive work settings, but which also suggested that good management requires a great deal of continuing federal attention to what goes on at work and training sites.

One thrust of Youth Employment and Training Programs (YETP) under the Comprehensive Employment and Training Act (CETA) has been to enrich work experience with occupational information and with counseling efforts to overcome sex stereotyping and the like. It is unproven whether these enrichments add to the impact of the experience although the conventional wisdom is that they do. Vocational exploration programs in which youth receive either classroom exposure to private sector requirements, field trips, and other periodic experiences, or actual job shadowing and rotation, were tested in the 1978 summer program. The evidence from the 1978 summer program documents only modest impacts on labor market knowledge, aspirations, and awareness. Since the enrichments typically account for only a minor part of expenditures and activities, it is innately difficult to separate their impact from that of work experience alone.

There has been little success in creating "meaningful" jobs in the sense of new career opportunities for teenagers. There is a broad array of work options available under youth programs, but the preponderance of them remain entry-level work, such as clerical and maintenance positions, positions in conservation work, and positions as social service aides. The efforts to link jobs to youth aptitudes and aspirations are limited, and evaluators of YEDPA programs have questioned the whole concept because of limitations in available work options and the uncertainty of participants about what they want to do until they have gained some work experience. The evaluators have suggested that career planning should be based on *past* experience rather than just test-based employability plans for the future. Potential job progressions within programs have not been fully utilized because of the categorical nature of intake, assessment, and assignment. In some prime sponsors with a limited number of low-income youth who are known on an individual basis by program operators, the progression may occur, for instance, with increasingly responsible jobs from summer to summer. But this is the exception rather than the rule.

More sophisticated work experience programs for youth characterized by linkages to education and apprenticeship, more skilled supervision, and greater expenditures for materials can be and have been structured and are attractive where successful. Youth benefit more in the long run from such successful projects and they are more productive in terms of output per man-hour. However, the failure rate in the project rises with the complexity. Participant hours per dollar of program expenditure are reduced by supervisory and material costs. Such projects rarely emerge in local settings because they require too long a gestation period and concentrate resources to a greater degree than is usually programmatically or politically feasible. Whatever the relative benefits and costs of more elaborate work projects, they have accounted for and are likely to account for only a small proportion of all work experience activities for youth at the local level.

The quality of these work experience activities is difficult if not impossible to judge from pre/post status changes of participants. There is a good deal of recent evidence, however, that summer employment modestly increases the chances of return to school as well as the likelihood of part-time work in school. Arrest rates are reduced during the summer months.

The aggregate impacts of work experience on short-term employment and earnings are difficult to measure because of the frictional unemployment associated with leaving a program. If impact measurement cannot be done with large samples over entire programs, it certainly cannot be done for individual projects. The only dimensions that can be measured are whether youth are working hard, are supervised, feel they are productive, and perform according to labor market standards of time attendance and behavior.

While basic work experiences of limited duration predominate in serving young people, CETA also provides some transitional or career-entry employment opportunities that give access to permanent jobs. A small portion of project-type work experience positions have apprenticeship linkages. More broadly, Public Service Employment provides career-entry opportunities for some of the youth who represent a fifth of participants (although the majority of youth in Public Service Employment positions are in project-type work which is indistinguishable from preparatory work experience). Perhaps the best indicator of the potential of such programs comes from the Public Employment Program in 1972, which placed a heavy emphasis on the transition into permanent employment. The postprogram earnings gains for younger participants were about 60 percent higher than for older participants. However, there was also evidence of "creaming," and those most likely to make a transition to employment were those who were most employable. The experience of the New Careers program, also of the 1970s, suggested the difficulties of rearranging job structures permanently and the need to institutionalize the transition process to assure that the new career ladders had more than one or two rungs. In other words, where career-entry employment can be arranged, young adults can benefit greatly. But significant effort must be exerted to assure a transition from the subsidized job to a permanent job, to promote subsequent upward mobility, and to avoid "creaming." There needs to be careful structuring of career-entry experience to assure multiple steps and subsequent access to regular jobs as well as control over the assignment into these positions.

INTENSIVE REMEDIATION

Intensive remediation efforts are premised on the belief that individuals failing in or failed by the mainstream developmental institutions and processes can, through concentrated training, education, and other assistance, become more employable and will, as a result, have greater future success in the labor market. The fifteen years of Job Corps experience provide more information about this approach than any other component of the employment and training program. The most important lesson is that the future can be redirected by such interventions. Perhaps the most sophisticated and dependable assessment of many manpower programs to date has revealed that Job Corps enrollees experience statistically significant increases in labor force participation, full-time employment, and weekly earnings. Arrests are markedly reduced during and after participation. Residential mobility for economic reasons is increased and dependence on welfare and on social insurance declines. The current value of these benefits exceeds social costs under conservative methods of estimation.

Evidence suggests that skill- or occupation-specific vocational training in an institutional setting works best for young adults who are mature enough to stick with a course over the time necessary for its completion and who have a fairly stable notion of what they want to do so that they will continue in a training-related occupation. Youth also must be old enough so that employers will hire them when they complete the training course.

This is most easily documented in the Job Corps program. In fiscal 1978, only a fourth of enrollees who entered at age sixteen completed their course of training, compared to two-fifths of those who entered at age nineteen and over. Among completers, those who were eighteen or under had a recorded placement rate of 70 percent, with half of these in a training-related job. The placement rate of graduates twenty-one and over was 77 percent, of whom two-thirds found a training-related job.

The experience is consistent across all institutional training—teenagers tended to have higher termination rates and lower training-related placements than young adults. Even in vocational education, the body of evidence does not suggest that secondary vocational education increases subsequent employment and earnings. Rather, it is postsecondary vocational education that produces most of the gains. There are doubtlessly many youth who are mature and directed enough in the teens to complete and benefit from specialized training, but this must be determined on an individualized basis; on the average, their retention and placement rates are not high enough to justify the investment at this point.

This reality is, in fact, recognized by decision makers in the employment and training system. In 1978, there were only 62,500 youth nineteen years of age and under in classroom training activities in local programs under Title II (then Title I) of CETA.

Most of this training was in basic skills and world-of-work type courses. In Job Corps sixteen- and seventeen-year-olds are usually placed in generalized training such as maintenance or cooking, which can be applied even if they drop out early; if they stay longer, they are usually shifted into more specific training occupations. Job Corps advanced training programs operated by unions frequently have an age requirement.

The same pattern apparently holds true for intensive remedial education. In Job Corps, for instance, the proportion of those who entered at age sixteen or seventeen lacking a high school diploma and who subsequently attained a certificate of General Education Development is 10.9 percent compared to 12.9 percent among those eighteen or nineteen even though education is stressed as the major component for younger enrollees and even though older youth tend to be more anxious to get on with vocational training. The experience with the Career Intern Program of alternative education suggests that those youth who have left school and are ready to return voluntarily do better than those who are identified as having problems in high school and are referred directly into the program. Finally, early results from the mixed services demonstration project, which randomly assigned out-of-school youth to work, work mixed with remediation, and classroom training, showed significantly greater dropout rates in the latter case, suggesting that young people may need some aging before they are ready to return to the classroom. Nevertheless, participants in training components were significantly more successful after termination than participants in work components.

Another lesson is the importance of alternative settings for such intensive remediation. The Job Corps provides a structured and positive environment away from home. The decision to leave home is frequently a demonstration of maturity or a sorting process. It has proved difficult under the Youth Incentive Entitlement Pilot Projects (YIEPP) to attract dropouts back into regular school; the dropout enrollment at local sites only increased when separate educational components were introduced. The common elements in successful intensive remediation appear to be self-paced learning and individualization. Remediation is necessary in the first place because the youth could not move at the average of their peers, so that return to the same environment is demeaning. Likewise, simply being slotted with all those who have fallen behind is not helpful because the achievers are dragged down by the less committed youth. In a separate setting, with self-paced learning that does not emphasize comparative deficiencies, a positive dynamic can be achieved.

DEVELOPMENT OF BASIC EMPLOYABILITY SKILLS

There is a broad assortment of activities which aim to provide youth with greater knowledge of career options, how to search and apply for jobs, the demands of the workplace, motivation and self-confidence to enter the labor market, a helping hand to overcome personal barriers, and follow-up on the job to reduce the chances of failure. The activities include basic life skills training, job search assistance, counseling, special efforts to overcome sex stereotyping, vocational exploration, and cluster skills training. The term "preemployment" assistance is sometimes used to describe such activities, but they may be integrated with work, may be needed at several stages of development, and may include follow-up after employment. Basically, however, the activities aim to provide a minimum set of competencies or coping skills with which youth can then make it on their own in the workplace. For youth aged fourteen and fifteen, this assistance is quite generalized and limited in scale. Usually it is offered in the school and summer under the rubric of school-to-work transition services. For out-of-school and older youth with more severe problems, more intensive assistance is required.

There is almost no hard evidence about the impact of assistance in the development of employability skills, the most effective delivery approaches, or the different mechanisms for dealing with different groups. The reason is that the services tend to be of limited duration and cost, so that their impact is by nature modest and, therefore, difficult to measure. The activities have the aim of changing knowledge and behavior which will not necessarily be reflected in immediate changes in employment and earnings, making evaluation a tenuous exercise.

In the absence of rigorous evidence, policy decisions must rest on the judgments of practitioners who deal with youth on a day-to-day basis. Employability skills development has been given extensive emphasis under local programs, and is also the major focus for non-CETA programs dealing with special needs groups. Practitioners generally agree that assistance is necessary before most disadvantaged youth can successfully enter jobs and that a helping hand is needed when failure is encountered in the labor market or a personal problem disrupts progress. Practitioners stress the need for role models and peer support networks, as well as arrangements that provide continuity of support for individuals so that their positive experiences become more cumulative. There are also those who emphasize the importance of intensive follow-up on the job, since for teenagers entrance into a job is only the beginning of a sequence rather than a career decision. Most observers agree that there has been inadequate emphasis on follow-up with employers and youth under CETA programs.

ACCESS TO THE PRIVATE SECTOR

There is a fundamental perception that youth participants in employment and training programs should receive a set of discrete services and then be placed in "real" private sector jobs. In fact, placement rates into unsubsidized employment are quite low. In fiscal 1978, less than a fifth of the terminees of the principal CETA youth programs entered private employment, with the rest returning to school or other programs or nonpositively terminating. Less than 4 percent of all YETP participants were in private sector on-the-job training. This is characteristic of all youth programs that serve teenagers primarily.

This has led to an active effort to find mechanisms of private sector involvement and access through new intermediaries and through financial incentives. On the assumption that red tape is an impediment to hiring and training low-income youth, and that reimbursement is needed for the extra costs, the Targeted Jobs Tax Credit provides half the first year wage for the hiring of certified low-income youth as well as students in cooperative education programs. The Youth Incentive Entitlement Pilot Projects (YIEPP) program provides for 100 percent wage subsidy to the private employer, with payrolling from the prime sponsor. Private Industry Councils have been created through CETA to mediate with employers. In addition, under the discretionary authority of YETP, there have been tests of a wide range of techniques for accessing private sector jobs. The lessons are not all in, but there are some preliminary indicators that are consistent with past experience.

First and foremost, it is unrealistic to expect high direct placement rates for programs that provide short duration or seasonal and in-school work experience, where participants are selected because of their labor market difficulties, and where funds are concentrated in areas where there are significant job deficits in the private sector.

The impediments are not just red tape nor can they be overcome by "bribes" to employers. YIEPP provided the first test of the full wage subsidy. In the seventeen project sites, a very substantial effort was made to line up business commitments to provide part-time and summer jobs. After a year and a half of operation only 15 percent of the jobs were in the private sector. This is four times the percentage under YETP, but the private sector remained only a modest component of the effort to fill the job deficit for the in-school poor youth in the YIEPP case, accounting for only one in seven of the needed employment opportunities. Anecdotal evidence suggests that even the 100 percent subsidy may not cover the costs of supervising these youth. There has been no evidence of increased hiring for the sake of subsidies. The proportion of YIEPP youth in private sector jobs has stabilized. Likewise, there has not been a massive surge in the use of the Targeted Jobs Tax Credit. Through July 1979, only 1,400 economically disadvantaged youth aged sixteen to eighteen had been hired under this mechanism, and only 6,300 nineteen- to twenty-four-year-olds.

Employers and the public complain about red tape in government programs, but it is not necessarily dysfunctional. In private sector subsidy programs, restrictions are necessary to protect against abuse. Under the JOBS program in the late 1960s, early subsidy contracts had few strings attached, but in many cases participants were similar to those who would have been hired anyway and there was little on-the-job training. Procedures were then tightened by putting more requirements in the contracts. The result was that fewer employers were willing to participate, but there was also less "windfall" subsidization. On the other hand, other restrictions might not be worth the effort. Attempts to reduce subsidy levels in private sector YIEPP jobs after participants stayed for a period of time were not successful. Either the youth are job ready and will be picked up by the employer or they are not, and a reduced subsidy formula creates red tape that discourages continued participation by the employer.

There has been a continuing search for model private sector approaches. But considering all the funds available under CETA and the fairly consistent pressure to place participants in the private sector, it is surprising how few "models" have emerged. In certain circumstances, those models are tautological in the sense that motivated employers have taken an initiative which is then called a model simply because it occurred. There are few easily replicable packages.

Finally, it must be realized that private sector access is inversely related to age. While rhetoric stresses placing youth in the private sector, it is really older participants in longer-term activities where linkages can be established for whom this is a feasible option.

For younger participants residing in job deficit areas, immediate private sector placement is unrealistic. The aim should rather be to provide teenagers a cumulative track record to improve their competitive prospects in the future. Employment and training programs do not do a very good job because there is no way to tell whether a participant has had positive or negative experiences. Private employers have a negative perception of those who have participated in CETA, so much so that motivated youth are better served by downplaying their participation in that program so that they will not be typecast as "disadvantaged" individuals.

Underlying Approaches

Youth employment and training programs and policies rest on a foundation of assumptions and understandings that are only rarely questioned. Targeting, participation standards and requirements, the structuring of services for individuals over time, and the tradeoff between the goals of income maintenance, employment, and the development of human resources are the crosscutting issues. Recent experience in youth programs suggests the need for reexamination and perhaps modification of some of the underlying approaches to these issues.

SORTING VERSUS SUPPORT

A predominant but unstated theme of employment and training programs is to provide a supportive environment for disadvantaged youth so that they will not reencounter the failure they have experienced in the schools or the labor market. It is assumed that the longer they can stay in structured activities, the more likely they are to benefit. For instance, Job Corps has found a significant relationship between length of stay and postprogram employment and earnings, so that retention has been emphasized and performance standards for centers are keyed to retention rates. Local efforts aimed at discouraging early leaving or promoting return assume that the best thing for youth is to remain in school, again because of the correlation between the diploma and subsequent earnings. Moreover, youth programs are judged by turnover and positive termination rates, so there is an incentive to keep participants as long as possible. In the summer youth employment program, local operators have an incentive to retain youth who are not performing, because the summer will be over soon, there are few other constructive options, and any vacant slots cannot be easily refilled.

It is not clearcut, however, that the youth who on the margin are most likely to drop out of programs will necessarily benefit from a longer stay. The average experience of completers versus noncompleters may not be predictive of the experience of a likely noncompleter who is coaxed to stay.

The Job Corps experience suggests that if youth are forestalled from dropping out for personal and nonrecurring reasons, they can complete training and be successfully placed. It is not at all clear, however, that coercing others who have continuing difficulty adjusting or are not ready for the Job Corps experience really produces a positive outcome for them. The 40 percent ninety-day dropout rate in Job Corps works as a sorting mechanism, and those who stay are then a better bet for more expensive continuing training. In a system like CETA, where a youth may be coaxed to stay in an activity for ninety days, the individual may still not be ready for intensive remediation because the sorting process may not have been allowed to occur.

Sorting does not mean that youth who do not perform are abandoned. In Job Corps, there are second chances to reenter after a period calculated to allow some maturation. Youth who cannot move forward into advanced components are given special remediation tailored to their needs. Likewise, in well run and smaller summer programs, there is a progression of jobs from summer to summer. The youth who are effective move up from year to year while the others continue in the more menial positions until they can prove themselves. The aim is to provide an individual incentive for performance and options for those who have more serious problems.

The emphasis on retention has several negative consequences. It tends to undermine standards in all activities. Youth who do not produce are retained alongside those who do. The discipline that is an important part of the work experience is lost. There is no chance for the individual to respond to increasing responsibilities and to mature when there is no expectation of performance.

Evidence suggests that structured and demanding activities have the greatest success. Worksite assessments under YEDPA and SYEP combining interviews of participants and supervisors with assessments of outside reviewers have consistently found that all parties consider the best worksites to be those with clear standards and enforcement of rules. In Job Corps centers that operate most effectively, Corpsmembers socialize new recruits into a standard of individual performance. Peer support tends to work.

There have been some efforts in recent programs to increase performance standards. Under YETP, a "service agreement" approach has been widely used in which services are prescribed for each youth on an individual basis with roles and responsibilities explained. Worksite agreements setting work standards and expectations have been required under YETP, SYEP, and the Youth Community Conservation and Improvement Projects (YCCIP). In the Entitlement program, the job guarantee is conditional upon school attendance and performance. The notion of academic credit for work experience assumes completion of a set of learning activities on the job. In the summer program, the theme in fiscal

1979 was to demand "a day's work for a day's pay," and although there were still cases of slack standards, the demands were greater than ever before and much more like those in private sector jobs.

Sorting by activity completion is straightforward where individual standards of performance are enforced in the activities. Sorting by acquisition of measured competence is more complex and rests on identification of a reasonable set of benchmarks of employability development. There has been very little effort outside Job Corps to document competencies attained as opposed to registering completion of service units. In Job Corps, there is a complete and detailed system for measuring demonstrated vocational skills. There is also extensive use of the Certificate of General Education Development. The certificate and positive performance ratings are needed in Job Corps for entry into advanced career training options. The aim has been to provide credentials, and to create an internal progression of experiences and rewards based on performance.

However, the underlying view that has to be changed is the notion that it is wrong to sort disadvantaged youth by identifying and referencing achievement. As programs reach an expanding portion of the universe of need, it is critically important that they provide opportunities like those in the private sector. The requirement for performance and the risk of failure are necessary parts of any opportunity. As the opportunities for positive experiences are equalized (for instance, when disadvantaged minority youth come to have the same chances of employment in school and out during the teen years as nondisadvantaged nonminority youth), then the application of labor market standards of success or failure, with rewards and punishments, becomes more feasible. The option for the youth who fails is not so bleak and the failure cannot be blamed as much on previously limited opportunities. It is necessary to provide second and third chances and a helping hand, but there is a need to tighten performance requirements and to utilize programs as a proving ground as well as a developmental opportunity.

DURATION AND SEQUENCING OF ACTIVITIES

The 1978 CETA amendments limited the period of work experience in CETA to 1,000 hours in a single year, 2,000 hours in any five years, and thirty months overall. There are exemptions for in-school work experience and a number of other loopholes, but the basic concept was to limit dependence so that "remedial" activities do not become continuing alternatives. This is based on the reasonable notion that persons should receive employment and training services and then become employable. However, it does not square with the needs of youth in the labor market. Youth may require several years of "aging vat" work experience (cumulated perhaps over summers or in short doses while in school), which may not immediately increase employability enough to guarantee placement, particularly in areas where there are significant job deficits and where the participants are the victims of discrimination. It is estimated, for instance, that the Summer Youth Employment Program already provides two-fifths of the employment for fourteen- to nineteen-year-old nonwhites in the summer months. To reduce the job gap would require further expansion of summer components. In turn, youth in need would be working primarily in the public sector because that is where the majority of jobs would be for the eligible population. Participants would run up against the hours limitation before they matured to the point where career investments would be feasible.

Simply put, the limitation in service should begin once the youth enters career training or has an opportunity for employment leading to a career, not during the developmental sequence. At current funding levels, or at any realistically projected funding levels, there will not be enough resources to provide continuing treatments from age fourteen to twenty-one for all youth in need. This is not intended nor is it necessary. However, some youth with particularly severe problems may require such continuity of treatment. Stricter standards in the programs, and careful progressions will discourage "CETA junkies." Individualized prescription of services, rather than arbitrary limits, should help to determine who needs what.

If activities occur over a continuum, it is important that experiences be sequenced so far as possible so that they cumulate maximally. Sequencing needs to be both "ex ante" and "incremental." "Ex ante" sequencing means that a plan is developed for an individual, mapping out a structured series of activities over a span of time. "Incremental" sequencing means that at each point the youth reenters the system (assuming periodic entry and exit), the activity prescribed at that point is based on past experience. The notion of implementing long-term plans for the development of employability is not realistic for younger teenagers, because they have so many options that only sort out over a period of years. However, "ex ante" sequencing becomes possible and necessary as youth mature, their career goals and options stabilize, and they are ready to begin intensive remedial investments or career entry. Here, training is best linked directly to jobs with no discontinuities. It is important to clear the obstacles so that the occupation-specific investment pays off. Put another way, the sequencing should be retrospective early in the development and transition process and more prospective later.

TARGETING RESOURCES

There is general agreement with the principle that scarce public resources should be utilized for persons most in need, but there is disagreement about the degree of such targeting and the best mechanisms for achieving it. Youth programs use a range of approaches both in allocating resources among areas and in determining eligibility within areas. The allocation formulas are varied. YCCIP divides resources among areas according to the unemployed population. YETP uses a weighted formula of unemployment, excess unemployment, and poverty. The summer program uses poverty and unemployment, along with a "hold-harmless" clause, which has retained the concentration of resources in central cities that was characteristic of the War on Poverty. YIEPP sites were decided by competition. Discretionary resources under YETP and YCCIP can be utilized anywhere and have been concentrated in urban and rural poverty areas. YACC sites are required to be near areas of substantial unemployment, but essentially they mirror the distribution of federal lands. Job Corps expansion was planned to balance slot distribution with the regional shares of unemployed poor youth.

The effects of these different area allocation approaches are substantial: poverty factors in the allocation formulas emphasize rural areas; unemployment shares spread resources evenly, while excess unemployment factors concentrate in a few cities; population density yields a very heavy concentration in the urban centers while the population factor distributes evenly across the country. Discretionary dollars are most effective in targeting to poverty areas. Finally, tying sites to the distribution of federal lands under YACC completely mismatches need.

There are also varying income requirements for eligibility. Entitlement is most restrictive, with poverty as the measure. SYEP uses 70 percent of the Bureau of Labor Statistics Lower Living Standard, while Job Corps uses this standard supplemented by an out-of-school requirement and several other conditions. YETP uses 85 percent of the BLS Lower Living Standard for work experience components but has no income restriction on low-cost services. YCCIP is open to all unemployed youth with first consideration to the economically disadvantaged. YACC is not targeted and is designed for a "good mix" of all youth.

There are problems in the application of both allocation formulas and the eligibility standards. There is little correlation between area adult unemployment and youth unemployment, and youth employment/population ratios would be preferable because of uncertainties about the meaning of unemployment measures for youth. However, neither youth employment nor unemployment data are available by prime sponsor as a basis for allocation. From an equity or efficiency perspective it makes no sense whatsoever to adjust youth allocation shares of prime sponsors each year based on adult employment changes, since youth employment needs of areas do not correlate well with adult changes or levels.

The income eligibility criterion is fraught with hidden problems. Vertical inequities occur since income is a poor descriptor of individual need and employment obstacles, given the wide range of potential and experience within any income or demographically defined youth cohort. Family status arrangements can make all the difference in the world. Just by declaring independence, an unemployed youth can meet the disadvantaged requirement. The use of school dropout status for eligibility creates incentives for school leaving, while the use of long-term unemployment may be reasonable for self-supporting youth out of school for several years, but is meaningless for teenagers who are in and out of the labor force. A long-term unemployment restriction would encourage some youth to remain unemployed in order to establish eligibility. Some special needs groups are already exempted from the income standards—the handicapped and offenders. However, relative to any income criterion, there are hundreds of thousands of ineligible youth who, by an individualized comparison, need help more than many who are eligible.

The preceding analysis of youth labor market problems has implications for targeting. Because there is such wide variation within cohorts, and because permanent problems emerge more clearly only after cumulative experiences, it makes less sense to target early interventions according to income. Labor market status variables such as being unemployed or long-term unemployed are ineffective mechanisms for identifying youth with severe needs. Analysis suggests that the most productive variables are those related to previous, longer-term patterns in the labor market and to participation in developmental activities. For instance, the fact that a youth had three periods of unemployment in the last year is more reflective of problems than the fact that he or she is currently unemployed. The most effective targeting could be done if there were an individualized multiyear record of experiences to determine patterns of success or failure. Because deficits are concentrated in certain geographic areas, and because it is not just the the individuals with problems at a particular time who are affected, targeting by area makes more sense than targeting by individual characteristics. And because multiple problems accumulate to more than the sum of the parts, extra weight must be given to intensity factors in these allocation formulas.

INCOME MAINTENANCE ELEMENTS

The wages and allowances paid in employment and training programs for low-income youth have important income maintenance effects. An in-school and summer combination of work for a poor youth can provide wages equal to two-fifths of the poverty threshold for an urban family of four. The problem comes when income maintenance objectives are stressed over objectives regarding employment and the development of human resources. For instance, when public work experience programs pay youth more than their productivity level and more than can be obtained in the private sector, society loses and the individual, while getting needed income, may develop unrealistic work behavior and be deterred from seeking employment in the private sector. Approximately half of the cost for classroom training goes for allowances, which are required by law to equal the minimum wage. Obviously, the more that is paid in allowances, the fewer the persons who can receive training.

There are several shortcomings in present wage practices. First, the minimum wage is more than what most fourteen- and fifteen-year-olds can earn in the private sector, and more than could be earned by many older youth without work experience. In the May 1978 Current Population Survey, the following percentages of working youth in various age groups reported earning less than the then current minimum of $2.65: ages fourteen and fifteen, 69 percent; ages sixteen and seventeen, 35 percent; ages eighteen and nineteen, 14 percent; and ages twenty and twenty-one, 8 percent. The government jobs clearly provide attractive options to private sector employment for some of these youth. To the extent that public work experience programs are less demanding than private sector employment, the disincentives are exacerbated.

Second, there is a classic case of "wage illusion" in public perceptions. A significant group in the population will oppose paying fourteen- and fifteen-year-olds $3.35 per hour. When the minimum goes up, so does the public opposition to activities for fourteen- and fifteen-year-olds that pay the minimum. This is particularly true when public service employment programs, which may employ the parents of these youth, are limited to wages only slightly above the minimum. There is pressure, then, to exclude fourteen- and fifteen-year-olds from programs they need simply because of the inflexibility relative to wages.

Third, allowances create special problems where disadvantaged and nondisadvantaged youth are slotted into the same training or remedial education, with one group getting paid for the effort and the other not. This disparity is one of the major barriers to co-ordination noted by educators and vocational educators.

Fourth, with scarce resources, the wages and allowance floor tend to become the ceiling so that everyone is paid the minimum.

This eliminates incentives for good performance, and limits the steps that are available within the public work experience sector.

Fifth, reduced allowances can help to differentiate between those who simply want income and those who are mature enough to devote themselves to investments in career development. The experience with programs of the Opportunities Industrialization Centers in the 1960s indicated that the absence of allowances provided a way to screen in participants who were highly motivated, so that a program dynamic could be created. The Job Corps allowance, now $50 monthly for new Corpsmembers, is equal to only a tenth of what would be earned monthly at full-time minimum wage employment. While full Job Corps services such as room and board may be valued at more than the minimum, the $50 is what the Corpsmember sees in his or her pocket. Youth who simply want income would tend to choose work experience positions rather than the Job Corps. This natural sorting of those committed to investment in human resources would be even greater if opportunities for work were equalized for disadvantaged and nondisadvantaged populations so that poor youth really had work options.

The wage issue is complex and fraught with political implications. There is general agreement that workers should get paid relative to their productivity. The minimum wage law provides for a 15 percent differential for fourteen- and fifteen-year-olds and for certain older students on the assumption that they lack the experience to be fully productive. A benchmarking system assessing employability on an individualized basis could provide a basis for applying such differentials. An individualized approach would be far better than any comprehensive youth differential which might lead to some fully employable and productive youngsters being forced to accept wages less than their productivity warrants.

CHAPTER XII

Problems of Cooperation and Coordination in Vocational Education

HARRY F. SILBERMAN

There is increasing concern over the lack of cooperation and coordination among the many different sectors of society that influence vocational education. For example, during the Carter administration, a multiagency review of vocational education was launched in preparation for the reauthorization for fiscal year 1983 of the Vocational Education Act. The review was to examine ways of improving the cooperation of vocational education with CETA programs and with the private sector. The demand for greater coordination is partly due to the belief that vocational education ought to take better account of labor market conditions.

Problems of coordination exist along many dimensions. One line of fragmentation cuts across levels of government, with very loose coupling between federal, state, and local organizations. Farrar, De Sanctis, and Cohen likened the evolution of federal programs in local settings to a lawn party wherein the federal program is the occasion for a gathering, and the local guests do pretty much as they please.[1] For example, Experience Based Career Education, a federally developed program involving community-based exploration of potential careers, was designated an exemplary vocational education program by a Joint Dissemination Review Panel and was made available for national dissemination with federal funding under the Vocational Education Act, Part D. The local implementation

---

The writer is indebted to Robert Rossi and Kevin Gilmartin for obtaining some of the reports cited in this paper.

1. Eleanor Farrar, John E. De Sanctis, and David K. Cohen, "The Lawn Party: The Evolution of Federal Programs in Local Settings," *Phi Delta Kappan* 62 (November 1980): 167-71.

of the program soon took its own form, however, and in some cases was hardly recognizable as the same program.

Other lines of fracture cut across types of schools (public versus private, secondary versus postsecondary), along management lines (CETA versus the Employment Service), and along curricular lines (academic versus vocational). Whether interorganizational agreements are able to mend these various splits is questionable, but most policy makers agree that the effective development of vocational skills in both young and adult members of our society cannot succeed through the lone efforts of the public schools. The very nature of the task requires the cooperative efforts of employers, unions, government, education, and other community-based organizations, each performing what it does best. The requirement is especially salient in the face of scarce resources and an attitude among legislators that waste and inefficiency exist in publicly supported programs at all levels.

In this chapter, case studies of cooperative efforts are described. The descriptions are followed by discussion of several factors that emerge from the case studies: indicators of cooperation, potent variables that influence cooperation, unresolved issues, and explanatory models of the cooperative process. Those findings and summary conclusions are presented in subsequent sections of the chapter. Because of the different and often inconsistent uses of the terms "cooperation," "coordination," and "collaboration" in the literature, those terms are used interchangeably in this chapter.

Case Studies

REGIONAL AND ADULT VOCATIONAL EDUCATION COUNCILS

In 1976, the California legislature established a network of Regional Adult and Vocational Education Councils. The main purposes of these councils were to reduce duplication of courses, promote better articulation among schools, delineate functions of the participant schools, and approve courses in restricted areas of adult and vocational education. A 1978 joint report to the California Legislature by the State Department of Education and the California Community Colleges, after seventy-one councils had completed their first year of operation, revealed that few councils were aware of all the agencies within their area that offered educational programs for adults. An inventory of courses and programs was prepared to help decide what programs contained unnecessary duplication, but the lack of a uniform course code made even this initial task difficult.

In 1976-77, sixty-six councils throughout the state reported 51,374 courses to review and recommend for approval. Only sixteen courses were found to be unnecessary duplications and only eight of these were eliminated, though some councils reported they had eliminated courses in anticipation of the review process. In some cases, the review process served to identify gaps and led to the development of new courses.

The councils were required to appoint advisory groups, a mandate that created some problems since no particular responsibilities had been outlined for such groups. The major problems of the councils pertained to council representation and to lack of authority commensurate with their responsibility. For example, all school districts served by the councils were not represented on the council, and no one in that body specifically represented regional occupation centers. Some members had controlling votes over others' programs, yet there was no reciprocity of control. Councils also reported that they found it frustrating to have no effect on the often duplicative CETA offerings in the area.

According to recent testimony by the State Vocational Education Director, "the councils did not have course approval authority for community college credit courses, regular high school vocational education courses, or courses provided by prime sponsors or private schools." [2] In other words, the councils spent most of their time on adult education programs. If they did have authority to reduce duplication, that authority would conflict with the prerogatives of the elected boards of the participating agencies. Without the ability to enforce their recommendations, the councils were reduced to the status of a debating society. Nevertheless, there was evidence that the discussions at council meetings were of value, and the survival of the councils suggests the existence of increasing trust among agency representatives. For example, even after Proposition

2. Sam Barrett, "Testimony for the Senate Select Committee on Occupational Preparation and Placement," November 6, 1980, San Diego, Calif.

13 eliminated state funding for the Councils, some 40 percent of them continued to meet regularly on a voluntary basis.

An evaluation of fifty community advisory councils in the Los Angeles School District confirms the importance of assigning meaningful tasks to advisory groups.[3] Most respondents agreed that the council should be more involved in setting goals and priorities, in planning and evaluating the education program, and in planning budget allocations. The respondents from more affluent areas (with less ESEA Title I support) were less supportive of councils. To explain this, one area office administrator said that lack of involvement in the council may be due to their having "no real responsibility in anything serious." Council members in Title I schools have specifically defined tasks for council members, such as budget sign off, program planning and evaluation, and recruitment of parent aides, which serve to organize and give them purpose, and engage them in meaningful roles.

ARTICULATION BETWEEN COMMUNITY COLLEGES AND AREA VOCATIONAL SCHOOLS

In 1976, the American Vocational Association and the American Association for Community and Junior Colleges sponsored a nationwide survey to identify factors that facilitate or impede cooperation among institutions.[4] A sample of twenty-two locations throughout the country was drawn from among 203 institutions nominated as having established exemplary cooperative relationships. Approximately 300 interviews were conducted to document a series of case studies on successful articulation among area vocational schools, community colleges, and other agencies engaged in vocational education. Of the twenty-two sites visited, nine community colleges and five area vocational schools were found to be cooperating effectively with their neighboring institutions. Five case studies were prepared from these nine locations.

The motivation for much of this cooperative effort was scarcity

3. Harry Silberman, "An Evaluation of Decentralization in a Large School District" (Paper presented at the annual meeting of the American Education Research Association, New York, 1977).

4. David S. Bushnell, *Education and Training: A Guide to Interinstitutional Cooperation*, Final report (Washington, D.C.: U.S. Office of Education, 1978).

of resources and mutual interest in reducing competition and securing added funding. Major barriers to articulation included the stereotyped perceptions of the limited roles of competing institutions, and conflicting educational values.

COMMUNITY WORK EDUCATIONAL COUNCILS AND
INDUSTRY EDUCATION COUNCILS

A wide variety of council arrangements have been established at local, regional, and state levels to bring employers and schools together. A decade ago such councils were often ceremonial in nature, with activities limited to an annual banquet at which a featured speaker would extoll the virtues of cooperation between education and industry. Some councils did support an annual career day and sponsored a few well-publicized career exploration programs. More recently, the council role has expanded from business education cooperation to community-wide collaboration in solving educational problems. The National Institute for Work and Learning (NIWL), formerly the National Manpower Institute, was funded by the Department of Labor to serve as an intermediary in working with a number of community work education councils to learn how effective community action can ease the transition between school and work. The assumption underlying this effort is that much of the transition process is outside the reach of schools, and that a collaborative arrangement among the key institutions of the community would be more effective than the usual passive advisory groups whose members are selected by the schools as sounding boards on school affairs.

The work of these councils was assessed by an independent group of observers who found that the various councils are quite similar.[5] They all act as catalysts rather than taking direct action themselves. All have successfully involved at least two groups: educators and employers. Much of the activity of the councils was already underway prior to the NIWL grant. For example, the Industry Education Council of California had been established in the late 1950s.

In general, personalities of individuals on such councils were of

5. Curtis Aller et al., *An Assessment of Community Work Education Councils: 10 Case Studies*, November 1977. Report to U.S. Department of Labor, contract 81-11-71-09.

central importance. Consequently, the observers discouraged the dissemination of prepackaged council start-up procedures in favor of building on personal relationships already in place in a given community. The attitudes prevalent among existing members largely determined the potential role of the council. For example, attitudes toward the disadvantaged generally suggest there is little likelihood that these councils would be able to include the efforts of CETA prime sponsors or other employment and training organizations that focus exclusively on low-income, disadvantaged groups. The employer representatives on these councils are, for the most part, content with focusing on school problems and do not wish to expand their role to that of hiring the disadvantaged. In part this attitude stems from a desire to avoid government interference and additional paperwork.

Corroborative evidence of such attitudes is cited in a recent survey of 620 Employer Advisory Group members concerning the use of job tax credits to encourage placement of hard-to-employ applicants.[6] A substantial majority of respondents believed that employers did not hire tax-credit-eligible applicants because such applicants did not have the basic abilities to do the job, were not motivated to work, and had too many personal problems.

These people only come to work to satisfy free money regulations. They are absent, most claim job injury, most fight with other employees who try to work, give poor work results. Lucky if they work three hours out of the eight! (p. 6)

In general, all eligible participants get into an affirmative action category. Once hired, if they are not satisfactory, they bring suits, hassle us through EDD, and in general cost an enormous amount to terminate. They arrive with a chip on their shoulder and an attitude of "you can't fire me because I can cause you trouble—with EEOC, AAP, FEPC, EDD." More employers would participate if they knew that an unsatisfactory employee could be fired without undue jeopardy. (p. 13)

In recognition of the importance of private sector participation in hiring the hard-to-employ, the Congress wrote the Private Sector

6. *Jobs Tax Credit Survey of Employer Advisory Group Members* (Sacramento, Calif.: Employment Service Division, Operations Branch, Employment Development Department, 1980).

Initiatives legislation, in which every CETA prime sponsor is required to organize a Private Industry Council (PIC). The intention behind this program is to ensure that CETA works closely with private employers, since most available jobs are located in the private sector. Though the intention of the PICs is to increase cooperation with the private sector, it is too early to evaluate their impact on CETA. Some concern has been expressed about proliferating councils with vague objectives and minimal authority.

CETA LINKAGES

Federal system reforms in the early 1970s decentralized the administration of employment and training programs to local prime sponsor agencies (CETA). But employment services are still centrally managed through state-run job service agencies with funding and policy direction from the Department of Labor. With the decentralization of manpower programs by the CETA legislation, the need for cooperation with employers, the employment service, and vocational education became more obvious. For example, the employment service is funded by a resource allocation formula, specified in federal regulations, that provides funds to states according to how many placements are made. This formula serves as an incentive to the employment service to concentrate on quick, easy placements, and to avoid time-consuming investment in collaboration with welfare, CETA, or vocational education programs.

On-site interview studies were conducted at nine specially funded CETA/Employment Service "linkage demonstration" projects.[7] These two agencies are ripe targets for collaborative effort since CETA is troubled with low placement rates and the employment service has limited access to hard-to-employ target populations. There is room for service integration where personnel from both agencies collaborate in the sharing of functions and for delegation of specialized functions in an equitable division of labor. While the linkage study found no discernible differences in effectiveness between integration and delegation procedures, delegation

7. *Evaluation of CETA/SESA Linkage Demonstration Project*, Final Report (Minneapolis, Minn.: Institute for Manpower Program Analysis Consultation and Training, Inc., 1978).

was easier to achieve and seemed to produce relationships that were more stable than was true for integration. Even though delegation presented fewer problems and resulted in a more immediate reduction in duplication of effort, most projects selected an integration strategy. The majority of CETA prime sponsors were not willing to delegate functions and become dependent on the employment service. Some impediments to collaboration were differences in goals and incentives, planning and budgeting cycles, definition of terms, data requirements, reporting forms, and operational procedures. Overall, the nine projects did tend to reduce the level of distrust between the officials governing the agencies, and have improved coordination in some cities.

In another study, Lecht and Matland prepared case studies of nine prime sponsors that had records of successful cooperation with business firms.[8] Findings revealed that the smaller companies were more likely to hire the hard-to-employ CETA trainees; the larger establishments, those employing 500 or more persons, were seriously underrepresented in placements in most of the sites visited. There was also considerable evidence of enrollee selectivity in that non-whites and economically disadvantaged persons frequently made up a smaller percentage of the on-the-job training enrollment (the program with maximum employer participation), than in Title I CETA programs generally. Not surprisingly, those employers who had been involved in the on-the-job training programs held a more favorable view of the CETA program than those without such involvement. The primary incentives for employer participation were the subsidies and labor shortages. Smaller employers favored larger subsidies, while larger employers wanted greater tax incentives. One of the strongest impressions in most of the sites visited was a sense of the low visibility of the CETA program in the business community.

In examining the practices of prime sponsors in the Philadelphia area, with respect to involvement of private industry with CETA sponsors, Northrup found that such participation depended on the attitude of employers and sponsors toward each other and their

8. Leonard A. Lecht and Marc A. Matland, *Involving Private Employers in CETA Programs: A Case Study*, R and D Monograph 75 (Washington, D.C.: Employment and Training Administration, U.S. Department of Labor, 1979).

past experience in working together rather than on the presence of employers on advisory councils.[9] In fact, most companies represented on the councils did not hire CETA enrollees. There was also reluctance on the part of prime sponsors to involve the private sector actively. Some CETA staff members had inadequate knowledge of the business environment; this was a handicap in attempts to place the disadvantaged in private sector jobs.

YOUTH EMPLOYMENT AND DEMONSTRATION PROJECTS ACT

When the Labor Department assisted the Congress in passing the Youth Employment and Demonstration Projects Act of 1977 (YEDPA), it was well aware of the difficulties experienced by CETA in establishing links with other systems. This new piece of legislation was used to initiate changes in the old CETA system. A much broader set of local institutions participated in YEDPA, which used its discretionary funds as a catalyst for change. The youth program was more flexible in the type of projects that could be funded. It reemphasized the importance of coordination with vocational education and laid the groundwork for the President's 1980 legislative proposal on youth.

The YEDPA experience suggests that the 22 percent set-aside funds have fostered significantly increased interaction between local education agencies (LEAs) and CETA prime sponsors.[10] The interim review of YEDPA projects by Butler and Darr led them to surmise that the expanded connections between prime sponsors and the private sector, and to a lesser extent, the public schools, may have had an indirect effect on the quality of the CETA programs, due to exposure of those programs to the expectations of the other two parties.

In a study of twenty-four projects in nineteen states, Rist found that linkages work best where mutual reciprocity is evident,

9. Herbert R. Northrup, "Feasibility Study to Develop a Model for Furthering the Involvement of Private Industry with CETA Sponsors, Especially in Training," abstracted in *Research and Development: A 16-Year Compendium, 1963-1978* (Washington, D.C.: Employment and Training Administration, U.S. Department of Labor, 1979), p. 337. ED 178-782.

10. Erik Payne Butler and Jim Darr, *Lessons from Experience: An Interim Review of the Youth Employment and Demonstration Projects Act,* Report for the Vice-President's Task Force on Youth Employment (Waltham, Mass.: Center for Public Service, Brandeis University, 1980).

and where the linkage system is not too complex.[11] His data show that interagency collaboration is exceedingly difficult and few successful linkages were generated. Where successful linkages were established, however, distinct improvements were noted in the delivery of services.

Wurzburg reported ten case studies of YEDPA in thirty-seven prime sponsorships in twelve states.[12] Among the results the following seven findings pertain to problems of cooperation and coordination:

1. Youth councils are required by the program but these councils are often "mere figureheads" with little participation by youths. Other forms of youth participation are needed.

2. Local education agencies have become more involved with the prime sponsors. There is also some evidence that LEAs may play a key role in mediating stronger links between CETA and the private sector by lending credibility to the CETA programs.

3. A mismatch or uneven partnership exists between CETA sponsors and the non-CETA agencies, such as local schools, with which they must collaborate. The non-CETA agencies are not controlled by a centralized agency with the authority to require them to cooperate, while the prime sponsors do operate under such federal control. The mismatch creates problems. Department of Labor can mandate collaboration of the prime sponsors, "but must rely on persuasion and the creation of credible incentives to get non-CETA agencies involved."[13]

4. There has been too little time or incentive for much participation by unions or private employers. Such participation is limited by the perceived powerlessness of the YEDPA Councils.

11. Ray Rist, *Patterns of Collaboration: The CETA/School Linkages* (Ithaca, N.Y.: Youthwork National Policy Study, Cornell University, 1980).

12. Gregory Wurzburg, *Improving Job Opportunities for Youth: A Review of Prime Sponsor Experience in Implementing the Youth Employment and Demonstration Projects Act* (Washington, D.C.: National Council on Employment Policy, U.S. Department of Labor, 1978); idem, *Youth and the Local Employment Agenda: An Analysis of Prime Sponsor Experience Implementing the Youth Employment and Demonstration Projects Act,* Final Report (Washington, D.C.: Youth Evaluation Project, National Council on Employment Policy, 1980).

13. Wurzburg, *Youth and the Local Employment Agenda,* p. 5.

Community-based organizations, however, have actively participated.

5. Incentives for encouraging new institutional linkages were not very successful because they were introduced at the same time as the formula-funded programs. The incentive grants thus became simply more money for which to apply. Incentive grants should be administered after the formula-grant program has stabilized; otherwise the incentive value of the grant is lost.

6. One point of contention between prime sponsors and local schools concerned the level of CETA funds. At least 22 percent of Youth Employment and Training Program funds are to be reserved by prime sponsors for local education agencies subject to agreement on the LEA programs to be implemented. Though most sponsors came to satisfactory agreements, in a few cases the sponsors felt that the schools were trying to use CETA resources to replace local revenues. School officials were afraid the CETA set-aside was being used by county and city governments to influence independent school districts.

7. A second point of contention between prime sponsors and local schools was the awarding of academic credit for work experience. School officials were protective of their authority to grant credit, but most are now awarding credit for work experience. Community colleges have been especially willing to award credit for work experience and have been quite willing to develop alternative classroom activities to complement the work experience.

Indicators of Cooperation and Coordination

The case studies cited above are illustrative of the type of reviews that have accompanied systematic efforts to encourage greater cooperation and coordination among vocational education, training, and employment services. Different studies use different indicators to judge the extent of cooperation and coordination being observed. These studies used interview procedures and report the results of their findings in general narrative form. Most studies focus on process indicators, but a few emphasized product or outcome.

PROCESS INDICATORS

By far, the majority of case studies report changes in cooperative procedures or linkages. For example, in evaluating local cooperative planning processes among employment and training agencies in three California counties, Rossi and Gilmartin observed the following twenty-one linkage procedures: [14]

1. *Referral.* Staff at one agency advise persons with needs to seek services at another agency.

2. *Case Consultation.* Staff at one agency ask advice from staff at another agency regarding the needs of particular clients.

3. *Case Conferences.* Staff from two or more agencies discuss the needs of clients they have in common, informally and as needed.

4. *Case Management (by one agency).* Staff at one agency are given responsibility for coordinating the services provided by several agencies to meet the needs of particular clients.

5. *Case Team.* Staff from two or more agencies coordinate services to meet the needs of a particular client through continuous and systematic interaction.

6. *Colocation.* Two or more agencies have staff and separate facilities at the same location; coordination of activities is optional.

7. *Staff Outstationing.* Staff from one agency are assigned to do their work in the facilities of another agency; coordination is necessary.

8. *Staff Transfer.* Staff from one agency are assigned to work (temporarily) under the direct supervision of another agency, to carry out activities for that agency.

9. *Staff Team.* Staff from two or more agencies are assigned to work as a coordinated unit for a number of clients.

10. *Purchase of Services.* One agency pays for specific services from another agency (for example, outreach, intake, transportation, diagnostic services).

11. *Fund Transfer.* One agency provides funds to another agency for that agency's use.

12. *Joint Funding.* Two or more agencies commit funds to a particular effort.

---

14. Robert J. Rossi and Kevin J. Gilmartin, *Coordinated Planning Program Report No. 3: Project Timelines, Progress toward Objectives, and Changes in Procedures; Interagency Coordination of Activities; and Resource Usage* (Palo Alto, Calif.: American Institutes for Research, 1980).

13. *Joint Budgeting.* Two or more agencies share in decisions regarding the allocation of resources for a particular effort.

14. *Joint Program Development.* Two or more agencies work together to plan and find resources for an effort.

15. *Joint Program Operation.* Two or more agencies participate in the implementation of an effort.

16. *Joint Program Evaluation.* Two or more agencies work together to assess the effectiveness of an effort.

17. *Joint Information Exchange.* Two or more agencies share information that each collected independently, without joint planning concerning what information was to be collected.

18. *Joint Information Gathering.* Two or more agencies plan and participate in the collection of new data.

19. *Joint Public Relations.* Two or more agencies work together to plan and carry out information dissemination activities to other agencies and to the public.

20. *Uniform Record Keeping.* Two or more agencies use standardized forms (for example, client application forms) so that they can be easily interchanged and used to serve more than a single agency's purpose.

21. *Standardization of Procedures.* Two or more agencies use the same procedures to respond to particular client needs.

Such procedures can be observed and tabulated. Process evaluation of such procedures can be made on quantitative and qualitative levels.

Quantitative descriptions. Linkages appear in a variety of forms. The number of linkages may be tallied as an indicator of cooperation. For example, a vocational education program may have five linkages if it used the public employment service to put on job search workshops at the school, carried on a personnel exchange with industry wherein high school teachers would work in industry for short periods, had an apprenticeship arrangement with the local union, had a cooperative education agreement with city government, and participated in a community work education council.

The breadth of involvement may also be expressed in quantitative form. Some agencies may have many linkages, but all of them associated with a narrow set of functions. Other agencies may have a smaller number of links but the links may be dispersed over a broader array of functions and with a greater variety of agencies.

The amount of personal interaction or depth of involvement is another quantitative process indicator. For example, an agency may have established links with other agencies, but those links may not involve frequent direct contact among agency personnel (for example, transportation, support services, outreach). On the other hand, an agency may have a single link that is used as a source of continuous interaction by personnel from the agencies involved (for example, a company adopts a local high school and there is a continuing one-to-one interaction between employees and students).

The amount of resources that an agency donates to cooperative endeavors is another indicator of cooperation. For example, school facilities might be used for non-school-related services, or personnel may be offered, as when a union supports a representative to work on a joint council. Availability of personnel with time and energy often determines the degree of representation and participation on joint councils. Sometimes vocational education advisory groups appear to overrepresent employer interests, not because union representatives are excluded, but because union personnel with the time to invest are not available. For the same reason, state and local government staff often dominate membership on planning councils, and it is sometimes difficult to get citizen representatives to attend meetings.

Quality of observed linkages. Though more difficult to measure, quality of linkage is a more important indicator of cooperation than number of linkages. One important qualitative indicator is the institutionalization of linkages or the extent to which cooperative services are merely added on to existing services. Too often federal or state grants are made to stimulate collaboration and numerous linkages are established, but those links are added on simply to comply with the provisions of the grant and have no systemic effect on the participating agencies. The lead agency typically hires new staff to carry out the cooperative project, and representatives from the participating agencies delegate the bulk of the action to the "add-on" staff. The participating agencies carry out their normal business as usual, and the only change in the system is that the new staff working on soft "seed" money devote much of their time writing proposals to attract additional support beyond the period of their grant. If the staff succeed in obtaining additional funds, they will gradually become one more agency whose activities must be coordinated. Unless there is a real need for collaboration, organizing a cooperative project replete with joint steering council and staff will only change the titles, not services. The council will comply with the statement of work in a perfunctory manner without disturbing its existing fragmented base of continuing operations. Instead of service integration or coordination among participating agencies, the staff will probably add new service activities that no one provided before.

In a study of seventy service integration projects, Lucas, Heald, and Vogel[15] found the most common choice of projects were those that avoided changing the preexisting system. In 85 percent of the projects, the traditional service agencies continued to deliver services in much the same way as they did in the past. Seventy-seven percent avoided changing in any way the organizational structure of the existing agencies. Most new services filled gaps in the old service delivery system or expanded old services to new locales. There was only limited evidence that extensive planning or the pursuit of organizational change had any effect on organizational outcomes; one change strategy was no better than another. Almost all the seventy projects had established links to aid service delivery to clients, but few of them had adopted any form of linkage that would have altered in any way their organizational structure (for example, fiscal, personnel, administrative support). The most frequent strategies were those that offered no threat to agency autonomy (for example, centralized intake, referral and diagnosis of service needs, colocation, and outstationing of some personnel). Even when agencies collaborated on common intake or diagnosis and referral services, those services supplemented rather than replaced existing services, and such supplemental services were withdrawn when the seed money expired. The same add-on phenomenon occurred when common information systems were adopted. They always supplemented and never replaced existing information systems. Intake workers always gathered additional information or

15. William A. Lucas, Karen Heald, and Mary Vogel, *Census of Local Services Integration* (Santa Monica, Calif.: Rand Corporation, 1975), pp. 1-45.

filled out two separate forms with duplicating information. Thus, service integration efforts always increased cost and reduced efficiency because coordinated services were overlaid on top of existing practices; the roles, expectations, and working relationships within the agencies that were party to the collaborative agreements were unchanged.

The extent of the add-on phenomenon described above is an important qualitative indicator. Another qualitative indicator of cooperation is the level of trust and trustworthiness exhibited in personal interactions. Usually, the first year of a cooperative venture is devoted to establishing trust among representatives of the participating agencies. Generally the representatives organize themselves into some form of council through which linkage agreements are established. It takes at least the first six meetings of the council to get through the sterile dialogue and establish some kind of a group. At first, the greatest barrier to open communication is the fear of losing autonomy.

The suspicions on the council are also likely to be exacerbated if the representatives are not at approximately the same rank within their respective organizations or of sufficient stature within their own agency to make decisions. For example, if community-based organizations that subcontract training functions from a CETA sponsor are threatened by proposals to have the local community colleges perform the same function, the officials of those organizations who have the authority and ability to resolve the conflict must be present, willing to discuss the idea, and able to negotiate a settlement. If such officials are not present, lower-level representatives who see the proposals as threatening to their turf will take refuge in endless discussion of unimportant or meaningless issues, a form of foot-dragging without vocal dissent.

To be successful, the council must have sufficient stability and authority to enforce participation and to impact policy and budgetary decisions within the member organizations. In addition, if the council is to be more than mere window dressing, the meetings must establish an informal communication network, and the depth of involvement within that network must be sufficient to break down institutional identities and build enough trust among members to talk about the real problems within their organizations, to overcome institutional conflict, and to build a commitment to change within their own organizations. Trust in mutual reciprocity and equity must replace the initial feelings that some members may be taking more than they are giving. Some progress has been made in measuring such forms of interpersonal trust and trustworthiness. Rotter and his colleagues have conducted a series of investigations in the field of interpersonal trust during the past decade.[16]

PRODUCT INDICATORS

Past experiences with collaborative efforts have indicated that genuine collaboration is not easy. Institutionalization of linkages is rare; integration only seems to happen during the period of the temporary "seed" grant or only when the law demands mixing of funds, personnel, and management. When integration does occur, the ultimate product indicators usually include increased efficiency (less cost and duplication) and improved services to clients (more accessible services, stable placement in desirable jobs, ample labor supply for industry).

In general, process indicators are more likely to be discussed than product indicators in reports of cooperative ventures. Perhaps products or outcomes are too far removed from the cooperative process itself to allow for unequivocal interpretation of observed changes in outcomes. For example, a cooperative project involving interagency training and placement services may be associated with lowered unemployment rates, but those unemployment rates may be accounted for by a variety of alternative explanations such as changes in aggregate demand for labor, seasonal variation, or structural changes in the labor market.

Variables That Influence Cooperation

Most of the case studies provide abundant information on types of linkages among organizations, but they do not factor out the essential variables that contribute to successful cooperation. In sifting through these reports it is possible to identify a few variables that reappear in many cooperative settings. An initial taxonomy of such variables is attempted here.

16. Julian Rotter, "Interpersonal Trust, Trustworthiness, and Gullibility" (Presidential address at the meeting of the Eastern Psychological Association, April 1977).

Variables that may influence the extent of cooperation among education, training, and employment providers can be clustered into three categories. By far the most significant category pertains to positive and negative *incentives*. A second major category pertains to the generalized *expectancy* among participants that genuine cooperation is possible and within their capabilities. A third category refers to the *composition* of the group of participants.

INCENTIVES TO COOPERATE

There are positive and negative incentives to cooperate. Positive incentives include grants, tax credits, wage subsidies, pass-through funds, categorical funds, an increased labor supply, additional staff, or any form of additional resource that an agency will seek to obtain. Negative incentives include anything that the agency will seek to avoid, for example, added paperwork, confusion, increased level of conflict, dissatisfaction with a current problem situation, group disapproval, censure by higher authority, penalties for disobeying a law or violating an agreement, removal of resources, or withdrawal of privileges.

The magnitude of an incentive is inferred by its potential for influencing cooperative effort. The value of an incentive, positive or negative, depends on other incentives with which it is associated. For example, seed money is valued because it buys time and staff to obtain added staff, space, visibility, and support. The value of an incentive is evident in the choices that are made in situations where a variety of incentives are operating. In times of great scarcity of funds, we can expect that the need for continued support will stimulate greater cooperation among agencies, especially those in greatest need, even in the presence of other disincentives. Such agencies are most likely to avoid doing anything that will have a negative effect on their continued support.

EXPECTANCY THAT COOPERATION IS POSSIBLE

The occurrence of cooperation among agencies depends not only on the incentives that are operating in a particular locale but also on the general attitude that prevails concerning the feasibility of such cooperation. If officials at various levels in the participating agencies have clear objectives for the type of linkage envisioned, if they have defined their roles and have successful models to observe, they are more likely to perceive the task of cooperative action as feasible. If they have a history of successful collaboration and respect the abilities of other members of the partnership, they are more likely to expect that cooperative efforts will improve client services. If the members of the partnership feel they are in control and have freedom to make and enforce decisions, they will expect that successful cooperative action is possible. On the other hand, if they feel they have no power and that events beyond their control govern their destiny, if they have no past experience with successful cooperation and have no success models to observe, they will not expect cooperation to work. If they do not expect cooperative action to be successful they are less likely to try it. Officials of agencies in urban centers, where existing staff are already overextended with too many local initiatives, are less likely to believe in the efficacy of joint action. They are too busy with daily survival.

Expectancy that particular linkages will improve client services will be determined by previous experience with those linkages, but also will be generalized from similar situations with other kinds of cooperative action. If those experiences have had positive outcomes and the participants feel free to engage voluntarily in the new collaborative venture, they are more likely to anticipate that it will also reach a successful conclusion.

COMPOSITION OF THE GROUP

Characteristics of participating agencies and the composition of the steering committee or council will affect the outcome of cooperative action. But such characteristics will probably have an indirect effect working through the other two factors: incentive value of cooperation, and expectancy that successful cooperation is possible.

The choice of lead agency is almost as important as the representativeness of the council. In a two-year comparative study of inner-city agencies, Rogers and Menzel found that an important feature of the most coordinated delivery system was that it existed outside city hall.[17] Continued conflicts between the mayor and suburban politicians, the short mayoral term of office, a city council representing various local neighborhood needs and interests that would delay and block citywide programs, and the general divisions between the city and county organizations, made it senseless to have the mayor and city hall as the center of a coordinated delivery system. Instead, an elite establishment base of metropolitan area employers and top officials of the public employment service, the board of education, and the city's public and private employment and training agencies initiated and sustained the necessary linkages that pulled together all the main "downtown" institutional participants. Those who were outside the direct line of fire were more effective.

Ideally the participating agencies should be represented by persons who can communicate with members of the other agencies at all echelons, from the highest level executives to the lowest level line employees. Unfortunately, such representation may increase the size of the council.

As the composition of the group becomes more representative of all the major power centers, the problem of group size emerges. The larger the group, the more unwieldly and difficult it is to reach consensus, especially in the formative stages of group development when trust has not been established. In a new group the conflict-resolution procedure may not be sufficient to sustain itself through differences in ethnicity, social class, and values. Complexity of interagency councils can seriously reduce their effectiveness.

Unresolved Issues

Implicit in the case studies of cooperative efforts are three unresolved issues: the primary goal of increased cooperation, the best method for achieving cooperation, and the most useful model of the cooperative process. No data are available to resolve such issues; the following discussion is openly speculative and more aptly described as hypothesis generation than as a report of facts obtained from previous studies.

17. David J. Rogers and Roslyn Menzel, "Interorganizational Relations and Inner-City Manpower Programs," abstracted in *Research and Development: A 16-Year Compendium*, pp. 335-36.

GOALS

Two goals dominate the literature on vocational education and employment and training policy: labor supply and educational growth. While most observers wish to have both, in an environment of diminishing resources one must usually choose between them. Resource allocations at the operational level depend on whether job preparation or personal development is primary. The two goals have different implications for program design and evaluation, staff selection, and budget.

Labor supply. The assumption that greater cooperation of education, training, and employment services with business and industry will reduce unemployment and better match the supply of skilled graduates to the needs of the labor market, makes education and training the servant of the labor market; it is education for work. Incentives are provided for worksite training and work experience, with the aim of providing short-term training to meet the needs of industry for large numbers of skilled entry-level employees. If the total number of jobs that can be created by the training is significantly increased (in excess of the number of positions created by the tax subsidy itself), then this view is defensible on grounds of economic development.

Competition between the Department of Labor and the Education Department focuses on this issue of job placement versus personal development. Although the bulk of educational funding is from state and local sources, the federal money provides the leverage to influence local policy. For example, the CETA legislation, administered by the Department of Labor, was implemented in a decentralized fashion, so that the initiative for purchasing job training services from schools would be in the hands of local prime sponsors. Thus, the employment and training agencies with their emphasis on job placement have been ascendant. They have used their funds to encourage schools to be more concerned with the work-experience needs of minority and disadvantaged youth. In support of this placement view, Farkas and Stromsdorfer cite references supplying evidence that the skill training is effective if specifically linked to labor market opportunities, work experience, and placement services.[18] They also conclude that programs aimed at changing personal values and personality traits, such as motivation, generally are not successful. Reubens has observed that countries that give a large role to employment and training agencies have been more successful than those with education-based programs in establishing genuinely cooperative planning and management between the schools and manpower agencies.[19]

Educational growth. The alternative view is that education is an end in itself and that the purpose of cooperative program planning and administration is to make better use of the broader community in the educative process. In this view, the primary purpose of vocational education is to promote full human development through exposure of the learner to work experience as part of the educational process, but the purpose of the work is to further the education of the student; the work is subordinate to the educational process; it is work for education.

In the long run the educational perspective may offer greater opportunity for economic development than the labor-supply approach, which uses work experience to impart job skills specific to a single company or family of companies. General behavioral competence may be more important than specific technical job skills, because general coping skills and personal competencies are common to all work organizations, indeed to life itself, for everyone must solve problems, make decisions, and communicate with others. Emphasis on specific job training may not be the best way of reducing youth unemployment or increasing productivity of labor. In the educational growth perspective, the purpose of community work-education councils is to provide a systematic way to involve members of the entire community in education. Councils can open doors to bring learning and earning together in the lives of students, and improve the attitude of businessmen, parents, and students toward schools.

18. George Farkas and Ernst Stromsdorfer, "Social Policies to Reduce Youth Unemployment: Lessons from Experience and the Potential of Recent Initiatives," in *Problems of Youth Employment*, U.S. Congress, Committee on Education and Labor, 96th Congress, 2d Session (Washington, D.C.: U.S. Government Printing Office, January 1980).

19. Beatrice G. Reubens, *Bridges to Work: International Comparisons of Transition Services* (Montclair, N.J.: Allandheld, Osmun and Co., 1977), p. 224.

In this educational view, unemployment is considered to be largely attributable to a lack of aggregate demand. Vigorous placement efforts may alter the identity of the unemployed, but are unlikely to increase the total number of jobs. Unemployment rates fluctuate with the business cycle and the size of the labor force rather than with the supply of employment and training services. Helping some people to get placed will neither increase the total number of jobs, nor reduce the unemployment rate.

METHOD

The debate on the best method of achieving whichever goals are selected has split over whether program planning and administration should be centralized or decentralized. This issue is sometimes referred to as the "top-down/bottom-up" question.

Decentralization. The argument for decentralization of authority posits that local program operators and administrators are closest to the problems, better understand the local concerns and issues, and need the authority to operate their program as they see fit. In a decentralized system the planning is "bottom-up" and cooperative. According to the recent Vice-President's Task Force on Youth Employment:

The most exciting and effective youth programs result when local actors work together, building on their experience and sense of local needs and opportunities. These are the programs which engage local institutions in doing what they do best. Schools teach, employers provide work experience, community organizations offer supportive services and the CETA system provides training. Taken together, harmonized by a common commitment and directed toward a common solution, powerful partnerships are being built.[20]

The dominant view here is that programs based upon local partnerships that link classrooms with work experience are the most cost-effective in educating and preparing students for work. This is essentially a local remedial approach to the jurisdictional problems that have been created by the multiple sets of overlapping federal legislation in the area of youth policy. The Carnegie Coun-

20. The Vice-President's Task Force on Youth Employment, *A Summary Report of the Vice-President's Task Force on Youth Employment* (Washington, D.C.: The White House, 1980), p. 44.

cil recommends creation of councils for work-education in every
sizable community where one does not exist.[21]

Centralization. The top-down argument is considered a preventive to the jurisdictional problems that now require so much local
coordination and persuasion. The cumulative effect of many pieces
of state and federal legislation that were made into law without
careful scrutiny of their impact on existing programs creates separa-
tions and jurisdictional problems. These problems are often dealt
with by simply adding some language to the new legislation to the
effect that local agencies should collaborate and avoid duplication
of effort. Much more will probably be required, however, to overcome the organizational barriers to cooperation. A centralized approach to the problem, though laden with political obstacles, would
have changed all the affected legislation so no problems of coordination would have arisen, or would even have created a new
institution to replace the existing institutions struggling for jurisdiction. Fragmented programs, wherein one needs local coordination
to put pieces together that should never have been separated in the
first place, require state and federal legislative reform.

McGowan and Cohen[22] view the social division of labor in
America as creating powerful barriers to any serious allocation of
responsibility among business, education, and labor and conclude
that inventing new community institutions may be preferable to
assuming that cooperation among schools, businesses, unions, and
other existing institutions can make up for deficiencies of the
system. In a critique of the concept of industry/education community councils, however, Walsh makes a strong case that before
any new institution is formed, an assessment should be made of
presently existing school-work linkages at the community level.[23]
Regardless of how the disagreement over decentralized or centralized approaches to coordination is resolved, there is little empirical

21. Carnegie Council on Policy Studies in Higher Education, *Giving Youth
a Better Chance: Options for Education, Work, and Service* (San Francisco:
Calif.: Jossey-Bass, 1979), p. 345.

22. Eleanor F. McGowan and David K. Cohen, "Career Education: Re-
forming School through Work," *Public Interest* 46 (Winter 1977): 28-47.

23. Paul E. Barton, Sue B. Bobrow, and John J. Walsh, *NIE Papers in
Education and Work, Number 9: Industry/Education Community Councils*
(Washington, D.C.: National Institute of Education, 1977).

evidence that cooperative planning has much impact on organizational change. At least there appears to be no evidence to support the establishment of extensive planning requirements.

MODELS OF THE COOPERATIVE PROCESS

At least two theoretical models of interorganizational relationships seem appropriate to the cooperative process: the exchange model and the expectancy model.

The exchange model. Citing material from Levine and White,[24] Baker describes the exchange model as "any voluntary activity between two organizations which has consequences, actual or anticipated, for the realization of their respective goals or objectives."[25] An exchange takes place when the leadership of participating agencies believe that cooperation will make better use of scarce resources than is possible through autonomous action. Scarcity of resources prompts an agency to confine itself to limited functions and to depend on other agencies for the performance of some functions within its domain that it cannot afford. Cooperative exchange is more likely when there is some overlap of functions. When there is complete overlap, agencies are more likely to compete, and when there is no overlap, there is no need for cooperation.

From the exchange model, one would predict maximum cooperation if it benefits all the participating institutions and a significant number of people within them; cooperation is more likely when it advances values and goals of the participants. If the exchange is unequal, the participants who benefit least will eventually seek other arrangements, perhaps forming alliances with other groups to improve their competitive position. As time goes by and contextual changes alter the benefits of cooperation, the partnership, with its explicit or implicit agreements, will also begin to grow or dissolve depending on the returns on the investment. The exchange is most fruitful when the partners specialize in tasks that are complementary and mutually interdependent. If educators understand

24. Sol Levine and Paul E. White, "Exchange as a Conceptual Framework for the Study of Interorganizational Relationships," *Administrative Science Quarterly* 5 (March 1961): 583-601.

25. Lynn E. Baker, *Perspectives on Interorganizational Relationships* (Bloomington, Ind.: National Inservice Network, Indiana University, 1980), p. 588.

how to improve basic skills and employment specialists understand the structure of the labor market and job search skills, one would expect that the two can cooperate effectively in helping students with the transition from school to work. But the schools and the employment service have not found joint effort easy. The exchange of mutual incentives is necessary but not sufficient for cooperation.

The expectancy model. In a decentralized system, cooperation is not automatic. There must not only be sufficient incentives to motivate the partnership, but in addition the potential partners must also believe, indeed *expect*, that such cooperation is possible. In some of the case studies the conditions which were most often associated with the initiation of coordination efforts by the local manager of CETA and employment services offices were the incentives (for example, a previously recognized operating problem, linkage demonstration money, and the state offices' requirement that they coordinate) *plus* an expectation that the problem could be mitigated by linkage. If the participants had experienced much failure in previous attempts to cooperate or if the goals for their collaboration were too difficult to accomplish, the expectation for successful cooperation may not have been sufficient for them to attempt, regardless of the magnitude of incentives. Thus there is an interaction between the value of the incentives that operate in the situation and the personal expectations of the participants. The potential for cooperative behavior is a product of the reciprocal interaction of the environmental incentives *and* the personal expectations of the participants. For example, if the participants had great need for the additional funding that was contingent on their collaboration and yet did not expect to be able to work together, the model would predict a high level of conflict.

The expectancy model would predict that the characteristics of the participants on the council will be associated with their expectations that cooperation is possible, and with the value placed on existing incentives. For example, a council that consists of officials of similar power and autonomy, who have had similar positive experiences with cooperative projects, are more likely to have the freedom of movement and the authority to expect their cooperative plans to be implemented. They are also more likely to be equally dissatisfied with the current situation and more likely to be similarly attracted or repelled by the incentives in the situation.

According to this model, the greater the expectation of successful cooperation and the more potent the incentives to cooperate, the greater will be the likelihood for increases to be observed in process indicators of cooperation (more linkages, more institutionalization of those links, greater interpersonal trust) and in product indicators (reduced cost, more client access to services, more positive placements).

The expectancy model is an adaptation from Rotter's theory of learning[26] and has not been empirically tested on cooperative efforts in vocational education, but it does offer a plausible explanation of them. The model would caution us against setting collaborative goals that exceed the limits of what participants expect they can accomplish, though this may mean minimal change (even successful projects have not accomplished much service integration). The model also suggests that before incentives are applied, they should be tried on a sample of the target population to test their adequacy. For example, voluntary incentives may be insufficient and may have to be increased.

Conclusions

1. The present climate of waste reduction and austerity in government will certainly accelerate the existing push toward greater cooperation among education, training, business, government, and labor, but exhortation and appeals for local cooperation and coordination have not fared very well in the past. Case studies of cooperative efforts are not encouraging. Cooperation is often too complex and not worth the effort. Where interagency cooperation has worked, and there are many positive examples, two essential conditions seem to exist: continuous incentives for the local agencies to participate, and a prior history of successful experience in cooperative ventures that causes the participants to expect it to work in the new situation.

2. Local cooperation and coordination can be more easily justified for educational purposes than for purposes of reducing the unemployment rate. Cooperative efforts to help some people get

26. Julian B. Rotter, *Social Learning and Clinical Psychology* (Englewood Cliffs, N.J.: Prentice Hall, 1954).

placed will not increase the total number of jobs; such efforts will only redistribute the unemployment.

3. If additional incentives are to be used to stimulate cooperation and collaboration, it is important to ensure that the local responses to the incentives are institutionalized as integral parts of their operation, and not simply added on to existing activities.

4. A centralized preventive approach to reducing fragmentation of programs is necessary; there is little hope that local cooperative action will remedy the jurisdictional problems ensuing from proliferating programs at the state and federal levels. Fragmented programs wherein one needs a local coordinating council to put pieces together that should never have been separated in the first place show the need for legislative reform at state and federal levels. If policy makers did a more thorough job, many local problems of cooperation and coordination would be avoided.

CHAPTER XIII

The Challenge to Vocational Education

HARRY F. SILBERMAN

The Sixty-fourth Yearbook of the National Society for the Study of Education, entitled *Vocational Education*, concluded with the optimistic observation that "the American people have at last learned to place value upon vocational education."[1] The general tone of that period was optimistic. The Manpower Development and Training Act (1962) and the 1963 legislation on vocational education promised a brighter future for all phases of vocational education. Though the lack of adequate research in the field was lamented and lack of adequate articulation and coordination among programs was cited by several authors, the atmosphere was filled with hopeful signs that such problems would tend to disappear.

In contrast, the 1980s present a more somber picture. Unemployment is up,[2] the economy is faltering, and the major problems in vocational education, in all of education, have not disappeared. Indeed, the issues of the 1960s seem to have grown more serious with time. Although it is not possible to describe all the problems that confront vocational education in a brief concluding chapter, I will discuss a few of the more salient issues.

Issues

THE QUALITY ISSUE

Questions of quality are hard to answer, partly due to the great variety of contextual and individual factors that affect the quality

---

1. Melvin L. Barlow, "A Platform for Vocational Education in the Future," in *Vocational Education*, Sixty-fourth Yearbook of the National Society for the Study of Education, Part 1, ed. Melvin L. Barlow (Chicago: University of Chicago Press, 1965), p. 291.

2. For example, the *U.S. Current Population Survey Data* (Washington, D.C.: Bureau of Labor Statistics, U.S. Department of Labor) reported a 3.8 percent unemployment rate in 1967 and a 7.1 percent rate in 1980.

of programs, but also because the primary purpose of vocational education has been preparation for jobs, a purpose that is very elusive. First, the portion of the total life experience of any student that is devoted to vocational programs is so small that it is very difficult to detect program effects.

Second, a student's occupational choice and the employer's selection of employees constitute a complex dynamic that encompasses the entire life of the person, his family, social status, personality, prior work experience, and unspecified chance factors. Most vacancies are filled by people already known to the employer, known by people who already work in the organization, and by those known by trusted acquaintances of the employer. Placement in preferred jobs is more like being accepted into a fraternity than being awarded a merit badge for job skills, except for those occupations that demand an exceptionally high level of training for which a college degree is usually required.

The transition from school to work is often likened to a bridge which must be crossed from one stage of life to another. Vocational training is the vehicle that transports the person across the bridge. If the person does not find suitable employment, the quality of training must somehow have been defective. This analogy ignores the true nature of both education and work, and while such simplistic images are plausible, they tend to confuse the policy process and make it difficult to evaluate program quality. To begin with, the analogy assumes a sharp distinction between education and work which does not bear close inspection. Education *is* a form of work and work *is* a form of education. Some parts of both are educative; some parts of both are sheer effort with little or no personal growth.

Both work and schooling may result in learning, but the learning outcomes of both will depend upon such conditions as the type of setting, the type of activities which occur in that setting, and the type of consequences of those activities. For example, a work setting, with a rich variety of expert adult role models who are friendly and willing to help someone learn, with activities of moderate difficulty for one's abilities but with considerable responsibility and opportunity for self-management, and with prompt candid feedback on one's performance by supervisors and others who are affected by one's work, is likely to help one grow and develop both as a person and as an employee.

There is no sudden change in the student as he attends school; nor is there a sudden metamorphosis when the student leaves school and accepts a full-time job. He has most likely worked for pay at part-time jobs while attending school. There is also no sudden disappearance of instruction when someone accepts a full-time job. True, much instruction received on the job is of an informal nature and related to rules of organizational conduct rather than to the formal discipline of subject matter, but instruction it is. Furthermore, the simultaneous enrollment in school while working is an increasingly common occurrence.

Determining the transferability of schooling experiences to work settings is simply a special case of the more general problem of determining the transferability of one work setting to another. When someone moves from one job to another, or from school to work, the similarity of skills required in the two settings is only one of the variables that influence the person's transferability from the first setting to the second, and perhaps not the most important one. Geographic distance may be a more important factor; people are often unwilling to move away from friends and family to take work. One's social network often determines the direction of the move. Someone knows someone who knows of an opening, or one wishes to work with friends or relatives. Wage level is another factor determining where someone will work, and most jobs that do not require an advanced degree can be learned on the job. Perhaps the most critical variable affecting transferability is the job vacancy rate. In good times people are more transferable. When jobs are plentiful people can be more selective; but when jobs are scarce one will take a job with less pay, farther away, with novel skill requirements, poorer working conditions, and without knowing anyone in the organization.

It is not the fault of the training programs that shifts in the economic cycle reduce the demand for their graduates. Though vocational policy has always advocated the use of labor market information to plan what programs to offer, such data are quite unpredictable—witness the many plant closures that have been occurring across the country during the past few years where the dominant motive for the move was to find cheaper sources of labor. The vocational program also cannot alter the number of available jobs nor their location. For example, attempts to increase the number of vocational schools in the impoverished Appalachian region, as an inducement for industry to enter the area, caused instead an outmigration of young people because they had acquired skills that were not needed in that region but were salable in other areas.

One way of improving the job preparation function of vocational education is to establish close linkages between schools and the private sector. The attempt at enlisting the private sector in short-term, open-entry, open-exit training programs capitalizes on industry's interest in maintaining an adequately trained labor pool. However, the investment is likely to be confined to narrowly company-specific technical skills that are, by design, nontransferable to other competing firms. So, if the criterion for a quality vocational program is the extent to which the trainee attains occupational versatility with transferable skills, such short-term private sector programs may not be very successful.

The problems of using job placement as a criterion of program quality are sufficiently intractable to warrant alternative indicators. A more useful alternative to job preparation is general education or personal growth and development. To be effective, teachers must believe that students benefit from their teaching, and in their daily interactions with students they must find evidence to confirm these beliefs. Such evidence is both a reward and an incentive to further effort, and those who have reasonable expectations about their influence on students are more likely to feel successful. Consequently, it is better for teachers to focus on attainable goals that are intrinsic to the educational process itself than on extrinsic goals such as employment and earnings over which they have little or no control.

In this viewpoint, the primary purpose of vocational education is to promote full human development through exposure of the learner to activities that are intrinsically meaningful and absorbing. These activities may utilize various forms of exploratory work experience as part of the educational process, but the purpose of the work is to further the education of the student; the work is subordinate to the educational process. This is work for education.

In the intrinsic perspective, vocational education activities are designed to enhance the quality of present experience, to engage learners in productive and creative ways that enrich the spirit. The emphasis is on the playful aspects of work. The criterion of success of the program is the personal growth of learners as revealed by their dedication to the tasks and by their level of voluntary participation in constructive activities.

To evaluate vocational education from an intrinsic perspective, one must ask what immediate benefits are obtained by students in such programs compared with students in purely academic programs. In the intrinsic perspective, income and future placement are secondary concerns; human development and personal satisfaction with the experiences provided in the program are primary. Although extrinsic concerns with economic progress are important, there is little that can be done by the vocational educator to alter the social class and general occupational status of students. The important objective within the control of the vocational educator is to improve the quality of the learning environment for students in the program.

Casual observation of vocational students at work on school and community projects generally reveals that these are popular activities. Students seem to enjoy their individual and collective efforts because they result in a tangible product or accomplishment. Whether they are building a house, a dune buggy, or whatever, the activity itself is totally absorbing. They may never choose construction as an occupation and never live in the house they are building, but its existence is their own creation. The process itself is sufficient to sustain the activity. In most vocational activities, as with sports, music, and the arts, students seem to participate more for the intrinsic properties; they are forms of play.

PROMOTING HUMAN DEVELOPMENT

But beyond making students happy, emphasizing the intrinsic qualities of vocational education can lead to a well-designed vocational program that promotes human development along at least five dimensions. First, vocational projects provide an arena in which we can provide students with a sense of personal competence. Students become aware of how things work, whether it be how one's television or automobile works, how a business operates, or how newspapers are published. There is a natural opportunity within vocational education for the demystification of modern technology. One may acquire a sense of control over one's physical and social environment by participating in a wide variety of community projects where one may test oneself and discover one's areas of competence.

A second dimension for personal growth is aesthetic expression. Most people take pleasure in doing a job well. The satisfaction and fulfillment of creative expression is not limited to the traditional arts. One may also feel creative when repairing a broken piece of furniture, installing a garage door opener, raising a prize-winning animal, typing at high speed, or cooking a gourmet meal.

A third dimension for personal growth is integrity. Implicit in craftsmanship is a way of life that may be modeled for the student. If you cut corners and fail to do the job right, it does not work, and one generally has to start over again. A poorly programmed computer is unforgiving. After tearing apart a project several times and wasting one's earlier careless effort, one begins to keep the effort honest from the outset, especially with help from quality role models who exemplify such discipline and integrity.

A fourth dimension for personal growth is cooperativeness. In most vocational activities one is dependent on others working on the same project. There is intrinsic pleasure to be derived in teamwork and collaboration. One can acquire improved interpersonal skills in communicating and negotiating with others in cooperative vocational projects, especially in age-integrated field settings.

A fifth dimension of personal growth is a heightened sense of altruism. Vocational projects offer an exceptional opportunity to provide real service to the community and to obtain visible evidence of one's accomplishment in the form of improved facilities, satisfied customers, and respect and appreciation from the recipients of the services.

In short, the intrinsic benefits of vocational education may contribute to the growth of students' personal qualities along many dimensions. Such growth is sought in the immediate process of project participation and is not deferred to an unpredictable future.

In the long run, such personal qualities may be as vital to the attainment of extrinsic economic benefits as the acquisition of technical skills. More often than not people fail to be admitted into the primary labor market or are fired or fail to be promoted on their jobs because they lack those personal qualities rather than because of technical deficiencies.

Emphasis on the intrinsic benefits of vocational education does not require the student to sacrifice economic gains for self-fulfillment. It is simply a more indirect way of getting there. The focus is on improving the quality of existing vocational programs over which educators have authority and control rather than emphasizing future job placements over which they exercise little control.

Increasingly, vocational services should move off-campus for a variety of reasons. Rapid obsolescence of equipment and limited funds offer certain cost advantages to using the facilities of existing organizations in the community; the community offers a greater variety of adult role models, provides greater age heterogeneity and a more communal learning environment; and realistic work settings can offer students opportunities for authentic responsibility with which to test themselves.

This is educational work experience, not to be confused with part-time jobs that students use to earn spending money. Too often such jobs offer little or no intellectual challenge and hardly any interaction with mature adults. In many cases youth employment may be worse than high school.

Such vocational education experience should be provided for *all* learners and should not be stigmatized as the exclusive preserve of special groups. The prospective engineer as well as the technician, the future surgeon as well as the orderly, should be involved in vocational education. Allocating sufficient resources for groups with special needs should be possible without compartmentalizing vocational education.

To evaluate intrinsic results one must use measures of personal growth rather than employment statistics or salary records. The types of questions to be answered from an intrinsic perspective include some of the following: Are students acquiring the technical skills? Are they enjoying themselves? Do they learn to talk easily with adults? Do they learn to speak out on their own behalf? Do they learn to ask for help when it is needed? Do they appreciate the beauty of their products? Are they more willing to risk making a mistake? Do they learn to help each other? Do they learn to accept responsibility and regulate their own actions?

Unfortunately, research has not provided much information on the intrinsic effects of vocational education. The comparisons of vocational, general, and academic students in the major longitudinal surveys describe differences among these groups but do not explain them.

What the longitudinal studies *do* show, is that we have a tracking system. The vocational education students are different from those in general or academic programs. They come from lower socioeconomic families, have less academic ability and lower school performance. They value occupational security and desire more practical vocational courses, have more faith in the school's ability to help them prepare for a job, and on leaving high school are more likely to work full-time than general and academic students who are more likely to have part-time, temporary jobs while they attend college.

Research has not provided much information on the effects of vocational education. In general, the longitudinal studies say more about tracking, inequality, and social stratification than about particular program effectiveness. Indeed, in her chapter, Berryman has drawn an interesting conclusion from the longitudinal studies. She attributes the lack of negative attitudes of vocational students to their having been provided with a niche in the high school and a future direction with which they can identify. That such findings may simply reflect initial differences in expectations of students in the three curricula needs to be tested. We need true experiments of alternative instructional strategies using both intrinsic and extrinsic measures of effects. We also need more naturalistic ethnographic studies that will allow us to observe more closely the full variation among vocational programs and to learn how they are perceived by the students.

Perhaps the best indicators of the quality of vocational programs are to be found in the statements made by those who have been involved in such programs. Such comments as the following, collected in an unpublished series of interviews of high school students by Ellen Lees, a graduate student at the University of California (Los Angeles), reveal how some young people feel about their vocational work experience. The following are typical responses:

"My job makes me feel important—more like an adult."

"When I am at work, I do what I want. No one is looking over my shoulder. I feel more responsible."

"It is easier to learn on the job. Nobody wants to learn when you're pushed into it. At work, you learn what you need—that's all. That's enough. Working with older people makes me feel different—makes me feel like an adult."

"At work, I act more serious. I'm alone and more responsible. School and work can never be the same because at school you're surrounded by your friends and you can act any way you want and at work, you're surrounded by adults. You act different which is OK. I like that."

Owen and Owens studied job site characteristics that students perceived as contributing the greatest learning experiences for various types of youth.[3] They found that what students considered most valuable was the opportunity to work closely with adults at the job site, taking on genuine responsibility for tasks that were moderately challenging. The students want to try out the work on their own; they want to talk to the adults on the job and get along with them; they want clear directions to follow and like being given an adult responsibility. They like the challenge and find it helpful to observe skilled adults doing the job, and the students benefit from adult encouragement when they are doing the tasks well. Designing such programs is the challenge for vocational education.

THE EQUITY ISSUE

Evaluations of vocational education as preparation for jobs is also difficult because the students who enroll in vocational education are different from those who enroll in academic programs. The vocational education student is less likely to go on to achieve a higher education and occupational status in professional and man-

3. Sharon K. Owen and Thomas R. Owens, "Insuring Quality Learning in Employer Site Placements" (Paper presented at the annual meeting of the American Educational Research Association in Los Angeles, 1981).

agerial fields than those who enroll in college preparatory or four-year academic college transfer programs. The "best" students take the college preparatory route. Consequently, it *appears* as if the most effective preparation is provided by the academic program. The doctors, lawyers, engineers, and managers move into the best paying jobs and suffer the least unemployment. The segregation of students into two groups (one going on to obtain a college degree and moving to the front of the hiring queue, the other taking a vocational program in preparation for lesser jobs) creates, by association, an inequality between vocational and academic programs. It is a self-fulfilling prophesy. As the degree holders get better jobs, the superior students are more likely to choose the academic programs and distance themselves from the vocational program stigma, thus confirming the lowered public assessment of the vocational programs. The absence of the best students from the vocational program also deprives those programs of the most essential ingredient in any form of quality instruction, a critical mass of pro-achievement role models who show others by their example what it is like to be involved in the learning process.

As the bifurcation between the vocational and college preparatory programs has widened, legislators have increasingly provided categorical aid for vocational programs aimed at special target populations. Legislators have levied substantial appropriations for programs to assist minorities and the poor who are usually at the rear of the certification line. It is assumed that if such persons are given skills for less preferred occupations they will have a better chance at obtaining employment. There may be some evidence to support this assumption, but there is an inherent contradiction in attempting at the same time to integrate the disadvantaged into mainstream society and simultaneously targeting funds for segregated programs for such groups. Mangum has noted that targeted programs do not work as well as programs that are not too highly segregated.[4] When working with concentrations of poorly motivated and underachieving youth who are lacking in success models, it is difficult to generate a program atmosphere conducive to rein-

---

4. Garth L. Mangum, *Career Education and the Comprehensive Employment and Training Act* (Washington, D.C.: Office of Career Education, U.S. Department of Health, Education, and Welfare, 1978).

forcing desirable behaviors; thus failure, rather than success, becomes the norm. This is not to discount the need for assistance for such youth. "Rather, the experience to date indicates that these special needs should be met within a program context that permits close contact and socialization with persons from other backgrounds and other groups." [5] Other evidence collected by Oakes[6] showed that grouping students into tracks does not enhance learning and has negative effects on student achievement for students at the bottom—lowered self-concepts, lowered aspirations, increased delinquency, and more frequent school misbehavior. In addition, poor and minority students were found consistently in disproportionately large percentages in the lowest achieving groups in a study of thirty-eight schools in the United States. Homogeneous grouping is not necessarily forced; for the most part such grouping occurs as a result of students with similar interests and talents enrolling in the same classes.

Unfortunately much of the school-to-work transition in America is a tracking process. Those who come into school with advantages are very likely to hold those advantages in and beyond school, make a better transition to work, and enjoy better jobs for the rest of their working lives. Those at the low end of the social distribution move along a different track. They are more likely to drop out of school and become unemployed, have the lowest self-esteem, and become dependent on public assistance agencies. Variations among individuals in family background, amount of schooling, and level of employment are quite stable.

Inequities are maintained in many efforts to help the poor. For example, when special funds are allocated to immigrant populations with special needs, such populations have often been unfairly placed in the lowest track. Indochinese refugees were typically placed in the lower track on arrival in this country regardless of their background. This may have been an improvement for many who came from extremely impoverished backgrounds, and it may have been an ideal placement for those who made a quick and smooth adjustment, but it was a serious demotion for many of the early im-

5. Ibid., p. 28.

6. Jean Oakes, "Ability Grouping and Differences in the Education Experience of Students" (doct. diss., University of California, Los Angeles, 1981).

migrants who came from more favorable circumstances and who had already worked at higher status occupations within their native country.

It is not surprising that immigrants end up in the lowest track. They are separated from the mainstream American by language, culture, housing, schools, and employment. Such isolation precludes the establishment of social networks in the Anglo community. Such networks are necessary links to the better jobs for several reasons. First, in the preferred jobs, employer perceptions of the attributes of applicants affect their decisions as much if not more than the actual skill level of the applicant. Trustworthiness of applicants is judged by their prior experience in organizations familiar to the employer and by references to personal qualities by persons trusted by the employer. Second, Anglos with attractive jobs are more likely to have information about the best job opportunities. Third, geographic dispersion of the preferred jobs requires a wide network of contacts who may assist one in getting placed.

Credentialing barriers also hinder the assimilation of immigrant groups since licenses and credentials are generally nontransferable across national lines. This is partly a matter of protectionism; the greatest resistance to easing credentialing restrictions comes from those with whom the newcomers may be competing. As Hume noted, "all conflict springs from scarcity."

Inequities are maintained in many efforts to help the poor because of the way the public agency has been defined. Its historic mission has been to assist the disadvantaged and hard-to-employ. With increasing privatization of social services, the public sector increasingly becomes the exclusive domain of the have-nots. Unfortunately, such public agencies offer services that may serve as an incentive for sustained dependency among their clientele. For example, many Vietnamese refugees were encouraged to take the whole package of social services even though they only needed medical care. The tight funding of public agencies also tends to render them less responsive to individual differences among their clientele. Bureaucratic efficiency and strict literal compliance with standard procedures reduce uncertainty among overburdened administrative personnel at the risk of being nonresponsive to differences in ability and in client preferences, for example, allocation of clients to underenrolled service providers regardless of fit. Consequently programs administered by public agencies often become stigmatized as being of lesser quality and many employers avoid them.

The consequence of inequitable tracking systems for immigrants and other disadvantaged groups is increased underemployment. Problems of underemployment may seem better than those of unemployment, since underemployment gets job seekers jobs and reduces welfare roles. But such effects may have long-term aversive consequences. Socialization effects of the work environment may alter the expectations of the immigrant and build a sense of being locked into the menial job for life. The segmented nature of the labor market confirms that expectation since the potential for upward mobility is, in fact, very limited (for example, technicians do not become engineers). Of course one can go back to school for credentials for higher status jobs; but that is expensive and time consuming, the admissions procedures are very selective, and the need to compete in a labor market of highly educated people makes it risky. No doubt the competition for the more meaningful jobs will continue to grow and will stimulate increased tensions in the workplace, leading to demands for improvements in the quality of working life, and such tensions may accelerate the flight by industry to labor markets where workers make fewer demands, and consequently increase competition further.

Although the above example is in some ways peculiar to the Indochinese refugee problem, it has certain commonalities with other hard-to-employ groups such as displaced workers, minorities, older workers, disabled, and otherwise disadvantaged persons. The problems of inequity for all these groups derive from isolation from the main social networks that operate in the labor market and lack of credentials that provide entry into the more preferred jobs. Gordon and Trow make an interesting distinction between the deprived hard-to-employ minority youth and those merely disadvantaged youth who simply need better services to bridge the gap between school and work.[7] With help, the disadvantaged readily

7. Margaret S. Gordon and Martin Trow, *Youth Education and Unemployment Problems: A Study Prepared for the Carnegie Council on Policy Studies in Higher Education* (Berkeley, Calif.: Carnegie Council on Policy Studies in Higher Education, 1979).

make the shift to stable employment, but the deprived have great difficulty. An important distinction between these groups is the access by the merely disadvantaged to personal networks that provide references and sponsorship that impress potential employers. Such networks are seldom available to the deprived. Perhaps racial and social class segregation in housing and schooling reduces access to the information channels about job vacancies. If so, vocational education is unlikely to narrow the gap in employment between these two groups.

For the past decade, public policy for remediation of problems of the hard-to-employ has tended toward income maintenance, public service employment, and on-the-job training. There has been a plethora of legislation in response to the special needs of particular target groups. Yet, while the legislated programs provide some income transfer, they have been criticized for providing little education and training. The benefits last only as long as the training subsidy, and the targeted groups remain at the bottom of the occupational hierarchy. Clearly, people want to learn on the job. They want assurance that their training leads to something interesting. Most have creative talents that they would like to use; they dream for something more, but unless their training has growth-enhancing features, unless the problem of aggregate employment can be resolved, those dreams will not materialize and special aid programs will continue to be stigmatized.

With the Reagan administration, major cutbacks in the public services employment program have been made as a counterinflationary measure. The selection of that program for excision, however, stemmed partially from a belief that involving the private sector would help assimilate the hard-to-employ, and partly from a disenchantment with the administration of the publicly subsidized jobs program. Yet past efforts question whether the private sector can be expected to work outside the framework of its organizational goals to assume a genuinely educational function. The Targeted Jobs Tax Credit program failed because the private sector did not put up with members of the hard-to-employ group; they were considered troublesome and not worth the incentives that were being offered. There is also some question about whether the private employers are prepared to redesign their jobs and provide the close supportive supervision required by deprived workers. In most instances, the private sector has flourished precisely because it has screened out the hard-to-employ. Many deprived workers act in a manner antithetical to the orderly conduct of business. It is very hard to make a profit and be a social service agency at the same time.

Yet, if the vocational education and employment and training system is to be fair, it must assist older persons, refugees, the young, and the hard-to-employ in finding a place in the economy. Perhaps less emphasis on exclusive programs for special problem groups would yield programs that are more fair and effective. They would focus on goals related to human development and refinement of taste, manners, language, technical skills, dependability, and self-esteem. The new criteria would be used to determine whether program suppliers did their job and should be compensated. Such standards for all participants, including the hard-to-employ, associated with fiscal and administrative consequences if not achieved, would offer better protection for the hard-to-employ persons then categorical prescription of segregated training inputs for these groups.

Worksite training in the private sector is also seen as a desirable policy, but high quality supervision and redesign of the work may be necessary for such experiences to make a contribution to the independence of hard-to-employ persons. Undoubtedly, incentives for the private sector to participate under these conditions will have to be increased substantially over current levels, but the long-term benefits in improved equity and productivity may be well worth the investment. The advent of such measures would go far in legitimizing public equal opportunity efforts and pose another challenge for vocational education in the 1980s.

THE FUNDING ISSUE

Another current issue is the uncomfortable matter of allocating resources in an era of scarcity. Vocational education must compete for limited resources with basic education programs that have greater legitimacy because of their generalizability and relevance to continued education. Vocational education programs also compete among themselves for funding. The postsecondary programs have gained greater credibility in requesting their portion of the total budget than secondary programs because the older graduates of the postsecondary programs are more readily employed.

All education and training systems inevitably consist of power relationships among their component subsystems. It is rare for all components to be equally effective and well regarded. One is bound to have more status or be more vulnerable than another. The more preferred, more legitimate components are granted the power position, even if only by a small amount. Such components have a preferred claim on the budget, attract the most competent staff and students, and offer greater opportuity for staff advancement. Vocational education programs at the secondary level are always described in the policy papers as being integral parts of the traditional comprehensive high school curriculum to avoid the stigma of being lesser alternatives to the college preparatory programs. One reason for insisting that vocational education be viewed as an integral part of the educational system is to protect its share of the common budget. For example, there is concern that in a period of scarcity the vocational education program will have its budget reduced in favor of maintaining the level of support for the basic skills portion of the budget. The funding problem also divides public and private vocational programs, vocational and CETA programs, and even subject matter areas within vocational education (for example, agriculture versus homemaking).

The solution to the funding issue generally includes more prudent management of existing resources. At best, different programs should be required to cooperate to reduce duplication and waste, At worst, different vocational programs may be totally integrated and no longer regarded as separate. This latter alternative is difficult to implement because the management of each of the several programs has a vested interest in maintaining its own identity. Genuine service integration is fraught with political and administrative obstacles. Legislative exhortations for collaboration result in perfunctory cooperative efforts that conceal basic jurisdictional differences that are only amenable to system-wide structural reforms in delineating program functions, and in the management and allocation of resources. For example, if equity is an important policy goal, a greater share of the federal funds for vocational education should be allocated to the secondary rather than to the postsecondary level for college grants and loans, since most hard-to-employ youth do not enroll in postsecondary institutions, loan or no loan.

If service integration is an important policy goal, it will be necessary to revise completely the federal legislation that created separate programs. For example, if greater collaboration between vocational education programs and CETA programs is desired, the vocational education legislation and the CETA legislation may have to become a single piece of legislation that merges the management, incentives, and evaluative criteria for the two programs. But since bold initiatives are fraught with political consequences, it is more likely that the federal role in vocational education will eventually be lessened by transferring the problem to state and local levels via block grants. That would be a reasonable move if the interests of all socioeconomic strata were represented in local and state decision-making bodies. Unfortunately, some minority groups are not confident that their interests will be represented at the local level if the federal government relinquishes its leadership in vocational education. Funds might be channeled where political pressure is greatest rather than where the need is greatest.

There is a close relationship between the quality-equity issues and the scarcity issue. If the schools had successfully developed a program of sufficient quality there would conceivably be no need for the provision of second-chance opportunities via expensive compensatory employment and training programs. When resources are plentiful it is feasible and administratively expedient to set up elaborate employment and training programs as a safety net for those who do not benefit from the school's vocational education programs. In times of scarcity, however, the tendency is to challenge the public school's ability to do the job in the first place and to hold it accountable rather than extending added resources to compensatory programs. In times of scarcity, there has been retrenchment in the income transfer features of the CETA legislation; the public service employment programs have been severely curtailed.

When funds are scarce, tradeoffs between vocational education programs and alternative methods of addressing youth unemployment are considered. For example, one asks, is it more effective to put an increment of resources into vocational education or to use that money as incentive for private employers to hire deprived youth and train them on the job? If enough funding is not available, neither option may be effective.

The problems of youth unemployment and separation of schooling and work may have to get much worse before the public gives sufficient priority to these issues to warrant the level of effort required, regardless of the options that are chosen to get the job done. The status of vocational education influences the priority assigned to it by the public. So long as the jobs associated with vocational training are associated with less prestige and income than those associated with college preparation, the status of vocational education will suffer. Only when there is an extreme shortage of appropriately trained persons will it be given priority. Even when qualified workers are scarce it is hard to determine whether such shortages can be attributed to insufficient occupational preparation or to such poor wages and working conditions in those jobs that trained persons have quickly abandoned them in favor of more attractive alternatives. For years, high schools across the nation have trained many more auto mechanics than there are jobs. But there is a high turnover rate among auto mechanics due to low wages and unsatisfactory working conditions. By contrast, there are no shortages among well-paid supervisors in those jobs. Similar arguments can be offered for the shortages among other occupations such as licensed vocational nurses, child care workers, and typists. As real shortages of technically trained personnel reach the stage where the pay and status of these occupations are at the level of jobs for which a college degree is required, vocational education will achieve higher priority and adequate funding, but not before.

In chapter 2, Swanson notes that vocational education budget allocations have been steadily falling behind as a percentage of the GNP, the total education budget, the total employment and training budget, and the total federal budget outlays. Recent recission decisions have also not been kind to vocational education and employment and training programs. Such policy actions imply reservations about the credibility of vocational education. Why else would there be disproportionate budget cuts? Yet, the research evidence is equivocal and clearly does not answer the question of whether vocational education is effective. Partly the lack of definitive evidence is due to poor definition of what vocational education is. Partly it is due to the self-selection bias of students who enroll in the various programs. Partly it is due to the differences among types of information on which one might make a judgment. It is one thing to show that programs are, or are not, associated with differences in student outcomes and quite another to understand why the differences occur.

The budget cuts in vocational education seem especially sad in the light of the absence of evidence and the testimonials by young people that such programs offer them for the first time the opportunity to prove what they can do, to help them become part of the mainstream society. Perhaps such budgetary decisions are not informed by empirical evidence of vocational education's deficiencies. It may simply be a judgment by decision makers that vocational education is the least prestigious and most expensive part of the curriculum. Or, vocational education may be receiving some of the blame for the high rates of minority youth unemployment, or perhaps the state and local educational authorities have come to believe that support for vocational programs is a federal responsibility and federal withdrawal is a reaction to that expectation. We simply do not have enough information. We need much better research on the allocation of education resources, especially about the interaction between centralized decisions and client reactions to those decisions at the local level.

Conclusion

A variety of policy proposals have been offered in response to the three issues described above. For examples: greater involvement of the private sector; short-term worksite learning opportunities; emphasis on basic skills; improved labor market information; closer matching of labor supply to demand; and greater collaboration among agencies that provide services. Most of these policy proposals are not described with sufficient specificity to ascertain their probable feasibility and impact. Unless the policies are feasible their objectives will never be achieved; they must at least be capable of implementation. For example, I have argued that program quality can be improved if we focus on intrinsic benefits. We must design programs to promote human development and evaluate them on their noneconomic returns. The test of the intrinsic approach resides in the consequences of its implementation, but if its implementation is too complicated for the staff to understand, it will not be implemented. For such a proposal to be effective, there must be specifications for the preparation of a cadre of personnel with sufficient skills to appreciate and to capitalize on the fact that in most vocational activities, as with sports, music, and the arts, students participate more for their playful properties—and therein lies their educational value. To improve the quality of vocational education, teachers must be committed to enhancing the intrinsic properties, believe in their efficacy, and be willing to execute the approach faithfully.

I have also noted that the equity issue can be alleviated if we can avoid tracking students, for tracking generates inequality where it did not exist before. Schools may not be able to eliminate inequity altogether, but at least they need not contribute to it. We should evaluate our programs on their effects on equity. For example, how important are they in enhancing the personal dignity and independence of the student? Do they segregate students by restricting eligibility to the most disadvantaged? The stigma resulting from such practices can only have a deleterious effect in the long run.

Finally, I have indicated that the funding issue is partly the result of undesirable side effects of ill-considered legislation. If training programs do not have sufficient local support to offset political opposition to their implementation, they will fail. If legislation merely adds new training programs on top of existing ones that are not considered effective, the result will be more duplication, waste, and fragmentation. The jurisdictional disputes over turf will further obstruct the successful implementation of the new program. Exhortation and legislative appeals to coordinate and collaborate will not alleviate these disputes.

The funds appropriated for the implementation of training programs must match the magnitude of the problem. To underfund a program is to reduce it to a service delivery operation, from what may have been a problem-solving operation. Excessive caution in budget allocation is the best way to doom the program to fail at the outset.

In conclusion, we must ask whether vocational education policies attempt to solve long-standing, deeply rooted problems with quick and easy, one-time, popular remedial services, without addressing the social contexts or the organizational structures that sustain the problems.

Name Index

Subject Index

Academic Growth Study, 174-76, 178

Academic learning time, research on, 161-62

Academic skills: effect of vocational education on, 192; importance of, in hiring decisions, 8, 191. *See also,* Basic skills.

Agricultural Extension Service, 23

Agriculture, decline in employment in, 71

All Volunteer Force, 188

American Association for Community and Junior Colleges, 208, 281

American Bar Association, 105

American College of Life Underwriters, 93

American Federation of Teachers, 11

American Society for Training and Development, 220

American Vocational Association, 5, 11-12, 153, 281

Anti-poverty acts, initiated by President Kennedy, 118

Apprenticeship training, 16, 26

Association of Independent Colleges and Schools, 215

Attitude toward school, among "low-track" students, 241-42

Basic skills: comparison of performance of vocational and nonvocational students in, 155; effectiveness of career education programs in promoting learning of, 156-57; issue of responsibility for teaching of, in vocational education, 165-68; programs in, for out-of-school youth, 157-59; research on factors related to learning of, 161-65; study of different approaches to instruction in, 159-60. *See also,* Academic skills.

Black youth: inadequacies of "supply-side" factors as explanation for unemployment among, 246-48; increasing enrollment of, in schools, 235; reasons for high unemployment rates among, 239-40; tensions between, and their employers, 252-53; uncertain prospects of, for transition to better jobs, 250-51; unemployment rates among, for high school graduates and for dropouts, 237-38

Black workers, position of, in labor force, 82

Career education: aspects of, in relation to vocational guidance and vocational education, 125-27; effectiveness of, in promoting learning of basic skills, 156-57; Minnesota model of, 124; summary of perspectives on theory of, 121-23; work competencies as basis for curriculum of, 125

Career behavior, variables related to, 123

Career Intern Program, 264

Carnegie Council on Policy Studies in Higher Education, comments on report of, regarding vocational education, 45-46

Certification, definition of, 92

Certifying agencies, 111-15

Civil Rights Act (1946), 102

Commission on the Humanities, report of, 46-47

Commission on Vocational Education (1914), 1, 3, 6, 7, 11

Community and Junior College Journal, 207-8

Community work education councils, efforts of, to improve relations between employers and educators, 282-84. *See also,* Work Education Councils.

Competency-based tests, as indicators of employability, 145-47

Comprehensive Employment and Training Act (CETA), 1, 28, 260, 263, 266, 279, 280, 283, 303, 321; curtailment of public service employment programs under, 322; decentralized administration of, 298;

INFORMATION ABOUT MEMBERSHIP IN THE SOCIETY

From its small beginnings in the early 1900s, the National Society for the Study of Education has grown to a major educational organization with more than 4,000 members in the United States, Canada, and overseas. Members include professors, researchers, graduate students, and administrators in colleges and universities; teachers, supervisors, curriculum specialists, and administrators in elementary and secondary schools; and a considerable number of persons who are not formally connected with an educational institution. Membership in the Society is open to all persons who desire to receive its publications.

Since its establishment the Society has sought to promote its central purpose—the stimulation of investigations and discussions of important educational issues—through regular publication of a two-volume yearbook that is sent to all members. Many of these volumes have been so well received throughout the profession that they have gone into several printings. A recently inaugurated series of substantial paperbacks on Contemporary Educational Issues supplements the series of yearbooks and allows for treatment of a wider range of educational topics than can be addressed each year through the yearbooks alone.

Through membership in the Society one can add regularly to one's professional library at a very reasonable cost. Members also help to sustain a publication program that is widely recognized for its unique contributions to the literature of education.

The categories of membership, and the dues in each category for 1982, are as follows:

>*Regular.* The member receives a clothbound copy of each part of the two-volume yearbook (approximately 300 pages per volume). Annual dues, $20.
>
>*Comprehensive.* The member receives clothbound copies of the two-volume yearbook and the two volumes in the current paperback series. Annual dues, $35.
>
>*Retirees and Graduate Students.* Reduced dues—Regular, $16; Comprehensive, $31.
>The above reduced dues are available to (a) those who have retired or are over sixty-five years of age and who have been members of the Society for at least ten years, and (b) graduate students in their first year of membership.

Life Membership. Persons sixty years of age or over may hold a Regular Membership for life upon payment of a lump sum based upon the life expectancy for their age group. Consult the Secretary-Treasurer for further details.

New members are required to pay an entrance fee of $1, in addition to the dues, in their first year of membership.

Membership is for the calendar year and dues are payable on or before January 1. A reinstatement fee of $.50 must be added to dues payments made after January 1.

In addition to receiving the publications of the Society as described above, members participate in the nomination and election of the six-member Board of Directors, which is responsible for managing the business and affairs of the Society, including the authorization of volumes to appear in the yearbook series. Two members of the Board are elected each year for three-year terms. Members of the Society who have contributed to its publications and who indicate a willingness to serve are eligible for election to the Board.

Members are urged to attend the one or more meetings of the Society that are arranged each year in conjunction with the annual meetings of major educational organizations. The purpose of such meetings is to present, discuss, and critique volumes in the current yearbook series. Announcements of meetings for the ensuing year are sent to members in December.

Upon written request from a member, the Secretary-Treasurer will send the current directory of members, synopses of meetings of the Board of Directors, and the annual financial report.

Persons desiring further information about membership may write to

KENNETH J. REHAGE, Secretary-Treasurer
National Society for the Study of Education

5835 Kimbark Ave.
Chicago, Ill. 60637

PUBLICATIONS OF THE NATIONAL SOCIETY FOR THE STUDY OF EDUCATION

1. The Yearbooks

NOTICE: Many of the early yearbooks of this series are now out of print. In the following list, those titles to which an asterisk is prefixed are not available for purchase.

*Fifteenth Yearbook, 1916, Part II—*The Relationship between Persistence in School and Home Conditions.* Charles E. Holley.
*Fifteenth Yearbook, 1916, Part III—*The Junior High School.* Aubrey A. Douglass.
*Sixteenth Yearbook, 1917, Part I—*Second Report of the Committee on Minimum Essentials in Elementary-School Subjects.* W. C. Bagley, W. W. Charters, F. N. Freeman, W. S. Gray, Ernest Horn, J. H. Hoskinson, W. S. Monroe, C. F. Munson, H. C. Pryor, L. W. Rapeer, G. M. Wilson, and H. B. Wilson.
*Sixteenth Yearbook, 1917, Part II—*The Efficiency of College Students as Conditioned by Age at Entrance and Size of High School.* B. F. Pittenger.
*Seventeenth Yearbook, 1918, Part I—*Third Report of the Committee on Economy of Time in Education.* W. C. Bagley, B. B. Bassett, M. E. Branom, Alice Camerer, J. E. Dealey, C. A. Ellwood, E. B. Greene, A. B. Hart, J. F. Hosic, E. T. Housh, W. H. Mace, L. R. Marston, H. C. McKown, H. E. Mitchell, W. V. Reavis, D. Snedden, and H. B. Wilson.
*Seventeenth Yearbook, 1918, Part II—*The Measurement of Educational Products.* E. J. Ashbaugh, W. A. Averill, L. P. Ayers, F. W. Ballou, Edna Bryner, B. R. Buckingham, S. A. Courtis, M. E. Haggerty, C. H. Judd, George Melcher, W. S. Monroe, E. A. Nifenecker, and E. L. Thorndike.
*Eighteenth Yearbook, 1919, Part I—*The Professional Preparation of High-School Teachers.* G. N. Cade, S. S. Colvin, Charles Fordyce, H. H. Foster, T. S. Gosling, W. S. Gray, L. V. Koos, A. R. Mead, H. L. Miller, F. C. Whitcomb, and Clifford Woody.
*Eighteenth Yearbook, 1919, Part II—*Fourth Report of Committee on Economy of Time in Education.* F. C. Ayer, F. N. Freeman, W. S. Gray, Ernest Horn, W. S. Monroe, and C. E. Seashore.
*Nineteenth Yearbook, 1920, Part I—*New Materials of Instruction.* Prepared by the Society's Committee on Materials of Instruction.
*Nineteenth Yearbook, 1920, Part II—*Classroom Problems in the Education of Gifted Children.* T. S. Henry.
*Twentieth Yearbook, 1921, Part I—*New Materials of Instruction.* Second Report by Society's Committee.
*Twentieth Yearbook, 1921, Part II—*Report of the Society's Committee on Silent Reading.* M. A. Burgess, S. A. Courtis, C. E. Germane, W. S. Gray, H. A. Greene, Regina R. Heller, H. J. H. Hoover, J. A. O'Brien, J. L. Packer, Daniel Starch, W. W. Theisen, G. A. Yoakam, and representatives of other school systems.
*Twenty-first Yearbook, 1922, Parts I and II—*Intelligence Tests and Their Use,* Part I—*The Nature, History, and General Principles of Intelligence Testing.* E. L. Thorndike, S. S. Colvin, Harold Rugg, G. M. Whipple, Part II—*The Administrative Use of Intelligence Tests.* H. W. Holmes, W. K. Layton, Helen Davis, Agnes L. Rogers, Rudolf Pintner, M. R. Trabue, W. S. Miller, Bessie L. Gambrill, and others. The two parts are bound together.
*Twenty-second Yearbook, 1923, Part I—*English Composition: Its Aims, Methods and Measurements.* Earl Hudelson.
*Twenty-second Yearbook, 1923, Part II—*The Social Studies in the Elementary and Secondary School.* A. S. Barr, J. J. Coss, Henry Harap, R. W. Hatch, H. C. Hill, Ernest Horn, C. H. Judd, L. C. Marshall, F. M. McMurry, Earle Rugg, H. O. Rugg, Emma Schweppe, Mabel Snedaker, and C. W. Washburne.
*Twenty-third Yearbook, 1924, Part I—*The Education of Gifted Children.* Report of the Society's Committee. Guy M. Whipple, Chairman.
*Twenty-third Yearbook, 1924, Part II—*Vocational Guidance and Vocational Education for Industries.* A. H. Edgerton and others.
*Twenty-fourth Yearbook, 1925, Part I—*Report of the National Committee on Reading.* W. S. Gray, Chairman, F. W. Ballou, Rose L. Hardy, Ernest Horn, Francis Jenkins, S. A. Leonard, Estaline Wilson, and Laura Zirbes.
*Twenty-fourth Yearbook, 1925, Part II—*Adapting the Schools to Individual Differences.* Report of the Society's Committee. Carleton W. Washburne, Chairman.
*Twenty-fifth Yearbook, 1926, Part I—*The Present Status of Safety Education.* Report of the Society's Committee. Guy M. Whipple, Chairman.
*Twenty-fifth Yearbook, 1926, Part II—*Extra-Curricular Activities.* Report of the Society's Committee. Leonard V. Koos, Chairman.
*Twenty-sixth Yearbook, 1927, Part I—*Curriculum-making: Past and Present.* Report of the Society's Committee. Harold O. Rugg, Chairman.
*Twenty-sixth Yearbook, 1927, Part II—*The Foundations of Curriculum-making.* Prepared by individual members of the Society's Committee. Harold O. Rugg, Chairman.
*Twenty-seventh Yearbook, 1928, Part I—*Nature and Nurture: Their Influence upon Intelligence.* Prepared by the Society's Committee. Lewis M. Terman, Chairman.
*Twenty-seventh Yearbook, 1928, Part II—*Nature and Nurture: Their Influence upon Achievement.* Prepared by the Society's Committee. Lewis M. Terman, Chairman.
*Twenty-eighth Yearbook, 1929, Parts I and II—*Preschool and Parental Education,* Part I—*Organization and Development.* Part II—*Research and Method.* Prepared by the Society's Committee. Lois H. Meek, Chairman. Bound in one volume. Cloth.
*Twenty-ninth Yearbook, 1930, Parts I and II—*Report of the Society's Committee on Arithmetic.* Part I—*Some Aspects of Modern Thought on Arithmetic.* Part II—*Research in Arithmetic.* Prepared by the Society's Committee. F. B. Knight, Chairman. Bound in one volume.
*Thirtieth Yearbook, 1931— Part I—*The Status of Rural Education.* First Report of the Society's Committee on Rural Education. Orville G. Brim, Chairman.
Thirtieth Yearbook, 1931, Part II—*The Textbook in American Education.* Report of the Society's Committee on the Textbook, J. B. Edmonson, Chairman. Cloth, Paper.

*Thirty-first Yearbook, 1932, Part I—*A Program for Teaching Science.* Prepared by the Society's Committee on the Teaching of Science. S. Ralph Powers, Chairman.
*Thirty-first Yearbook, 1932, Part II—*Changes and Experiments in Liberal-Arts Education.* Prepared by Kathryn McHale, with numerous collaborators.
*Thirty-second Yearbook, 1933—*The Teaching of Geography.* Prepared by the Society's Committee on the Teaching of Geography. A. E. Parkins, Chairman.
*Thirty-third Yearbook, 1934, Part I—*The Planning and Construction of School Buildings.* Prepared by the Society's Committee on School Buildings. N. L. Engelhardt, Chairman.
*Thirty-third Yearbook, 1934, Part II—*The Activity Movement.* Prepared by the Society's Committee on the Activity Movement. Lois Coffey Mossman, Chairman.
*Thirty-fourth Yearbook, 1935—*Educational Diagnosis.* Prepared by the Society's Committee on Educational Diagnosis. L. J. Brueckner, Chairman. Paper.
*Thirty-fifth Yearbook, 1936, Part I—*The Grouping of Pupils.* Prepared by the Society's Committee. W. W. Coxe, Chairman.
*Thirty-fifth Yearbook, 1936, Part II—*Music Education.* Prepared by the Society's Committee. W. L. Uhl, Chairman.
*Thirty-sixth Yearbook, 1937, Part I—*The Teaching of Reading.* Prepared by the Society's Committee. W. S. Gray, Chairman.
*Thirty-sixth Yearbook, 1937, Part II—*International Understanding through the Public-School Curriculum.* Prepared by the Society's Committee. I. L. Kandel, Chairman.
*Thirty-seventh Yearbook, 1938, Part I—*Guidance in Educational Institutions.* Prepared by the Society's Committee. G. N. Kefauver, Chairman.
*Thirty-seventh Yearbook, 1938, Part II—*The Scientific Movement in Education.* Prepared by the Society's Committee. F. N. Freeman, Chairman.
*Thirty-eighth Yearbook, 1939, Part I—*Child Development and the Curriculum.* Prepared by the Society's Committee. Carleton Washburne, Chairman.
*Thirty-eighth Yearbook, 1939, Part II—*General Education in the American College.* Prepared by the Society's Committee. Alvin Eurich, Chairman. Cloth.
*Thirty-ninth Yearbook, 1940, Part I—*Intelligence: Its Nature and Nurture. Comparative and Critical Exposition.* Prepared by the Society's Committee. G. D. Stoddard, Chairman.
*Thirty-ninth Yearbook, 1940, Part II—*Intelligence: Its Nature and Nurture. Original Studies and Experiments.* Prepared by the Society's Committee. G. D. Stoddard, Chairman.
*Fortieth Yearbook, 1941—*Art in American Life and Education.* Prepared by the Society's Committee. Thomas Munro, Chairman.
*Forty-first Yearbook, 1942, Part I—*Philosophies of Education.* Prepared by the Society's Committee. John S. Brubacher, Chairman. Paper.
Forty-first Yearbook, 1942, Part II—*The Psychology of Learning.* Prepared by the Society's Committee. T. R. McConnell, Chairman. Cloth.
*Forty-second Yearbook, 1943, Part I—*Vocational Education.* Prepared by the Society's Committee. F. J. Keller, Chairman.
*Forty-second Yearbook, 1943, Part II—*The Library in General Education.* Prepared by the Society's Committee. L. R. Wilson, Chairman.
Forty-third Yearbook, 1944, Part I—*Adolescence.* Prepared by the Society's Committee. Harold E. Jones, Chairman. Paper.
*Forty-third Yearbook, 1944, Part II—*Teaching Language in the Elementary School.* Prepared by the Society's Committee. M. R. Trabue, Chairman.
*Forty-fourth Yearbook, 1945, Part I—*American Education in the Postwar Period: Curriculum Reconstruction.* Prepared by the Society's Committee. Ralph W. Tyler, Chairman.
Forty-fourth Yearbook, 1945, Part II—*American Education in the Postwar Period: Structural Reorganization.* Prepared by the Society's Committee. Bess Goodykoontz, Chairman. Paper.
*Forty-fifth Yearbook, 1946, Part I—*The Measurement of Understanding.* Prepared by the Society's Committee. William A. Brownell, Chairman.
*Forty-fifth Yearbook, 1946, Part II—*Changing Conceptions in Educational Administration.* Prepared by the Society's Committee. Alonzo G. Grace, Chairman.
*Forty-sixth Yearbook, 1947, Part I—*Science Education in American Schools.* Prepared by the Society's Committee. Victor H. Noll, Chairman.
*Forty-sixth Yearbook, 1947, Part II—*Early Childhood Education.* Prepared by the Society's Committee. N. Searle Light, Chairman. Paper.
Forty-seventh Yearbook, 1948, Part I—*Juvenile Delinquency and the Schools.* Prepared by the Society's Committee. Ruth Strang, Chairman. Cloth.
Forty-seventh Yearbook, 1948, Part II—*Reading in the High School and College.* Prepared by the Society's Committee. William S. Gray, Chairman. Cloth, Paper.
Forty-eighth Yearbook, 1949, Part I—*Audio-visual Materials of Instruction.* Prepared by the Society's Committee. Stephen M. Corey, Chairman. Cloth.
*Forty-eighth Yearbook, 1949, Part II—*Reading in the Elementary School.* Prepared by the Society's Committee. Arthur I. Gates, Chairman.
*Forty-ninth Yearbook, 1950, Part I—*Learning and Instruction.* Prepared by the Society's Committee. G. Lester Anderson, Chairman.
*Forty-ninth Yearbook, 1950, Part II—*The Education of Exceptional Children.* Prepared by the Society's Committee. Samuel A. Kirk, Chairman.
Fiftieth Yearbook, 1951, Part I—*Graduate Study in Education.* Prepared by the Society's Board of Directors. Ralph W. Tyler, Chairman. Paper.
Fiftieth Yearbook, 1951, Part II—*The Teaching of Arithmetic.* Prepared by the Society's Committee G. T. Buswell, Chairman. Cloth. Paper.
Fifty-first Yearbook, 1952, Part I—*General Education.* Prepared by the Society's Committee. T. R. McConnell, Chairman. Cloth, Paper.

Fifty-first Yearbook, 1952, Part II—*Education in Rural Communities*. Prepared by the Society's Committee. Ruth Strang, Chairman. Cloth. Paper.

*Fifty-second Yearbook, 1953, Part I—*Adapting the Secondary-School Program to the Needs of Youth*. Prepared by the Society's Committee: William G. Brink, Chairman.

Fifty-second Yearbook, 1953, Part II—*The Community School*. Prepared by the Society's Committee. Maurice F. Seay, Chairman. Cloth.

*Fifty-third Yearbook, 1954, Part I—*Citizen Cooperation for Better Public Schools*. Prepared by the Society's Committee. Edgar L. Morphet, Chairman.

*Fifty-third Yearbook, 1954, Part II—*Mass Media and Education*. Prepared by the Society's Committee. Edgar Dale, Chairman.

*Fifty-fourth Yearbook, 1955, Part I—*Modern Philosophies and Education*. Prepared by the Society's Committee. John S. Brubacher, Chairman.

Fifty-fourth Yearbook, 1955, Part II—*Mental Health in Modern Education*. Prepared by the Society's Committee. Paul A. Witty, Chairman. Paper.

*Fifty-fifth Yearbook, 1956, Part I—*The Public Junior College*. Prepared by the Society's Committee. B. Lamar Johnson, Chairman.

*Fifty-fifth Yearbook, 1956, Part II—*Adult Reading*. Prepared by the Society's Committee. David H. Clift, Chairman.

*Fifty-sixth Yearbook, 1957, Part I—*In-service Education of Teachers, Supervisors, and Administrators*. Prepared by the Society's Committee. Stephen M. Corey, Chairman. Cloth.

Fifty-sixth Yearbook, 1957, Part II—*Social Studies in the Elementary School*. Prepared by the Society's Committee. Ralph C. Preston, Chairman. Cloth. Paper.

Fifty-seventh Yearbook, 1958, Part I—*Basic Concepts in Music Education*. Prepared by the Society's Committee. Thurber H. Madison, Chairman. Cloth.

*Fifty-seventh Yearbook, 1958, Part II—*Education for the Gifted*. Prepared by the Society's Committee. Robert J. Havighurst, Chairman.

*Fifty-seventh Yearbook, 1958, Part III—*The Integration of Educational Experiences*. Prepared by the Society's Committee. Paul L. Dressel, Chairman. Cloth.

Fifty-eighth Yearbook, 1959, Part I—*Community Education: Principles and Practices from World-wide Experience*. Prepared by the Society's Committee. C. O. Arndt, Chairman. Cloth. Paper.

*Fifty-eighth Yearbook, 1959, Part II—*Personal Services in Education*. Prepared by the Society's Committee. Melvene D. Hardee, Chairman.

*Fifty-ninth Yearbook, 1960, Part I—*Rethinking Science Education*. Prepared by the Society's Committee. J. Darrell Barnard, Chairman.

*Fifty-ninth Yearbook, 1960, Part II—*The Dynamics of Instructional Groups*. Prepared by the Society's Committee. Gale E. Jensen, Chairman.

Sixtieth Yearbook, 1961, Part I—*Development in and through Reading*. Prepared by the Society's Committee. Paul A. Witty, Chairman. Cloth.

Sixtieth Yearbook, 1961, Part II—*Social Forces Influencing American Education*. Prepared by the Society's Committee. Ralph W. Tyler, Chairman. Cloth. Paper.

Sixty-first Yearbook, 1962, Part I—*Individualizing Instruction*. Prepared by the Society's Committee. Fred T. Tyler, Chairman. Cloth.

Sixty-first Yearbook, 1962, Part II—*Education for the Professions*. Prepared by the Society's Committee. G. Lester Anderson, Chairman. Cloth.

Sixty-second Yearbook, 1963, Part I—*Child Psychology*. Prepared by the Society's Committee. Harold W. Stevenson, Editor. Cloth.

Sixty-second Yearbook, 1963, Part II—*The Impact and Improvement of School Testing Programs*. Prepared by the Society's Committee. Warren G. Findley, Editor. Cloth.

Sixty-third Yearbook, 1964, Part I—*Theories of Learning and Instruction*. Prepared by the Society's Committee. Ernest R. Hilgard, Editor. Paper. Cloth.

Sixty-third Yearbook, 1964, Part II—*Behavioral Science and Educational Administration*. Prepared by the Society' Committee. Daniel E. Griffiths, Editor. Paper.

Sixty-fourth Yearbook, 1965, Part I—*Vocational Education*. Prepared by the Society's Committee. Melvin L. Barlow, Editor. Cloth.

*Sixty-fourth Yearbook, 1965, Part II—*Art Education*. Prepared by the Society's Committee. W. Reid Hastie, Editor. Cloth.

Sixty-fifth Yearbook, 1966, Part I—*Social Deviancy among Youth*. Prepared by the Society's Committee. William W. Wattenberg, Editor. Cloth.

Sixty-fifth Yearbook, 1966, Part II—*The Changing American School*. Prepared by the Society's Committee. John I. Goodlad, Editor. Cloth.

Sixty-sixth Yearbook, 1967, Part I—*The Educationally Retarded and Disadvantaged*. Prepared by the Society's Committee. Paul A. Witty, Editor. Cloth.

Sixty-sixth Yearbook, 1967, Part II—*Programed Instruction*. Prepared by the Society's Committee. Phil C. Lange, Editor. Cloth.

Sixty-seventh Yearbook, 1968, Part I—*Metropolitanism: Its Challenge to Education*. Prepared by the Society's Committee. Robert J. Havighurst, Editor. Cloth.

Sixty-seventh Yearbook, 1968, Part II—*Innovation and Change in Reading Instruction*. Prepared by the Society's Committee. Helen M. Robinson, Editor. Cloth.

Sixty-eighth Yearbook, 1969, Part I—*The United States and International Education*. Prepared by the Society's Committee. Harold G. Shane, Editor. Cloth.

Sixty-eighth Yearbook, 1969, Part II—*Educational Evaluation: New Roles, New Means*. Prepared by the Society's Committee. Ralph W. Tyler, Editor. Paper.

*Sixty-ninth Yearbook, 1970, Part I—*Mathematics Education*. Prepared by the Society's Committee. Edward G. Begle, Editor. Cloth.

Sixty-ninth Yearbook, 1970, Part II—*Linguistics in School Programs*. Prepared by the Society's Committee. Albert H. Marckwardt, Editor. Cloth.

Seventieth Yearbook, 1971, Part I—*The Curriculum: Retrospect and Prospect*. Prepared by the Society's Committee. Robert M. McClure, Editor. Paper.

Seventieth Yearbook, 1971, Part II—*Leaders in American Education.* Prepared by the Society's Committee. Robert J. Havighurst, Editor. Cloth.

Seventy-first Yearbook, 1972, Part I—*Philosophical Redirection of Educational Research.* Prepared by the Society's Committee. Lawrence G. Thomas, Editor. Cloth.

Seventy-first Yearbook, 1972, Part II—*Early Childhood Education.* Prepared by the Society's Committee. Ira J. Gordon, Editor. Paper.

Seventy-second Yearbook, 1973, Part I—*Behavior Modification in Education.* Prepared by the Society's Committee. Carl E. Thoresen, Editor. Cloth.

Seventy-second Yearbook, 1973, Part II—*The Elementary School in the United States.* Prepared by the Society's Committee. John I. Goodlad and Harold G. Shane, Editors. Cloth.

Seventy-third Yearbook, 1974, Part I—*Media and Symbols: The Forms of Expression, Communication, and Education.* Prepared by the Society's Committee. David R. Olson, Editor. Cloth.

Seventy-third Yearbook, 1974, Part II—*Uses of the Sociology of Education.* Prepared by the Society's Committee. C. Wayne Gordon, Editor. Cloth.

Seventy-fourth Yearbook, 1975, Part I—*Youth.* Prepared by the Society's Committee. Robert J. Havighurst and Philip H. Dreyer, Editors. Cloth.

Seventy-fourth Yearbook, 1975, Part II—*Teacher Education.* Prepared by the Society's Committee. Kevin Ryan, Editor. Cloth.

Seventy-fifth Yearbook, 1976, Part I—*Psychology of Teaching Methods.* Prepared by the Society's Committee. N. L. Gage, Editor. Paper.

Seventy-fifth Yearbook, 1976, Part II—*Issues in Secondary Education.* Prepared by the Society's Committee. William Van Til, Editor. Cloth.

Seventy-sixth Yearbook, 1977, Part I—*The Teaching of English.* Prepared by the Society's Committee. James R. Squire, Editor. Cloth.

Seventy-sixth Yearbook, 1977, Part II—*The Politics of Education.* Prepared by the Society's Committee. Jay D. Scribner, Editor. Paper.

Seventy-seventh Yearbook, 1978, Part I—*The Courts and Education,* Clifford P. Hooker, Editor. Cloth.

Seventy-seventh Yearbook, 1978, Part II—*Education and the Brain,* Jeanne Chall and Allan F. Mirsky, Editors. Cloth.

Seventy-eighth Yearbook, 1979, Part I—*The Gifted and the Talented: Their Education and Development,* A. Harry Passow, Editor. Cloth.

Seventy-eighth Yearbook, 1979, Part II—*Classroom Management,* Daniel L. Duke, Editor. Cloth.

Seventy-ninth Yearbook, 1980, Part I—*Toward Adolescence: The Middle School Years,* Mauritz Johnson, Editor. Cloth.

Seventy-ninth Yearbook, 1980, Part II—*Learning a Second Language,* Frank M. Grittner, Editor. Cloth.

Eightieth Yearbook, 1981, Part I—*Philosophy and Education,* Jonas F. Soltis, Editor. Cloth.

Eightieth Yearbook, 1981, Part II—*The Social Studies,* Howard D. Mehlinger and O. L. Davis, Jr., Editors. Cloth.

Eighty-first Yearbook, 1982, Part I—*Policy Making in Education,* Ann Lieberman and Milbrey W. McLaughlin, Editors. Cloth.

Eighty-first Yearbook, 1982, Part II—*Education and Work,* Harry F. Silberman, Editor. Cloth.

Yearbooks of the National Society are distributed by

UNIVERSITY OF CHICAGO PRESS, 5801 ELLIS AVE.,
CHICAGO, ILLINOIS 60637

Please direct inquiries regarding prices of volumes still available to the University of Chicago Press. Orders for these volumes should be sent to the University of Chicago Press, not to the offices of the National Society.

2. The Series on Contemporary Educational Issues

In addition to its Yearbooks the Society now publishes volumes in a series on Contemporary Educational Issues. These volumes are prepared under the supervision of the Society's Commission on an Expanded Publication Program.

The 1982 Titles

Improving Educational Standards and Productivity: The Research Basis for Policy (Herbert J. Walberg, ed.)

Political and Social Foundations of Education: The Changing Politics of Schooling (Michael W. Kirst and Frederick M. Wirt)

The 1981 Titles

Psychology and Education: The State of the Union (Frank H. Farley and Neal J. Gordon, eds.)

Selected Issues in Mathematics Education (Mary M. Lindquist, ed.)

The 1980 Titles

Minimum Competency Achievement Testing: Motives, Models, Measures, and Consequences (Richard M. Jaeger and Carol K. Tittle, eds.)

Collective Bargaining in Public Education (Anthony M. Cresswell, Michael J. Murphy, with Charles T. Kerchner)

The 1979 Titles

Educational Environments and Effects: Evaluation, Policy, and Productivity (Herbert J. Walberg, ed.)

Research on Teaching: Concepts, Findings, and Implications (Penelope L. Peterson and Herbert J. Walberg, eds.)

The Principal in Metropolitan Schools (Donald A. Erickson and Theodore L. Reller, eds.)

The 1978 Titles

Aspects of Reading Education (Susanna Pflaum-Connor, ed.)

History, Education, and Public Policy: Recovering the American Educational Past (Donald R. Warren, ed.)

From Youth to Constructive Adult Life: The Role of the Public School (Ralph W. Tyler, ed.)

The 1977 Titles

Early Childhood Education: Issues and Insights (Bernard Spodek and Herbert J. Walberg, eds.)

The Future of Big City Schools: Desegregation Policies and Magnet Alternatives (Daniel U. Levine and Robert J. Havighurst, eds.)

Educational Administration: The Developing Decades (Luvern L. Cunningham, Walter G. Hack, and Raphael O. Nystrand, eds.)

The 1976 Titles

Prospects for Research and Development in Education (Ralph W. Tyler, ed.)

Public Testimony on Public Schools (Commission on Educational Governance)

Counseling Children and Adolescents (William M. Walsh, ed.)

The 1975 Titles

Schooling and the Rights of Children (Vernon Haubrich and Michael Apple, eds.)

Systems of Individualized Education (Harriet Talmage, ed.)

Educational Policy and International Assessment: Implications of the IEA Assessment of Achievement (Alan Purves and Daniel U. Levine, eds.)

The 1974 Titles

Crucial Issues in Testing (Ralph W. Tyler and Richard M. Wolf, eds.)

Conflicting Conceptions of Curriculum (Elliott Eisner and Elizabeth Vallance, eds.)

Cultural Pluralism (Edgar G. Epps, ed.)

Rethinking Educational Equality (Andrew T. Kopan and Herbert J. Walberg, eds.)

All of the preceding volumes may be ordered from

McCutchan Publishing Corporation
2526 Grove Street
Berkeley, California 94704

The 1972 Titles

Black Students in White Schools (Edgar G. Epps, ed.)

Flexibility in School Programs (W. J. Congreve and G. L. Rinehart, eds.)

Performance Contracting—1969–1971 (J. A. Mecklenburger)

The Potential of Educational Futures (Michael Marien and W. L. Ziegler, eds.)

Sex Differences and Discrimination in Education (Scarvia Anderson, ed.)

The 1971 Titles

Accountability in Education (Leon M. Lessinger and Ralph W. Tyler, eds.)

Farewell to Schools??? (D. U. Levine and R. J. Havighurst, eds.)

Models for Integrated Education (D. U. Levine, ed.)

PYGMALION *Reconsidered* (J. D. Elashoff and R. E. Snow)

Reactions to Silberman's CRISIS IN THE CLASSROOM (A. Harry Passow, ed.)

The 1971 and 1972 titles in this series are now out of print and are no longer available.